FV

Wordsworth and Philosophy

Empiricism and Transcendentalism
in the Poetry

Wordsworth and Philosophy
Empiricism and Transcendentalism in the Poetry

by
Keith G. Thomas

U·M·I Research Press
Ann Arbor / London

Produced and distributed by
UMI Research Press
an imprint of
University Microfilms Inc.
Ann Arbor, Michigan 48106

Library of Congress Cataloging in Publication Data

Thomas, Keith G., 1948-
  Wordsworth and philosophy : empiricism and transcendentalism
in the poetry / Keith G. Thomas.
    p. cm—(Nineteenth-century studies)
    Bibliography: p.
    Includes index.
    ISBN 0-8357-1880-8 (alk. paper)
    1. Wordsworth, William, 1770-1850—Philosophy.
2. Transcendentalism in literature. 3. Empiricism in literature.
4. Philosophy in literature. I. Title. II. Series: Nineteenth-century studies (Ann
Arbor, Mich.)
PR5892.P5T47   1989
821'.7—dc19   88-27287
                                                                         CIP

British Library CIP data is available.

To my parents, Kathleen and Leslie Thomas

Contents

Acknowledgments

For their encouragement, inspiring example, help and generosity, over the years and in numerous ways, I wish to thank especially Frances Ferguson, Carol Christ, Morton Paley, Peter Manning, Jerome Christensen and Susan Wolfson. I also wish to thank especially Jeffrey Robinson, chair of the English Department at Colorado, for allowing me to rearrange my teaching schedule at a crucial time during the writing of this book. Special thanks also go to my typist, Marjorie Urban, who got through a vast amount of work in record time. Many colleagues and friends at Colorado gave support and advice, and it is a pleasure to thank here John Stevenson, Robert Steiner, Gina Schwartz, Lesley Brill, Therese Jones, Jill Heydt, Mary Tanner, Bob Greer and all the guys at the "T."

Finally, I wish to thank The Wordsworth Trust, Grasmere, England, and Cornell University Press for permission to quote from Wordsworth's manuscripts, and Oxford University Press for permission to quote from the standard editions of the works of Wordsworth and Coleridge.

Abbreviations

CPW   *The Complete Poetical Works of Samuel Taylor Coleridge.* Ed. Ernest Hartley Coleridge. Poems are cited in the text by line number.

PW   *The Poetical Works of William Wordsworth.* Ed. Ernest de Selincourt and Helen Darbishire. Poems are cited in the text by line number, and other material by volume and page number.

PrW   *The Prose Works of William Wordsworth.* Ed. W. J. B. Owen and Jane Worthington Smyser. Quotations are cited by volume and page number in the text.

1850 *Prel*   William Wordsworth. *The Prelude: Or, Growth of a Poet's Mind.* Ed. Ernest de Selincourt. Quotations are cited in the text by line number, and other material by page number.

Prel   William Wordsworth. *The Prelude: Or, Growth of a Poet's Mind* (Text of 1805). Ed. Ernest de Selincourt. Rev. Stephen Gill. Unless otherwise indicated, all quotations are from this edition, and are cited in the text by book and line number.

Introduction

The topic of this book is the relation of Wordsworth's poetry to the philosophy of his time: specifically, empiricism, still the dominant philosophy in England when Wordsworth began his poetic career in the 1780s, as it had been throughout the eighteenth century, and German transcendental idealism, which he and particularly Coleridge were among the first to introduce into England in the early 1800s.

But why a book on Wordsworth and philosophy in 1988—especially when it would seem that the topic has been exhaustively treated over the years by a host of studies that have covered, one would think, every aspect and variety of philosophy influencing him? The answer, quite simply, is that the developments in literary theory and scholarly methodology that have occurred during the last decade or so—even during the last few years—make such a topic once again problematic and all the more in need of fresh examination.

These developments include both the particular and the general. The most important particular development is Harold Bloom's rethinking of the concept of influence in a trilogy of books published between 1973 and 1976.[1] The general developments have to do with the broader shifts in theory that have dominated critical practice since the mid 1970s. The most important is deconstruction, which has given us not only a theory of textuality and a method of textual analysis but in particular, from the point of view of my topic here, a theory of intertextuality and, at the heart of Derrida's work itself, an extensive rethinking of the whole relation between philosophy and literature. The latter endeavor began affecting American literary criticism in the early 1980s, and is today a major scholarly growth industry.[2] The second relevant general development, partly emerging in opposition to deconstruction, is the New Historicism (as well as Marxist historicism and materialism), which in establishing in new ways the importance of the historical context and material conditions of a writer's life has raised the question of influence—or, more broadly, causal relations—from a different perspective.[3] My treatment of Wordsworth and philosophy here will, to varying degrees, acknowledge these developments; but before showing how they have reshaped our understanding of the topic, we should review some of the traditional ways in which studies of Wordsworth and philosophy have proceeded.

As already implied, most studies have been studies of sources and influences. They have proved invaluable in first mapping the field, in establishing the nature and range of the philosophy affecting Wordsworth. One thinks here of the pioneering work of Arthur Beatty, Melvin Rader, M. H. Abrams, E. R. Wasserman, H. W. Piper, Jonathan Wordsworth and Alan Grob.[4] Such scholars have firmly established Wordsworth's relations to British empiricism, German idealism, pantheism and other philosophies. But as we have come to see (thanks to Bloom and others), the theory of source and influence itself has proved to be highly problematic and has given rise to some dauntingly restrictive assumptions. First, establishing an author's indebtedness can pose insoluble problems of mathematics. Beatty and Rader, for example, contradict each other absolutely, the former arguing that Wordsworth is a Hartleyan empiricist, the latter that he is from the start a transcendentalist. Is one right and the other wrong? Or are both right but in a different way or to different degrees? Of course, any decision will be a matter of interpretation; but interpretation must wrestle with the mathematical problem of estimating the depth of an author's debt and assessing its duration, or establishing proportionate indebtedness to several contemporaneous and probably conflicting sources. Granted, for example, that Wordsworth *is* a transcendentalist by 1804, is his transcendentalism closest to Kant's, as several scholars have argued, or Fichte's, as Daniel Stempel argues, or Schelling's, as E. D. Hirsch argues?[5] Or is it some amalgam of all three kinds (or two kinds), or a version all his own bearing only a glancing resemblance to one or more of these or other transcendentalisms? Second, as the case of Wordsworth shows, there can be an insoluble problem at the heart of source and influence study: for in Wordsworth's poetry of 1804 we can sense an influence but cannot find the source. In a letter to Henry Crabb Robinson (March 10, 1840), Wordsworth declared that he had "never read a word of German metaphysics, thank Heaven!"[6] Was Wordsworth telling the truth? Had he forgotten? Or was Coleridge his main conduit to German idealism? The absence of any determinate evidence (Wordsworth left very few records about his reading on any subject) presents a crucial problem of causal relations that scholars have tried to overcome usually in the manner of E. D. Hirsch and M. H. Abrams. Hirsch offers a "typological" study of Wordsworth and Schelling, establishing the parallelism between their philosophies regardless of its empirical provenance; Abrams argues that such parallelisms proceed from the *Zeitgeist,* that certain ways of thinking were simultaneously in the air in England and Germany in the early nineteenth century.[7]

Adjudicating several competing influences is one problem, then, and even identifying possible sources is another; a third, perhaps more difficult, problem arises when we can establish both the source and the influence, a problem that strains causal relations all the more. To argue the influence of philosophy on a poet is inevitably to assert the priority of the philosophical text and the secondariness of the poetic. The issue is then conceived to be one of congruence, as if at best there should obtain a one-to-one correspondence between the secondary text and its source. The philosophical text thus becomes the authority and the poetic text but a derivative restatement of it—of ideas and theories all presumed to be better articulated in the original. This is to argue cause and effect, however, with a self-vexing vengeance, for while effects are hereby directly related to their causes, many causes have no effects whatsoever or end up with effects that are evidently distorted: the poem deviates from its sources. We may recognize, for instance, certain theories and terms derived from Locke's *Essay concerning Human Understanding* in Wordsworth's *Prelude,* but we may wonder why these theories and terms and not others are there, or why Wordsworth may have stretched Locke's meaning in some cases or given a term a completely new or wrong meaning.

Harold Bloom has successfully addressed such problems of the theory of influence by recasting the author's deviation from his source as a question of "misprision," a "misreading" that is sometimes intentional and always creative, resulting in a text that is fundamentally "revisionary": the secondary text essentially revises its source, thereby becoming an authority in its own right—becoming even more authoritative, in fact, by reason of its very secondariness, than the precursor source text.[8] While one may look for other reasons for the poet's misreading than the ones Bloom gives (he offers a purely psychoanalytic explanation: an "anxiety" of influence, an oedipal struggle with a strong precursor, etc.), one is assuredly indebted to his salutary emphasis on the poet's acts of transformation, on the essential originality of the poet's adaptation and revision of his sources.

The work of Jacques Derrida, although less frontally aimed at this issue, has greater implications for the topic I am studying here. One of his concerns from the mid-1960s on has been to examine the relation between philosophy and literature—specifically, by calling attention to philosophy's textual and rhetorical dimensions, by treating philosophy *as* literature. Such a move essentially challenges philosophy's claim to an ontological "truth" superior to literature's merely "aesthetic" truth. Neither literature nor philosophy is really more authoritative than the other. In fact, by this approach, not only does philosophy cease to have exclusive rights to truth, but truth itself now becomes entirely subject to its modes of apprehension. The supposedly pure logic whereby philosophy attains to the truth is thus a textual mediation—and subject to all the maneuvers and errors that characterize any text. Questions of genre, formal structure, rhetorical strategy and tropology cease to be secondary or suppressed but become primary and constitutive. Metaphors in the philosophical text, for example, cannot be quarantined as merely superadded and expendable literary embellishments; instead, they permeate the argument because they are of the essence, enacting the unworkable logic of the very distinction between the literal and figurative, even prompting us to see, at a further remove, that "concepts," and even "metaphysics" itself, are tropes that have been deprived of their figurative force.[9]

The history of philosophy could indeed be rewritten as a literary history—a history that is as much the result of anxious reading and wilful misreading, of strong writing and revisionary rewriting, as Bloom argues is the case for literary history proper. But whereas Bloom focuses on the author and his psychological agon with strong precursors, Derrida confines himself more manageably to texts and their interrelations; he thus replaces "influence" with the heuristically more efficient concept of "intertextuality." Intertextuality places text against text, or "reads" one text "through" another, in order to uncover certain common problems and procedures.[10] This strategy may well encompass the same domain as influence, but it is as often concerned to bring widely disparate texts into relation (such as texts by Hegel and Genet in *Glas*) as texts where there is an ostensible causal relation. The important difference is that intertextuality produces close readings of *both* texts brought into relation—from our point of view here, both the philosophical and the poetic text—whereas traditional influence study does not "read" the source so much as take it at face value or treat it as textually unproblematic in order to establish it as authority and precursor for another text. Following an intertextual approach, we can see that philosophy and poetry (to borrow Wordsworth's words) become "joint-labourers in [the] work" of truth (*Prel,* 13. 438).

The advantages of an intertextual approach are enormous and have made their mark on many areas of criticism and scholarship and in several disciplines over the last ten years. One should cite, for example, the extensive amount of work done on the romantic and eighteenth-century sublime, which has offered readings of Burke and Kant as well as of the relevant poetry.[11] One should cite, too, studies like John J. Richetti's *Philosophical Writing: Locke, Berkeley, Hume* (1983), which was the first explicitly to treat these philosophers as writers. I mentioned at the start the growing interest in reading "philosophy as literature/literature as philosophy." But one should also stress that originally deconstructionist notions of text, intertextuality and reading, of the applicability of the textual model to technically nontextual phenomena that people nonetheless "read" (broadly speaking, "context" as well as "text," but without privileging one over the other), methodologically underlie the current, often interdisciplinary, study of culture and its representations.

Even so, despite its eminent success, the practice of intertextuality can itself become problematic. It can too easily foster an ahistoricism by letting actual causal links between two texts go unexamined in its very preoccupation with their complex consonances as texts. For example, in one of the two books published in the last two years explicitly on the topic of philosophy and romantic poetry, the author gives an exemplary exposition and reading of German idealism from Kant through Fichte to Schelling, showing how the "quest romance" emerges as a dominant philosophic and poetic mode, one which he then explicates in the poetry of Coleridge, Shelley and Byron; but the endeavor becomes suspect when we are offered a thoroughly Fichtean reading of Coleridge's "The Rime of the Ancient Mariner"—that is, of a poem written in 1797–98, approximately three years before Coleridge read Fichte. To ignore chronology and causality in this way is to stretch even the *Zeitgeist* too thin.[12]

Of course, there is no intrinsic reason why intertextuality should not be compatible with a scrupulous historicism. And indeed the historicist criticism that has come to the fore particularly in the last two or three years, even if largely opposed to deconstruction and its potential (or wilful) ahistoricism, can be seen as an implicit corrective and much-needed development, the next logical step, that nevertheless relies on deconstruction's close-reading practices in order to go beyond the margins of the text to social, political and economic conditions, to discourse and ideology in general, to the various historical factors, that is, that determined the production of those texts. Historical contextualization of this kind not only widens the field of possible causes but bids us recognize that the formal and thematic consonances that are the stuff of intertextuality may themselves be shaped by extratextual forces.

If anything, the new historicist criticism accentuates all the more the need for reexamining the topic of Wordsworth and philosophy. Standing at the center of the romantic ideology, philosophical idealism in general and transcendentalism in particular, which, in Wordsworth's case, are integrally linked to visionary insight and the solitary sublime, were the first to come under attack as elaborate evasions motivated by impinging socioeconomic conditions they pointedly elide.[13] If we might now see the situation as being more complicated than a direct defensive reaction, we at least appreciate more fully the effects of context and, as a result, how motivation and reference weave through romantic texts whose idealism was traditionally interpreted as pure, free-standing, "truthful" revelation. By restoring reference and reconstructing the interplay of external pressures and inner motives, this historicism nicely supplements deconstructive analysis of the various subversions and complexities structuring those same texts. But more than this, it is implicitly (and rapidly) leading towards a regenerated concept of biography—one in which material conditions are understood to exert as much of a determining influence on an author's work as individual psychology or literary history. If the first effect of this has so far been, in Wordsworth studies, a shift in our sense of his canon, away from the poetry of solitude and the sublime towards the sizable number of poems more engaged with the social and economic order,[14] then the time is not so far off when the new historicism will lead us back to Wordsworth's idealism to recuperate it for critical study. The philosophical biography that might result would seek to answer not only how particular historical circumstances motivated a certain literary-philosophical response but why the poet chose a particular form of response and not some other to address those circumstances. Why transcendental idealism, or pantheism, and not some other available philosophy, such as Neoplatonism?

My purpose in sketching the developments in literary theory over the last decade or so has been to show how they establish the need for reexamining the question of Wordsworth's relation to the philosophy of his time, to propose how we should answer those questions differently now from in the past, and to present possible ways of proceeding. A thoroughly historicist study would draw the causal links between socioeconomic conditions, the motives and reactions they might have prompted, and Wordsworth's turn to philosophy as evidenced in the poetry. But precisely because the *textual* relation of the philosophy to the poetry is still so problematic (the ways in which the philosophy is evidenced in the poetry), I propose trying to answer more immediate questions to do with "how" rather than trace farther-reaching, extraphilosophical causes in historical conditions as such in the hope of establishing "why." I follow here, then, an intertextual approach and I concentrate more on literature as philosophy than philosophy as literature, for reasons given below; but I proceed according to historicist principles insofar as I relate Wordsworth's philosophical development to its historical context: specifically, I attend here to the question of what philosophy "influenced" Wordsworth, how he had access to it, how he interpreted it and how it enters his poetry. In short, my province encompasses the immediate set of philosophical and textual causes, chronology in general and, on several occasions, the particular sequence of Wordsworth's composition of first drafts. My focus, approach, methods and reasons will become clearer if we turn to Wordsworth's poetry and its contexts in 1798. To do so will entail discussing Coleridge's poetry too, precisely because the close friendship and enthusiastic dialogue between the two poets resulted in the philosophical poetry which is my focus here.

When Wordsworth and Coleridge became friends in June 1797, they not only read their latest poems to each other but began discussing broad theoretical questions their poetry seemed to raise: theories of poetic language, theories of poetry, theories of what constitutes a fit poetic subject for poetic treatment—but above all *theories*. From June 1797 to July 1798, first in Racedown in Dorset and then in Nether Stowey and Alfoxden in Somerset, Wordsworth and Coleridge debated, besides such literary matters, a diversity of philosophical theories: pantheistic theories of the One Life in nature, epistemological theories of the workings of mind (such as Harleyan associationism) and Lockean empiricist theory in general, possibly Kantian philosophy insofar as it was becoming known in Britain, and probably more mystical as well as more orthodox theories of religious belief. Doubtless, as university-educated men who had eagerly immersed themselves in the political and ideological debates of their day (the French Revolution, the conservative English reaction to it, Godwinism), they found the philosophical theories they discussed important and compelling in their own right. But as poets, whose mutual recognition of each other's genius soon led to their collaboration on a volume of poems, they intended that their philosophical interests should serve an express poetic purpose. For from such answers as they could derive they hoped to formulate the ideological program for a long "philosophical poem"—"the *first* and *only* true Phil[osophical] Poem in existence," as Coleridge hailed it—which Wordsworth was to write and which would be called *The Recluse*.[15]

Looking back late in his life, Coleridge outlined the nature and scope of the project:

> Then the plan laid out, and, I believe, partly suggested by me, was, that Wordsworth should assume the station of a man in mental repose, one whose principles were made up, and so prepared to deliver upon authority a system of philosophy. He was to treat man as man—a subject of eye, ear, touch, and taste, in contact with external nature, and informing the senses from the mind, and not compounding a mind out of the senses; then he was to describe the pastoral and other states of society, assuming something of the Juvenalian spirit as he approached the high civilization of cities and towns, and opening a melancholy picture of the present state of degeneracy and vice; thence he was to infer and reveal the proof of, and necessity for, the whole state of man and society being subject to, and illustrative of, a redemptive process in operation, showing how this idea reconciled all the anomalies, and promised future glory and restoration. Something of this sort was, I think, agreed on. It is, in substance, what I have been all my life doing in my system of philosophy.[16]

Although this account may reflect Coleridge's own bias in 1832, it accords sufficiently closely with what Wordsworth announced in 1814 to be his poetic program in his preface to *The Excursion* for us to see what the "philosophical poem" would entail. There Wordsworth mentions his early "determination to compose a philosophical poem, containing views of Man, Nature, and Society; . . . as having for its principal subject the sensations and opinions of a poet living in retirement" (*PW*, 5: 2). And although he adds that it is not his "intention formally to announce a system" (as Coleridge would have him do), he nevertheless stresses that if he "shall succeed in conveying to the mind clear thoughts, lively images, and strong feelings, the Reader will have no difficulty in extracting the system for himself" (*PW*, 5: 2). Then, to inform the reader of "the design and scope of the whole Poem," he concludes his preface with the "Prospectus," which, like Coleridge's statement in his *Table Talk,* specifies what the philosophical foundation of "system" is to be:

> Paradise, and groves
> Elysian, Fortunate Fields—like those of old
> Sought in the Atlantic Main—why should they be
> A history only of departed things,
> Or a mere fiction of what never was?
> For the discerning intellect of Man,
> When wedded to this goodly universe
> In love and holy passion, shall find these
> A simple produce of the common day.
> —I, long before the blissful hour arrives,
> Would chant, in lonely peace, the spousal verse
> Of this great consummation:—and, by words
> Which speak of nothing more than what we are,
> Would I arouse the sensual from their sleep
> Of Death, and win the vacant and the vain
> To noble raptures; while my voice proclaims
> How exquisitely the individual Mind
> (And the progressive powers perhaps no less
> Of the whole species) to the external World
> Is fitted:—and how exquisitely, too—
> Theme this but little heard of among men—
> The external World is fitted to the Mind;
> And the creation (by no lower name
> Can it be called) which they with blended might
> Accomplish:—this is our high argument.
>
> (*PW*, 5: 4–5; lines 47–71)

While *Paradise Lost* prescribes the epic pattern that the philosophical poem is to follow, Wordsworth forswears Miltonic theodicy in favor of justifying the ways of "the Mind of Man" (40) to men, in favor of a "system of philosophy" founded on the "individual Mind" and deriving from its "contact with external nature." Paradise, redemption, "future glory and restoration," religious belief, imaginative faith, ethics and "principles"—that is, all the ideas, feelings and attitudes that go to make up "a system of philosophy"—are to result from sense experience of the phenomenal world and be, as Wordsworth sees it, the "creation" which mind and world "with blended might / Accomplish."

The Recluse was to have been a long four-part poem consisting of an introduction and then three epic-length parts. Wordsworth completed the introduction, part 2, and book 1 of part 1, but the rest of part 1 and part 3 were never written. Doubtless, in addition to the many other cogent reasons, the projected work was too vast, too comprehensive, too ambitious, to ever be realized. Nevertheless, the philosophic and poetic program behind it gave inspiration and direction to Wordsworth's writings throughout the larger part of his career. In late 1798, Wordsworth began work on what he would regard as the introduction: he began undertaking "a review of his own mind, . . . record[ing], in verse, the origin and progress of his powers, as far as he was acquainted with them" (*PW,* 5: 2)—both to ascertain his own adequacy to the task and to establish to his own satisfaction the "authority" of "his own mind" to deliver a system of philosophy (in Coleridge's version, to establish his own credentials as "a man in mental repose, . . . whose principles were made up"). *The Prelude,* the work which resulted, completed in 1805, is itself a long "philosophical poem" in its own right, effectively delivering the "system," if in an unsystematic, discursive way, in the very course of Wordsworth's determining his fitness to deliver it. Yet equally philosophical are the other completed parts of *The Recluse.* In 1800 Wordsworth began "Home at Grasmere" (the "Prospectus" forms the final part of it, and was written in 1800), completing it in 1806 and subtitling this thousand-line poem *"The Recluse.* Book I. Part I." In 1806 too, or perhaps as late as 1809 (but certainly long enough after completing *The Prelude*), Wordsworth began work on *The Excursion,* the narrative-dramatic central part of *The Recluse* (following "Home at Grasmere," the rest of the first part and the third would have been first-person meditations), completing and publishing this nine-book poem in 1814. This work comes closest to fulfilling the *Recluse* plans by explicitly offering a philosophy that is grounded in the experience of nature, and giving a lengthy critique of pastoral and urban society as well as recommending principled answers to the problems they pose. Moreover, in the preface to *The Excursion* (in which he outlines the *Recluse* project), Wordsworth figures the poem and all the other poetry he has written as a "gothic church": the introduction, *The Prelude,* is the "ante-chapel"; the three-part *Recluse* proper constitutes the main building; but added on to it are "little cells, oratories, and sepulchral recesses"—that is, all the "minor Pieces" he has written thus far (*PW,* 5: 2). Despite, then, the unfinished state of *The Recluse,* the cohesiveness of Wordsworth's image testifies to the all-pervasive power of the plans laid in 1797–98. For even if Wordsworth failed to complete the first and only true philosophical poem in existence, he nevertheless wrote between 1798 and 1814 many successful philosophical *poems* of major pretension and proportion. These achievements—the cells, ante-chapel, oratories and nave—are the subject of my study here.[17]

Coleridge's and Wordsworth's statements about the "philosophical poem" imply how the poem would be philosophical, what the philosophy is, and even what problems are likely to be encountered. A consideration of the first issue will lead us to the other two.

The project Coleridge and Wordsworth set themselves in 1797–98 is essentially epistemological, for at the center is the interaction of self with nature, the empirical ground on which to construct, and from which to deliver, "a system of philosophy." In their insistence on the primacy of epistemology Coleridge and Wordsworth follow the lead of Enlightenment philosophers—Descartes, Locke, Berkeley, Hume, Kant—for whom epistemology is "first philosophy," because how the mind knows and what it is possible for it to know are questions to be settled before assessing the possibility of systems of knowledge, whether already established sciences or customary, ordinary beliefs.[18] Whatever the problems of moving from epistemological foundational premises to systems— and clearly in Wordsworth's case they are immense, since the systems he wishes to embrace include not only ontology and metaphysics ("Nature") but psychology, ethics, politics and religion ("Man, . . . and Society")—this occupation of a central epistemological ground assuredly allows the poet to establish his own "authority" and the poem to establish its "authority" in relation to philosophy. By "treat[ing] man as man—a subject of eye, ear, touch, and taste, in contact with external nature," Wordsworth takes the speaker and his subjective situation as ground of the poem's philosophical discourse. Any philosophical statement will derive its authority from this speaker and his experience, conditioned as they will be by the contingencies of time and place and by the varying motions of the senses, the mind and external nature. As commentators have recognized, this is the salient feature distinguishing Wordsworth's and Coleridge's poetry during the late 1790s from that of their eighteenth-century predecessors;[19] and the first of the two poets to develop this innovation was Coleridge in his Conversation Poems.

Reflective in mood and imitating in blank-verse form the idioms and rhythms of conversational language, the Conversation Poem, as Coleridge perfected it in 1797–98, became a flexible poetic medium for presenting a wide range of thought and feeling expressed in the poet's own person. "The major achievement of the Conversation Poems," writes Mary Jacobus, "is its fusion of subjective experience and philosophic statement."[20] The "abstract theology" of pantheism, the "system of philosophy" consistently presented in these poems—and presented as bare theory in the earlier "Religious Musings" (1794)— is now "translated into the language of subjective experience,"[21] even, in fact, in the first Conversation Poem, "The Eolian Harp" (1795). Musing on the "desultory breeze" (14) and the harmony it elicits from "that simplest Lute / Plac'd lengthways in the clasping casement" (11–12), Coleridge senses the ubiquitous harmony in nature and then proceeds to "philosophic statement" when he playfully explores the concept of the windharp as an imaginative explanation of that harmony:

> And what if all of animated nature
> Be but organic Harps diversely fram'd,
> That tremble into thought, as o'er them sweeps

Plastic and vast, one intellectual breeze,
At once the Soul of each, and God of all?

(44–48)

Coleridge, of course, does not answer the question (even if he elaborates its implications) but abandons it, a response which, like the subjective conditions prompting him to ask the question in the first place, dramatically affects the status of the philosophical statement. Even if the statement is little more than "abstract theology" cast in question form, its emergence as the contingent utterance of a particular speaker on a particular occasion converts what might be accepted theory *outside* the poetic context into the speculation (and speculative answer) of the particular moment *inside* the poem. Admittedly, Coleridge actually asks a question. But the overt question is really the surface expression of a deeper questioning attitude characterizing the consciousness of this speaker, who, as a subject of eye, ear, touch and taste, in contact with external nature, seeks to inform his senses and what they report from the mind and its theories. Were we, then, to rewrite the question as indicative statement, the speculative character would nonetheless remain—because subjective conditions have become the arbiter of the "authority" of philosophic utterance.

During this momentous year, "Coleridge's work quite literally interbraids with Wordsworth's," writes Paul Sheats. "Themes, motifs, and technical innovations pass from one mind to the other and back again, enriched and transformed at each passage."[22] The Conversation Poem clearly influenced Wordsworth's development of the first-person philosophical mode that characterizes *The Prelude,* a mode that first emerged in January 1798 in fragmentary passages of blank verse in the Alfoxden Notebook and quickly reached perfection in *The Pedlar* (though written in the third person) completed sometime in March, and later in Wordsworth's own Conversation Poem, "Tintern Abbey" (July 1798). "Without Coleridge," Mary Jacobus claims, "Wordsworth could have written neither the great visionary poetry of *The Pedlar* nor the confessional poetry of 'Tintern Abbey.' "[23] The Conversation Poem embraced both styles of writing moving effortlessly from one to the other as it presented an experience which was to become typically Wordsworth's own. "Reflections on Having Left a Place of Retirement" (1795) was the first poem to present what Jonathan Wordsworth has called the characteristic "Wordsworthian progression from natural beauty, via a moment of deep emotion, to perception of the One Life"[24]—a movement evident in "This Lime-Tree Bower My Prison" (1797) and consistently articulated in Wordsworth's poetry of 1798.

While this "progression" firmly establishes the subjective basis of philosophic statement, it is his lyrics of the spring of 1798 that most attest to Wordsworth's mastery of this mode of subjective philosophic expression. While their simple language and ordinary everyday settings link them to Coleridge's own concern with biographical and domestic details in the Conversation Poems, lyrics such as "To My Sister," "Lines Written in Early Spring," and the paired "Expostulation and Reply" and "The Tables Turned" argue the One Life more boldly, even, than Coleridge's poems. Wordsworth presents both animate and inanimate nature as alive and full of feeling and love:

> There is a blessing in the air,
> Which seems a sense of joy to yield
> To the bare trees, and mountains bare,
> And grass in the green field.
> . . . .
> Love, now a universal birth,
> From heart to heart is stealing,
> From earth to man, from man to earth:
> —It is the hour of feeling.
>
> ("To My Sister," 5–8, 21–24)

Wordsworth claims, furthermore, that metaphysical principles informing all nature are automatically intuited via the senses:

> "The eye—it cannot choose but see;
> We cannot bid the ear be still;
> Our bodies feel, where'er they be,
> Against or with our will.
>
> "Nor less I deem that there are Powers
> Which of themselves our minds impress;
> That we can feed this mind of ours
> In a wise passiveness."
>
> ("Expostulation and Reply," 17–24)

All these philosophical ideas arise out of the excitement of the moment, or are consciously playful notions invoked to celebrate the joy of the moment. Exactly as in "The Eolian Harp," they are explanatory hypotheses or speculative propositions answering the questionings of sense or the promptings of feeling:

> The budding twigs spread out their fan,
> To catch the breezy air;
> And I must think, do all I can,
> That there was pleasure there.
>
> ("Lines Written in Early Spring," 17–20)

On the one hand, then, as these examples suggest, the poet appeals to philosophy as the authority that can explain the present moment; but on the other hand, as he applies the philosophy and examines whether experience corroborates it, he inevitably makes experience the authority—and makes philosophy that which is under question. As Keats remarks, "axioms in philosophy are not axioms until they are proved upon our pulses."[25] The text becomes the medium in which the poet tries to prove these axioms upon his pulses. Whatever its status outside the poem—"truth," axiom, or fanciful notion—philosophic theory, in entering the poem, becomes surmise, the speculation of the questioning poet responding to his senses, to external nature, in situ. It becomes a subjective utterance, conditioned by the particular situation and moment. The result, more-over, will as likely be adaptation and revision as corroboration, because proving upon the pulses may well uncover anomalies and discontinuities and urge the poet towards new theories. Process rather than product, the poem is, then, not a passive repository of experience, thought and reading, but an active medium in which all three interact creating a whole that exceeds its antecedent parts. (Hence the importance of Bloomian revisionism and the "literature-as-philoso-phy" axis of intertextuality.)

What I have outlined here not only describes how philosophy enters poetry but suggests how the poet might move from one philosophical position to an-other. Wordsworth's philosophical development is not a matter of reading one book and believing it until a more persuasive one is taken off the shelf or put into his hands, but a matter of continually testing reading, thinking and experi-ence against one another—all only finally proved upon the pulses in the writing of a poem (a proof that may well alter a belief in the very act of putting it down in writing). Wordsworth thus argues his way from one position to another through the medium of the text: that is, he *writes* his way from one position to another. Yet what the proving and re-proving upon the poetic pulses also imply is that no one position is likely to be permanent or absolute. Any "landing-place," as Coleridge calls it,[26] may be unstable; breakthroughs may cede to backsliding; an argument or a theory may be abruptly abandoned for another more agile or tantalizing; or a supposedly disproved persuasion may persist as some unacknowledged hankering, suddenly reasserting itself to disrupt newly affirmed theories. Wordsworth's philosophical development, then, by no means consists in a smooth, steady, clearly reasoned progress, but proceeds in this irregular discursive way.

The passages quoted from Wordsworth's "Prospectus" and Coleridge's *Table Talk* suggest, then, how the philosophical poem will be philosophical. Let us return to those passages to see how they synopsize the philosophical development that is my topic here as well as articulate some of the problems outlined above.

As already mentioned and as the subtitle of this book specifies, we are dealing with two very general and extensive philosophies, empiricism and tran-scendentalism, and the historical movement from the first to the second that occurred during the age and in Wordsworth's and Coleridge's careers.

Wordsworth's statement about "How exquisitely the individual Mind . . . to the external World / Is fitted" sets forth the empiricist position, more critically stated in Coleridge's version: the subject of eye, ear, touch and taste, in contact with external nature, is in danger of believing that his mind is compounded out of his senses, as if mind were simply a function or by-product of (the sensory experience of) nature. Coleridge counters this erroneous assumption with a transcendental insistence on the autonomy of an already existent mind: the mind will inform the senses and not be their compound. Wordsworth offers a less tendentious, more evenly balanced version of the same idea: "and how exquisitely, too— / Theme this but little heard of among men— / The external World is fitted to the Mind." To be sure, writing in 1832 after he had long held a distinctly Kantian position, Coleridge had the benefit of philosophical hindsight when looking back on the plans of those early years. Yet the same is also true of Wordsworth writing in 1800 in the first flush of enthusiasm for a newly won idea (he announces it as a "Theme . . . but little heard of among men"). But the counterturn of Coleridge's phrasing and the even balancing of Wordsworth's suggest that what each might propose as a simple progression from one theory to an opposite one is already threatened by the binarism in which the two theories exist in relation to one another. Coleridge's slightly waspish point about "informing the senses" and not "compounding a mind" alerts us to the persistent power of what he repudiates. Wordsworth, on the other hand, by resolving the antithesis as a both/and, half cancels the historical development in order to reinscribe the two philosophies as compatible and copresent persuasions.

Indeed, as Coleridge and Wordsworth testify, empiricism and transcendentalism, though historically consecutive, exist as a binarism, for the very sequence of their historical unfolding intimates that each is implicated in the other as an outside that makes its presence felt in the shape of the inside. Because transcendentalism superseded empiricism, the transcendental landing-place, once reached, permits one to look back and notice how transcendentalism was always implicitly present though necessarily unacknowledged. But the converse holds true as well. Empiricism persists as transcendentalism's other. Wordsworth's chiastic statement limns both possibilities—with startling consequences for his philosophical "biography." Traditionally we have had studies documenting his move from empiricism to transcendentalism,[27] but upsetting this plausible account are studies like Rader's, which argue that he was really a transcendentalist all along. I believe that Wordsworth certainly was an empiricist in the late 1790s but that his attempts to prove empiricist epistemology and metaphysics upon his pulses falter at the limits on what is as yet the transcendental outside. Traditional studies, moreover, take transcendentalism to be Wordsworth's enduring, mature position that only finally gives way to a stolid, unimaginative Christian faith. My argument here (setting aside that Christianity as another topic entirely) is that, precisely because of the fluctuations of the pulse, transcendentalism cannot prevent empiricism's disruptions: Wordsworth's philosophical development does not come to rest at transcendentalism but continues as an oscillating tension between that hard-won transcendentalism and a reemergent, reenergized, almost atavistic empiricism.

What, then, is the nature of Wordsworth's empiricism and transcendentalism? What is his understanding of these philosophies? It would seem that the best way to answer these questions is to rehearse the history of philosophy in the eighteenth century and review particular sources to show how certain theories filter down to Wordsworth while others are left out or get distorted. This approach would commit one to reading "philosophy as literature" on the way towards establishing Wordsworth's revisionary reading and rewriting—a task I eschew here (although I do offer "readings" of the philosophy at various points in the following chapters) not only because it would double the size of this book (shades of *The Recluse!*) but because the sources themselves are difficult to establish with any real certainty. As already mentioned, Wordsworth left almost no records of his reading, so that apart from the evidence of his poetry itself the only other evidence we have to go on is the books in his library at the time of its sale after his death and what we know of the undergraduate curriculum at Cambridge between 1788 and 1791 when he was a student there. Indeed, by reconstructing as far as we can Wordsworth's modes of access to philosophy we will gain a better sense of what his understanding of it might have been, since these would certainly have shaped its reception.

Although Wordsworth makes few references to the philosophy of his time, there is no reason to believe that his knowledge of it was not, in many cases, firsthand. His library (at the time of his death, at any rate) contained many works of philosophy that one might expect to see on an intellectual's shelves: for example, Plato, Aristotle, Bacon, Descartes, Leibniz, Newton, Locke, Berkeley, Hartley, Paley, Rousseau and Burke.[28] Moreover, there was in his possession one book popularizing German philosophy for an English audience, Willich's *Elements of the Critical Philosophy* (1798), which gives an accurate, succinct account of Kant's philosophy and major works in a hundred thirty pages—this book, like many others in his library, lent to him by Coleridge.[29] While we cannot know for certain whether or when he read this or other works of philosophy, we can be sure of some texts he did read—or else assimilated through general cultural osmosis. The undergraduate curriculum at Cambridge, as Ben Ross Schneider, Jr., has documented, included Newton's *Principia* and Locke's *Essay*. In the spring of 1789, at the end of Wordsworth's first year at St. John's College, "hard-working Johnians," Schneider writes, "concerned themselves with mechanics (levers, inclined planes, friction, falling bodies, and so forth), the Twenty-first Book of Livy's *History of Rome,* and Locke's *Essay on the Human Understanding.*" Wordsworth took the classics part of the June examinations, but with no records for the other subjects it is not clear "whether he read any, or all, or none of Locke's *Essay* at that time."[30] If he did not read "Locke's *Essay* when it was assigned to him, certainly at Cambridge, where Locke was the starting point of so much that was thought and said, Wordsworth could not have escaped its influence." The "materialist-mechanist Locke that he absorbed at Cambridge" would have prepared Wordsworth for Hartley's associationism (he may also have read Hartley's *Observations on Man* at Cambridge)[31] and certainly the necessitarian theory of his later Godwinism, but it would also have excluded rival philosophical traditions that he may not have become significantly acquainted with until he became friends with Coleridge in 1797, after his disengagement from Godwinism: "the arguments of the idealists and believers in innate ideas like Plato, Plotinus, the Cambridge Platonists and Berkeley, whose philosophies Locke had kept out of the Cambridge schools," and perhaps also the theories of "philosophers like Lucretius and Spinoza whose 'atheistic' concepts had been discredited at Cambridge" by Newtonian science.[32] Supplying new books and theories to support Wordsworth's growing interests, Coleridge would have emphatically broadened Wordsworth's philosophical education (the two of them doubtless arguing how materialism and mechanism might be synthesized with these various forms of idealism). Wordsworth's first-hand reading would have been considerably supplemented—and affected—by these secondary modes of mediation.

The role of Coleridge is not to be underestimated. He was a major fund of philosophical knowledge to which Wordsworth had direct, frequent access between 1797 and early 1804, when Coleridge left the Lake District to go to Malta. Coleridge would certainly have kept Wordsworth well abreast of his own philosophical development (which he recorded in his notebooks as it occurred, later turning it into an autobiography). We know that Coleridge eagerly communicated to Wordsworth his enthusiasm for Hartley and Spinoza, and he doubtless did the same for Berkeley, whom he took up in earnest in 1797, and Kant and Fichte, whom he began reading seriously in early 1801.[33] In short, it is fairly safe to say that Wordsworth's philosophical development up to 1804 is essentially Coleridge's—or at least so closely in step with it that the two made the move from empiricism to transcendentalism at the same time and together. Indeed, Wordsworth's plea in March 1804 to Coleridge (who was still in London before embarking for the Mediterranean) to send him his "notes for the Recluse" has always been interpreted as a request for the philosophy he was to write into the poem, the very urgency of his plea sounding the depth of his reliance on Coleridge's mediation.[34] That philosophy, had Coleridge sketched it out for him then, would doubtless have been Kanto-Fichtean.

With philosophy as much mediated to him by his culture and Coleridge as acquired firsthand—and then further domesticated by these conversations with Coleridge and by being proved upon the pulses of his own experience—Wordsworth developed an understanding of philosophy that seems by turns generalized, popularized, eclectic and synthetic. He may well have never really read Locke, for example, because he probably felt he did not need to (Coleridge did not study Locke's *Essay* seriously until February 1801, when Kant and Fichte had given him the required critical vantage point).[35] For Lockean theories, concepts and terms were as much part of everyone's understanding and vocabulary as are Freudian categories today (we all automatically use and understand such terms as "ego," the "unconscious," "repression," and so on). And the same would be true of other philosophies during the period: Newtonian science, of course, and possibly the barest rudiments of Berkeley's immaterialism and Hartley's associationism. Compounding together—though by no means necessarily reconciling—different ideas and theories from the various sources available to him, Wordsworth thus arrived at a popularized, generalized understanding of empiricism and transcendentalism. We can now summarize, as far as is possible, what his understanding of these philosophies was.

As will be shown in greater detail in the following chapters, empiricism, for Wordsworth, primarily means Lockean epistemology: the mechanistic psychology developed by Hartley into a thoroughgoing associationism, but also the more strictly Lockean account of sense perception involving substances, powers, primary and secondary qualities, sensations and ideas. Wordsworth subscribes in his early poetry to a passive theory of mind, largely ignoring Locke's equal emphasis on the mind's activities of reflection and judgement; but he also often insists on the necessitarianism of the Lockean-Hartleyan scheme: nature's sweet influences necessarily result in a self that is full of benign feelings and is morally good.[36] Nature is thus the source of all that is best in the self—the self being most receptive to nature during trancelike states of "wise passiveness." Wordsworth's empiricist epistemology thus tends towards a pantheist metaphysics in which the "One Life" in nature animates the self too. But sometimes a Berkeleyan strain is also evident in the metaphysics. Yet as we can see, there is so far no adequate concept of self or mind in Wordsworth's empiricism— which is precisely the problem that thwarts his poetic attempts to prove this epistemology and metaphysics on his pulses.

Transcendentalism offers answers to these problems, and we can see Wordsworth moving towards this position as he strives to elaborate empiricism. The mind's activity keeps asserting itself even if Wordsworth has no theory to accommodate it: it interferes with "wise passiveness" and brings trancelike moments to an end. In time, Wordsworth comes to recognize this activity as "creative sensibility," "a plastic power," "An auxiliar light" (*Prel*, 2. 387–97), from which he develops a workable theory of mind. His language and understanding may still be Lockean-empiricist, but they increasingly cede to more Kantian formulations. His transcendentalism consists first, then, in a theory of the mind's projective, creative power: the mind can not only "inform" the senses but direct them, making the external world fit its categories. This leads to a Kantian emphasis on the mind's architectonic structure, its a priori form, and to a more Platonic interest in the possibility of an a priori content. It also leads to speculation about another transcendent realm and more openly theological issues such as God and the immortality of the soul (as the Immortality Ode and the later poetry will show).[37] More immediately, Wordsworth's projectivist epistemology and metaphysics of the a priori switch the emphasis from nature and the senses to the mind, its autonomy and its separation from nature. In turn, these tendencies carry Wordsworth to a post-Kantian interest in the mind's essential "infinity" and in a nature made real again and equally infinite when seen to be the positing of a mindlike power.[38]

To summarize (and oversimplify), empiricism tends to reify nature and the senses, encourage belief in pantheism and the mind's ideal passivity. Transcendentalism reverses these tendencies, asserting a more capable theory of mind and its activity and casting nature less as "Life" or sensory surface than as a function and realization of mind. Furthermore, the binaristic interplay of empiricism and transcendentalism results in a dialectical argument that at times seems remarkably simple but that never reaches synthetic closure; instead, the tensions reinstate themselves, prompting Wordsworth to favor by turns one tendency over another, or let the tension persist unresolved, or abandon his argument altogether. That is, while empiricism turns the object, nature, into a subject so that it can constitute the self as a subject, transcendentalism counters (but repeats the process) by having the self as subject constitute the object—and constitute it as a subject. The dialectical argument here (and pursued through *The Prelude*) effectively reduces to a debate about subject/object priority, about which is prior to and constitutes the other (a problem that forms the centerpiece of chapter 12 of Coleridge's *Biographia Literaria* and in precisely these terms). The synthetic goal would seem to be the subject/subject resolution offered as analogy and "Resemblance" (*Prel,* 13. 87) in the Snowdon episode in the final book of *The Prelude,* and the mutual "fit" of the Crossing the Alps sequence in book 6, where the mind's efforts are usurped by the apparent "workings of one mind" in nature (*Prel,* 6. 578). But such transcendentalist resolutions founder, precisely because the object—phenomenal nature, sensory surface—at a certain point disrupts the subject/subject parity, its otherness challenging the sameness that transcendentalism would affirm. Appealed to as corroborative evidence and yet resisting conformity to the subject's schema, nature, in its sheer phenomenality, revives an empiricist attraction to the external object as origin. The result, as can be seen in *The Excursion,* with which I conclude this study, is a binarism that in circular fashion reproduces and reinscribes itself.

The chapters that follow trace in greater detail Wordsworth's engagement with empiricism and transcendentalism and the argument that develops in the philosophical poems written between 1798, when empiricism, pantheism and

Coleridge first inspired him to write a certain kind of philosophical poetry, and 1814, when, in *The Excursion,* transcendentalism on the one hand evolved into religious belief but on the other gave way to a new, thoroughgoing empiricism.

1

Inarticulateness and the Language of Nature: The Alfoxden and Christabel Notebooks

Quoting in a letter to Thelwall the climactic moment from "This Lime-Tree Bower My Prison," Coleridge complains that "It is but seldom that I raise & spiritualize my being to this height."[1] As Jonathan Wordsworth comments, "Coleridge had evolved the doctrine of the One Life, and had pointed the way toward 'Tintern Abbey'; but . . . it was left to Wordsworth to write the great poetry of response and mystical perception."[2] Inaugurated in the Alfoxden Notebook (January–March 1798), this "great poetry" culminates immediately in *The Pedlar* (March 1798). A few months later, it becomes the medium for sustained self-reflection in "Tintern Abbey" (July 1798), an achievement which sets the scene for autobiography proper in *The Prelude*. Developing the specific set of concerns fully elaborated in the thirteen-book *Prelude* of 1805, the Notebook fragments, *The Pedlar,* and "Tintern Abbey" delineate the steady evolution of Wordsworth's characteristic philosophic mode: a blank-verse form of meditation exploring self and nature and their interaction.

The scattered, fragmentary passages of blank verse in the Alfoxden Notebook show Wordsworth, as Geoffrey Hartman observes, "recording various impressions in situ: the fragments indicate that a present sensation has become the matter of his song. It is perhaps the first time a poet has kept his eye so steadily on the object (which is also a subject, himself) and attempted a direct transcription of his personal response to nature." The variety of his response allows Wordsworth to formulate the beginnings of a theoretical understanding of self and nature, and the modes of their interaction. In particular, Hartman argues, he "begins to see some of the 'curious links' mediating between his present emotion and the past. Even while he tries to seize a present joy, an understanding grows in him of the role of the involuntary memory, and he is led to introspection."[3] At Alfoxden, Wordsworth "learns that the present depends deeply on the past." He discovers that the continuity of the self is based in memory—"a discovery," according to Hartman, "which made *The Prelude* possible."[4]

The discovery, however, first made *The Pedlar* and "Tintern Abbey" possible. Wordsworth's exploration of the memory and of his response to nature gives him a sense of the self's "powers and habits,"[5] from which he develops an ideal theory of personal growth. Consolidating the insights and incipient theories of the Notebook fragments, Wordsworth organizes them into a full-scale biography in *The Pedlar,* in which he recounts the childhood and youth of the narrator of the already-written *Ruined Cottage.* In "Tintern Abbey," Wordsworth starts applying the insights and theories to himself. Focusing on the present moment and a particular moment in the past, he learns not only just how deeply the present depends on the past but how closely his own "powers and habits" are linked to his responses to nature and to perception of the One Life. Although these latter emphases suggest the poem's connections to *The Pedlar,* Wordsworth's anxious questioning of past and present (and future) anticipates the sustained autobiographical enterprise of *The Prelude.*

Perception and response, present and past, memory, nature, and the One Life all pose problems even as Wordsworth organizes them into manageable theories. For experience puts in his way counterexamples that he must somehow incorporate into his scheme. Response to nature often fails because of some sudden wilful tendency in the self or because nature suddenly seems like a blank, inanimate surface. At one time the One Life will seem like a true intimation of an unknown autonomous power; at another time it seems simply a wilful human fiction. Memory fades, or the past can be recalled only indistinctly. The present may usurp or even rewrite the past; or memory may be so strong as to direct perception of the present absolutely. All these differing possibilities emerge at various moments in this poetry of 1798, pushing Wordsworth in new directions, sometimes into inconsistent positions, but causing him always to revise as he sees the implications of his arguments. We should therefore interpret the inconsistencies, turns and counterturns as landing-places in his larger philosophical development.

Philosophically, the inconsistencies trace an increasing tension, in its most general terms, between epistemology and metaphysics, between what the mind knows and how it knows. Intuitions of the One Life in nature or of the meaning of nature's "language" will often get Wordsworth speculating about the workings of his own mind in such a way as to undercut his initial metaphysical claim. Conversely, "what" may overrule "how" when he passionately affirms a belief against all explanatory odds. Such epistemological problems also affect less local issues. They call into question larger teleological claims about design and purpose in nature, its "guidance" of the human self, or the relation of means to ends in the self's development.

In general, in the poetry of 1798, problems arise as Wordsworth seeks to elaborate empiricist theories of mind and nature and the pantheism to which he links them. Discovering that theory often exceeds, falls short of, or fails to square with, experience, he implicitly opens the way towards transcendentalism as he exposes the inadequacies of empiricism. These philosophical developments are discernible in the Notebook fragments that inaugurate Wordsworth's career as a philosophical poet. If the One Life is at the center of "the great poetry of response and mystical perception" and is the signal philosophical belief behind *The Pedlar* and "Tintern Abbey," the Notebook fragments in many ways preempt their achievement not only by examining the epistemological errancy that interferes with receptivity to the One Life but by positing the One Life simultaneously with that errancy.[6] Although his writing implicitly half-compromises the One Life from the start, Wordsworth does not fully recognize or address the issue until "Tintern Abbey." These experimental, exploratory fragments are thus philosophically more important than they may seem.

The fragments of philosophic blank verse in the Alfoxden Notebook (and in the Christabel Notebook, which I discuss here too) consistently present Wordsworth in a characteristic "stance of surmise."[7] They present him, as Geoffrey Hartman has observed, in situ in nature and engaged in speculation about nature and its influence on the self. As he moves from fragment to fragment, Wordsworth sets down—in a random, unsystematic, revisionary way—the fundamentals of his epistemology and metaphysics, formulating positions analogous to those he will develop in *The Prelude*. Whether written in the third person (and intended for *The Pedlar*) or the first person, the Notebook fragments not only give a preliminary sketch of Wordsworth's future preoccupations, but in many ways encapsulate the subsequent course of his career, thus affording a surprisingly comprehensive glimpse of the future "range of Wordsworth's vision."[8]

Most of the passages of philosophic blank verse in the Alfoxden Notebook describe instances of sense perception in a "presentational" mode, as Paul Sheats has called it,[9] that strives to render the experience as faithfully as possible. Concern with epistemological accuracy leads Wordsworth to specify all the circumstances contributing to the event: the condition of the perceiving subject, his attitude, degree of receptivity, the effect of the object, and so on:

> There would he stand
>   still
> ~~Beneath~~ In the ~~warm~~ covert of some [?lonesome] rock
>   Or
> Would gaze upon the moon untill its light
> Fell like a strain of music on his soul
> And seem'd to sink into his very heart.[10]

At first, it seems that Wordsworth is emphasizing the effect of sense perception on the self, for the synaesthetic description of moonlight falling "like a strain of music on his soul" adequately captures the perceiver's enchantment. Equally, as the moonlight continues to fall—*through* his soul, it seems—and "sink into his very heart," we realize that effect has carried into the "self-discovery" Hartman mentions. An unknown depth in the self has been discovered as the moonlight penetrates to the center of the perceiver's being, his *"very* heart" (emphasis added).[11] Yet this fragment describes more than only the effect of sense perception. Comparing the falling moonlight to a strain of music defines the moonlight as an object, its ethereality and elusiveness; while the details of the plot ("There would he stand . . . Or / Would gaze . . . untill . . .") specify the determining conditions: intentional activity yielding on the "untill" to passive receptivity.[12]

It is precisely this balance between activity and passivity that Wordsworth explores in a passage on the following page of the Notebook, as if the implication of these lines had suddenly become apparent to him:

> [T]here is a holy indolence
> compared to which our best activity
> Is oftimes deadly bane
>   They rest upon their oars
> Float down the mighty stream of tendency
> In the calm mood of holy indolence
> A most wise passiveness in which the heart
> Lies open and is well content to feel
> As nature feels and to receive her shapes
> As she has made them.
>
>   (16ʳ)

Wordsworth explicitly pits activity against passivity, and ascribes a different moral value to each state. His basically epistemological concern—how best to be receptive to nature—assumes a teleological dimension as he weighs the merits of means to ends: "They rest upon their oars / Float down the mighty stream of tendency." The "holy indolence," the "most wise passiveness," that he values as superior to "our best activity," is not a neutral epistemological state, therefore, but is itself motivated by an active intentionality. "Passiveness" constitutes a level of activity in that it must be intentionally achieved by the stilling of "best activity" and then maintained. The original dichotomy between activity and passivity is really a continuum, for one merges imperceptibly into the other. Indeed, it seems that it is only by stressing "wise," "best" and "deadly," which establish the *degree* of passivity and activity and their *distance* from one another on the scale, that passivity is kept from evolving into the activity that threatens it. How best to be receptive to nature is situated here by its negative, which it implies and attempts to ward off. The last four lines of the fragment imply that the heart very often does not lie open or feel as nature feels. Such counterpositions turn out to be not only a threat but the rule rather than the exception.

A complex description of sense perception is already beginning to emerge. We can tell that the various instances of sense perception in the Notebooks—such as gazing on the moon—constitute examples of "wise passiveness"; but as Wordsworth moves to consider them theoretically he discusses them in context of an implied wider range of perceptions that show an inhibition of response. More often, it seems the self interferes with or distorts a process that otherwise would be simple and straightforward, a direct influx of nature's forms into the self.

Direct influx, Locke's model of elementary perception, is the paradigm here. The inhibiting or distorting activity is presumably a product of the secondary qualities, as Locke calls them, which do not yield an "adequate idea" or "resemblance" of sensible phenomena.[13] Whether or not Wordsworth is actually invoking Locke, he has implicitly located something problematic about the self in its ability to obscure, transform, or block out altogether what is outside itself: nature's forms. In later fragments in the Notebook, Wordsworth will focus on this problematic barrier, but at this point his interest is more practical. He wants the outside to find unhampered access to the inside, the self.

But more is implied in the concept of direct influx, of receiving nature's shapes as she has made them, than only the idea of perception freed from distortions. Equally important, influx implies that nature is already complete in itself and that the self it affects is subordinate and secondary to it—a situation that suspends the general rule even as it names it: for all too often, it seems the self feels oblivious to nature. The lines immediately following those on "wise passiveness" give an example of an ideal, undistorted influx issuing from a self-complete nature:

> The mountain's outline and its steady form[?s]
> Gave simple grandeur to his mind nor less
> The changeful language of its countenance
> Gave movement to his thoughts and multitude
> With order and relation.

$$(16^r)$$

Nature imparts its own inherent qualities to the self: "grandeur," and "movement . . . multitude . . . order and relation." These qualities are as much substantive as formal, emanating as much from "shape" or "form" as from "outline." They thus give a form as well as a content to a consciousness that otherwise would be empty. And they constitute a self that not only feels as nature feels but even thinks as nature speaks.

These lines occur again in expanded form slightly later in the Notebook, where they appear as the concluding portion of a lengthy passage articulating a "discovery" that, more than any other in either Notebook, constitutes a founding insight of *The Prelude.* It is here that Wordsworth distinctly learns how "deeply the present depends on the past." Wordsworth obviously appreciated the significance of this passage in that he incorporated the first half of it into book 2 of *The Prelude* and used the concluding portion (containing the lines above) as a transition to close book 7 and lead into book 8. Furthermore, in MS. D of *The Ruined Cottage,* in which *The Pedlar* stands as an autonomous poem, this passage is also accorded that privileged status, where it is written out in fair copy and entitled "Fragment."[14]

This "Fragment" (beginning on 20ʳ in the Alfoxden Notebook) recapitulates and conflates some of the instances of sense perception recorded so far in the Notebook, but it becomes evident that it is not the phenomena of nature per se, its "shapes" or "forms," that command Wordsworth's attention but the "power" they communicate:

> he wanderd there
> In storm and tempest and beneath the beam
> Of quiet moons he wandered there and there
> Would feel whateer there is of power in sound,
> To breathe an elevated mood, by form
> Or image unprofaned—there would he stand
> Beneath some rock, listening to sounds that are
> The ghostly language of the antient earth
> Or make their dim abode in distant winds
> Thence did he drink the visionary power . . .
>
> (20ʳ)

In calling natural phenomena "shapes" and "forms," as he has consistently done so far, Wordsworth reduces the diversity of phenomenal content to its merest schematic outline. Here he furthers that tendency by emphasizing the nonrepresentational nature of sound, thus approximating understanding and response to immediate intuition. Sound here is merely the medium, the vehicle to convey power. Its adequacy, almost its transparency, is evident in that the self feels *"whateer* there is of power in sound, / To breathe an elevated mood" (emphasis added). All the power there is in sound the self feels; no power is lost in the transmission—as equally no power is lost in the reception, for the resultant "elevated mood" is "by form / Or image unprofaned," which might dissipate the power or append it to the more fixed forms of visual representations.

Even if sound is essentially nonrepresentational in character, it is nevertheless a signifying medium: Wordsworth calls sound "The ghostly language of the antient earth." The metaphor contains considerable implications. In calling the language "ghostly," Wordsworth implies that it is not only disembodied, emanating from an unapparent source (like those sounds which "make their dim abode in distant winds"), but supernatural as well. And in calling its speaker "antient," he also implies that the language is primordial, as if it were a dead language of antiquity that, unknown to Wordsworth until this moment, had continued to be spoken. In the mouth of the speaker, the earth, the language is obviously an efficient medium of expression. But to the ears of this attentive listener it is almost unintelligible. Meaning, syntax and grammar (as well as history and origin) are all obscure to him. As a signifying medium, sound is therefore opaque, despite its adequacy in conveying "power."

On the same page on which Wordsworth writes the first drafts of this passage he also writes some fragmentary lines that gropingly attempt to capture the physical phenomenon behind the notion that sound is a language making its dim abode in distant winds:

> Oh listen listen how ~~sounds~~ that wind away
> While the last touch they le[?vae] upon the sense
> Tells they [?have]
>   the firs
> ~~Hush they are coming—[?they] have passd~~
> ~~And [?run]~~

(15ᵛ)

The syntactical incompleteness of these lines may evidence the quick impulse of the creative flow,[15] but it also shows surmise stopping short before being able to specify any meaning: "listen how sounds that wind away" do what? "While the last touch they [leave] upon the sense / Tells they [have]" what? Wordsworth can indicate only *how* and not *what*. He can roughly indicate tendency (they "wind away," they leave) and origin ("they are coming they have passd the firs"), and he knows that sounds amount to speech ("the last touch they [leave] upon the sense / Tells they [?have]"); but he cannot catch the meaning—just as he cannot, as it were, catch the sounds themselves. They come out of the distance, pass over the firs and vanish before he has a chance to understand.[16]

The revised version of these lines in the fragment "In Storm and Tempest" preserves precisely this sense of marveling at "power" while being unable to specify meaning or content. The listener can assert that sounds are a language, but it is the "power" in sounds that really rivets his attention. As a system of signs, sounds constitute a language whose meanings he does not understand— although the differentials of their power he understands very readily. He certainly understands the "how," even if he does not understand the "what"—that is, the ostensible content, the accessible meanings into which this "language" might translate.

Yet translation, in fact, is precisely what all these passages are about: a translation of "power" into "grandeur" and "elevated mood" via a medium which Wordsworth predominantly conceives to be a language. Although the language is obscure to him, Wordsworth succeeds in translating "whateer" he understands of it into subjective feeling. This translation triggers an important self-discovery in this fragment, for as he recalls "these fleeting moods / Of shadowy exaltation" he now perceives the ramifications of "power" in the self. He now sees how the past is connected to the present, and hence the present to the future—an insight into the history and continuity of the self that certainly constitutes a cornerstone of *The Prelude*. Yet, equally important, Wordsworth now applies to the self the same heuristic process he has implicitly applied so far only to nature. Although he actually broaches here the operative distinction between "how" and "what," he has implicitly deployed it already in calling nature's sounds a language that he finds obscure. In this fragment "In Storm and Tempest," he now finds that the combination of the unintelligible with the more intelligible characterizes not only external nature but the self too. The soul can remember only "how she felt" and not "what she felt"—just as the listening self understands the power in sound but cannot make sense of any more of nature's language:

> I deem not profitless these fleeting moods of
> Of shadowy exaltation not for this
>
> That they are kindred to our purer mind
> And intellectual life but that the soul
> Remembring how she felt but what she felt
> Remembring not retains an obscure sense
> Of possible sublimity at which her [—?—]
> ~~Een from the very dimness of the [?things]~~
> With growing faculties she [?doth] aspire
> With facu l still growing, feeling still
> That whatsoever point they Gain, There still
> Is something to pursue.
>
> (20^r)

The soul's ability to remember only "how she felt" and not "what she felt" testifies to the preeminence of "power" over the contingent medium conveying it, the ghostly language attentively heard but not understood. Power has been Wordsworth's overriding objective, so that the function of the medium and its nature as a "what" have been entirely subordinated to their capacity to communicate power. Yet if function and nature have been subordinated, they have by no means been delimited or circumscribed. The phenomenon of sound, the play of its language, presents itself as always in excess of its communicative function; correlatively, the "what" that the soul does not remember is an implanted trace that continues to reside in the soul after yielding up its impulse of power.[17] Play and trace, the phenomenon and the unremembered "what" it deposits, directly contribute to the "obscure sense / Of possible sublimity" even if, again, it is "how," the way in which power elaborates in the soul, that ostensibly generates this "sense." Wordsworth's understanding of "how," of the mechanics of epistemological process, makes him understand how previously experienced sublimity is again possible. But "possible" also carries another meaning; it generously allows for a sublimity not (yet) known and not (yet) understood, and perhaps exceeding the sublimity experienced so far. Its as-yet-undetermined measure coordinates with what is not understood, not grasped in the play of the ghostly language Wordsworth hears. The deleted line firmly hints at this: "Een from the very dimness of the things"—as if it were the "dimness" of nature's language provoking the attempt at possible sublimity, a dimness referring both to the elusiveness of the language and to the "what" retained in the soul along with the better-remembered "how" overshadowing it (and, perhaps, also referring to sounds' "dim abode in distant winds"). The project of aspiring after sublimity becomes, then, not only that of feeling an "elevated mood" once more, a reactivation of power, but equally that of comprehending the lexicon of nature's language, of bringing "dimness" into the light of understanding.

The soul, then, aspires at "what": at sounds, at their language, and at the "what" they leave behind in the self. In this project, the understanding gains competence as it gains an increasing familiarity with "how," the workings of power that the soul remembers. Power and the memory of "how" foster the development of faculties. The self's "powers and habits," whose growth becomes the overt subject of *The Pedlar* and *The Prelude,* are seeded by repeated experiences of nature's power and nourished by recollection of the ways in which "how" subsequently elaborates in the self after the original "influence" (20^v, line 4) has passed. But although "how" now efficiently helps the self to understand "what," it never fully coordinates with it: the soul feels "still / That whatsoever point they [i.e., the faculties] Gain, / There still / Is something to pursue." The play of the language of sounds, the "what" of its meanings, continues to elude comprehension, and therefore powerfully augurs still more possible sublimity, even though the self may feel it now understands more of the lexicon than before.

Quite clearly, what this passage is focusing on is the play between retention and erosion. If Wordsworth discovers here the power of memory and how deeply the present depends upon the past, he nevertheless already knows how ephemeral, if not rare, these kinds of experience are that have afforded him insight and given him his obscure sense of possible sublimity. The trouble with fleeting moods of shadowy exaltation is that they are fleeting and shadowy. Wordsworth even begins to disparage them in favor of a more substantial, more lasting response:

```
                              But from these haunts
                    lonesome
              Of u̶n̶t̶a̶m̶e̶d̶ nature he had skill to draw
              A better & less transitory power


                    n  ⎫
              an i [?f] ⎬  fluence now he drew a better power
                    habitual
                 less transient   n ⎫
              An influence more permanet ⎬  t.
```

(20ᵛ)

In promoting this "better & less transitory power," this "influence more permanent," Wordsworth returns from sound to sight. The source of this power will not be eroded, the influence of the power on the self can be infinitely renewed, because the power derives from what Wordsworth calls in the 1800 preface to *Lyrical Ballads* an "hourly communicat[ion] with the best objects."[18] In this way, Wordsworth succeeds in coordinating "exaltation" and "sublimity" with the "habitual"—and even in grounding them in it, for the "habitual" elicits a response comparable to that elicited by the "transitory":

```
                              To his mind
              The mountain's outline and its steady form
              Gave simple grandeur and its presence shaped
              The measure and the prospect of his soul
              To majesty, such virtue had these forms
              Perennial of the aged hills nor less
              The changeful language of their countenance
              Gave movement to his thoughts and multitude
              With order & relation.
```

(20ᵛ)

"Grandeur" and "majesty" correlate with "shadowy exaltation" and "sublimity." "Simple grandeur" is something given, a content imbued by direct influx. But it communicates almost as much a sense of "how" as of "what" in that it resembles a "mood of shadowy exaltation," though of a distinctly moral kind. Even less contentlike, but equally as moral in its essentially teleological character, is the "majesty" to which the mountain's "presence shaped / The measure and the prospect of his soul." This quite closely coordinates with "possible sublimity" in that it demarcates the range of what there is to pursue— and which the self has, in part, already gained.

This passage is, of course, a slightly expanded (and reordered) version of the one on 16ʳ. But in its context in "In Storm and Tempest," and in particular in featuring as part of an argument on nature's language and its effect on the self, the passage now yields an altogether more complex account of influx than earlier in the Notebook, where it illustrated a straightforward case of receiving nature's shapes as she has made them. Admittedly, the implication of these lines is that the mind does not of itself possess "simple grandeur" or "majesty." These it must be given by nature. But insofar as nature is a source outside the self of what comes to constitute its inner being, it ceases to be an exclusively independent phenomenon and instead becomes a kind of supplementary extension of the self.[19] Outward "forms" supply the self with its own inner form; but the self perceives what it discovers to be its own form as already present in, or inscribed on, outward nature first. "The mountain's outline and its steady form," its "presence," function as an outer limit of the extent or range of the self, so that "The measure and the prospect of [the] soul," "shaped . . . To majesty" by the mountain, appear to be both external and internal, both literal and figurative.

Moreover, insofar as the "aged hills" exhibit on their "countenance" a "changeful language," they appear to be a writing that the self reads, an inscription in which it reads itself. The "movement . . . multitude . . . order & relation" that this "changeful language" "gives" to the self's "thoughts" become the spatialization—and temporalization—outside the self of a process, a consciousness, conducted inside. The changeful language of the aged hills writes down "With order & relation" the "thoughts" that, up to that moment of perception, are disorderly in the self. In nature, the self reads what it is thinking. Self-consciousness, "thoughts," a silent, internal hearing-oneself-speak, depends, then, on reading what one *is* to speak. What the self speaks (silently to itself in the form of "thoughts") it first of all reads.[20]

Language is a recurrent metaphor for nature not only in this fragment and in others in the Notebooks but throughout Wordsworth's poetry. Nature is either speech which the self hears or writing which it reads. But what the self hears or reads, as this passage reveals, is a text whose sense and referentiality are constituted by the self alone. The outward phenomenon of sound and the "changeful" play of light and shade on the hillsides are no more than a temporal or spatial series of marks displaying differential force. It is the auditor/perceiver who interprets them as exhibiting the spacing, structure and systematic features of a language. Nature provides no more than the marks composing the text: no more, that is, than "movement . . . multitude . . . order & relation." The auditor/perceiver contributes the meaning—or, as Wordsworth says, the "thoughts."

In this passage, then, nature is a supplement of the self, existing in the same relation to it as does writing to speech, as an outside to an inside.[21] This inevitably changes the nature of influx, however, for it is clear now that the flow from outside to inside involves a simultaneous commutation of inside to outside. By the same token, these instances of "wise passiveness" conceal the self's implicit activity. In the first part of the fragment Wordsworth mentions that "Thence did he *drink* the visionary power" (emphasis added), while in the transition to these lines on grandeur and majesty he stresses that the self "had *skill to draw"* (emphasis added) the "better & less transitory power" that mountain and hills offer. Not only is a level of intentional activity presumed as the precondition of "influx," but the influx itself, when it occurs, also implements the self's intentional activity. Influx itself essentially constitutes an act of reading (or hearing): the self coordinates movement, multitude, order and relation outside with the flow of "thoughts" inside—just as, earlier, it studiously extracted power from sound. The concept of language, then, which appears to be an innocent enough metaphor to apply to the play of natural phenomena, actually alters the epistemological configuration, creating a double action where previously it had seemed there was only a single one.

As an outside to an inside, nature's "language" in relation to the self's "thoughts" is a "what" that still remains obscure even after the self has derived from it, or correlated with it, its own more determinate sense of "how": moods of exaltation, grandeur, or majesty. This the fragment "In Storm and Tempest" has emphasized throughout. Yet while the metaphor of language has increasingly revealed the interdependence of inside and outside and the supplementarity of self and nature, it has nevertheless resulted in a reduction of the concept of nature, even if it began by enlarging it. Nature may be less the articulate speaker presenting an almost human "countenance" and voice than it at first seemed to be. It may, in fact, be no more than simple outward substance, inarticulate and nonsignifying in itself. Such a possibility is always implicit but it pointedly haunts several of the fragments following "In Storm and Tempest" in the Alfoxden Notebook. Attempting to ward off this problematic reduction of nature, Wordsworth asserts all the more emphatically the need to perceive nature as an articulate speaker, or at least as an entity approximating intelligible human form in its intrinsic attributes.

Two passages immediately following the conclusion of "In Storm and Tempest," though unrelated to it, develop the notion that an interdependence between inside and outside necessarily underlies the functioning of language:

> Why is it we feel
> So little for each other but for this
> That we with nature have no sympathy
> Or with such things as have no power to hold
> Articulate language
> . . . .
> And never for each other shall we feel
> [?find]
> As we may feel till we ~~have~~ sympathy
> With nature in her forms inanimate
> [?If ?such ?]

> With objects such as have no power to hold
> Articulate language. In all forms of things
> There is a mind

(20^v, 21^r)

Wordsworth makes sympathy between people dependent on sympathy "With nature in her forms inanimate / With objects such as have no power to hold /Articulate language." But sympathy explicitly includes the idea of linguistic communication, of speaking, hearing and understanding. If nature's "forms inanimate" are inarticulate, they are not without language. They only "have no power to hold / *Articulate* language" (emphasis added): that is, they cannot speak, although, presumably, they "have . . . power to" hear and understand, for, as Wordsworth states in conclusion, "In all forms of things / There is a mind."[22] Wordsworth thus conceives of sympathy as an intersubjective language dependent on an outward *substance* which does not immediately seem to signify or communicate. In fact, sympathy is not possible, Wordsworth declares in the second fragment, until "inanimate" nature is included in the circle of intersubjectivity. His conditional yet categorical way of stating his point argues that the failure of sympathy directly results not only from failing to include "inanimate" external nature but from failing to see that it does indeed signify.

A third passage shows Wordsworth exploring a corollary of the notion that "In all forms of things / There is a mind." Here, however, he does not so much surmise the presence of life or speech in the apparently inanimate or inarticulate as body forth a cosmic sense of connectedness out of airy nothing:

> Of unknown modes of being which on earth
> Or in the heavens or in the heavens & earth
> Exist by mighty combinations, bound
> Together by a link, & with a soul
> Which makes all, one.

(21^r)

What might be designated the indeterminate or inarticulate in other fragments discussed so far Wordsworth construes here as "unknown modes of being." Yet in attempting to body them forth via a basically Lockean rhetoric of modes and combinations, link and soul,[23] plurality and unity, he imparts to them quite a specific degree of metaphysical determination, for this rhetoric amounts to a "how" that allows surmise of "what." "Combinations," "link" and "soul" suggest that these modes of being are determinate in both a metaphysical and teleological sense—as if, supernatural as well as natural, they not only possess organization and design, but have been created to perform some secret ministry which may well become more palpable. Yet these unknown modes of being are determinate only to an extent: they remain an unknown "what" that can be grasped only in terms of "how," Wordsworth's sense of structure and organization.

By surmising that "In all forms of things / There is a mind," by surmising that there are "unknown modes of being" that exist in a certain way, Wordsworth can rescue "nature in her forms inanimate" from indeterminacy and inarticulateness. The One Life, which these surmises approximate and introduce, can be regarded as a metaphysical resolution that completes (and grounds) the epistemological project of understanding nature. Yet metaphysical resolutions of this kind—that is, surmises which imbue an obscure "what" with a determinate metaphysical content—transgress beyond the proper scope of epistemology, because a nonsignifying inarticulateness will continue to present itself to the self, making indeterminacy unavoidable and irreducible. The supplementarity between self and nature, the efficacy of language, of hearing, speaking and writing all depend, as we have seen, on the very existence of an outward that is nonsignifying in itself but whose play can be made to signify because it submits to (or accords with) human categories of "order & relation" and "thought." At the same time, this play is also always in excess of, and eluding, human system; a large measure of it cannot be determined. As the foundation upon which the self rears its human structures, the indeterminate and the nonsignifying at once constitute the ontological premise of their possibility and delimit their range and efficacy. Signification is always circumscribed in scope—while the nonsignifying, the indeterminate, the inarticulate, appears, in contrast, unlimited.

Even so, the heuristic strategies Wordsworth has engaged for epistemologically facing inanimate, inarticulate nature have succeeded to some degree in pushing back the margins of the indeterminate and rendering the inarticulate articulate. Through "how," as we have seen, Wordsworth has constituted "what." Hearing a "language," he constitutes nature as its speaker and ascribes to it an articulateness that it might otherwise lack. But hearing this language also suggests to him something of the constitution of the hearer, as "In Storm and Tempest" has already shown. The strategies for describing nature thus illuminate the self as well, since the hearer's inarticulateness is dispelled by hearing this language and his original visionary blankness is changed into visionary competence as nature teaches him the grammar of the sublime. In fact, the metaphor of language constitutes the hearer in precisely the same way as it constitutes the speaker. For in the self as well as in nature the articulate shades into the inarticulate, the determinate into the indeterminate, "how" into "what."

An important passage on 21ᵛ, on the next leaf after the lines on "unknown modes of being," directly focuses on the way in which the determinate opens onto "unknown modes of being" in the self. The self-discovery here is comparable to that in "In Storm and Tempest," except that this fragment treats explicitly some of the notions and processes featuring only implicitly in the earlier fragment. If "In Storm and Tempest" reveals influx to be a two-way process, this fragment begins exploring that notion by presenting the "ebb & flow" of consciousness as the self responds to external nature. The double action Wordsworth describes here gives a more complex account of supplementarity by focusing on the way the self rather than nature is constituted by the process. Yet at the same time, this fragment returns to a more straightforward notion of influx—largely, perhaps, because Wordsworth eschews the suggestive metaphor of language in favor of the stricter, more philosophical vocabulary of epistemology. In many ways, this passage could easily serve as a classic illustration of sense perception in Locke or Hume—as equally its present-tense description closely resembles the beginning of a Coleridgean Conversation Poem. Indeed, Coleridge's doctrine of the One Life features here again, but this time epistemologically rather than metaphysically: as something sensed via the medium of an all-pervasive "consciousness of life," a "life" that Wordsworth does not posit so much as discover through sense experience:

> To gaze
> On that green hill and on those scattered trees
> And feel a pleasant consciousness of life
> In the [?impression] of that loveliness
> Untill the sweet sensation called the mind
> ~~Into itself and all external things~~
> [?So]?
> Into itself by image from without
> Unvisited: and all her reflex powers
> Wrapp'd in a still dream forgetfullness
>
> I lived without the knowledge that I lived
> Then by those beauteous forms brought back again
> To lose myself again as if my life
> Did ebb & flow with a strange mystery

(21ᵛ)

The passage opens with a verbal flux which does not specify but only implies a perceiving self. The sense of suspension and vague unattachment this creates is pertinent, in that the epistemological presentation Wordsworth is concerned to give discloses the process whereby influx leads to self-discovery. Although he begins by indicating the outward objects of perception, his focus shifts immediately to their effect on the self, to what amounts to a subjective definition of the contents of influx: "a pleasant consciousness of life / In the impression of that loveliness." The "life" of which he is conscious is presumably that pervading "green hill" and "scattered trees," and is therefore a manifestation of the One Life—although "life" could be inner as much as outer too, implying (or at least prefiguring) the particular consciousness of self Wordsworth describes in the concluding four lines of the fragment. The determinate contents of influx—"consciousness of life," "impression of that loveliness," "sweet sensation"—conduct to a state of indeterminacy: mind "called . . . Into itself by image from without / Unvisited." This movement is familiar from previous fragments. As in the passage on 15^r and in "In Storm and Tempest," a determinate sense of "how," which the self extracts from external nature, results in a "what" that cannot be fully articulated, either because it is not remembered, or because it "still / Is something to pursue," a phenomenon felt to be meaningful but from which no determinate meaning can (as yet) be drawn. As before, "how" results in "an obscure sense," but one that does not yield ostensible content or "thoughts" but mind in itself emptied of content or "thoughts."

At first, the description of mind called into itself appears to corroborate a Lockean theory of mind.[24] Certainly this passage gives onto a peculiar blankness of mind, which is as far as the empiricist theory of mind can go. But Wordsworth's description presses beyond Lockean empiricism. He annexes this unknown mode of being by presenting it as the indeterminate continuation of the determinate. What is significant about this fragment in context of Wordsworth's philosophical position in 1798 is that it strives to deliver what is explicitly transcendental in almost the strict Kantian meaning of the term. Mind called into itself by image from without unvisited approximates, as it were, the a priori "what" that constitutes the mind before sense experience fills it with content—that is, something like pure mind, or the nature of mind in itself.[25] Like Kant, too, Wordsworth recognizes that this blankness does not, strictly speaking, amount to an object of experience; it is something which can be "thought" or "intuited" in only an "empty" or "blind" way.[26] It can be described more adequately in the negative rather than the positive—and only from the outside, not the inside.

Even more pointedly than other fragments discussed so far (including the final section of "In Storm and Tempest"), this fragment is concerned with outside and inside and the movement from one to the other. And here Wordsworth carries that movement farther inside than he does in other fragments in the Notebook, thereby showing how the outside becomes an inside and the inside an outside. This is evident in the way sensation mediates external nature to the self. Hill and trees are the originating outside, but Wordsworth describes them as subjective sense impressions. Yet "Impression," like "pleasant consciousness of life," constitutes an outside with respect to its object, hill and trees—as equally it then evolves into an outside with respect to the self, as Wordsworth becomes conscious of and savors the sweet sensation, loveliness and life. In this one movement, outside turns into inside but this inside then becomes an outside (as mind withdraws from its sensations into itself). In fact, this movement leaves the conscious self on the outside too as the influx continues toward the deeper inside of mind called into itself.

Sensation functions here in precisely the same way as language. As the mediator between hill and trees and the inner mind, it too is a phenomenal medium bearing an intelligible content inside: the consciousness of "life," "loveliness" and "sweet[ness]." In its mediating position as a surface at once inside and outside—or alternately one or the other according to how far the perceiving mind is called into or out of itself, sensation serves, therefore, as the medium of inscription; it bears the "impression" stamped on it (as Locke would say)[27] by hill and trees, a "changeful language" that the self reads and interprets.

Besides exemplifying the epistemological functioning of language, this fragment dramatizes the functioning of supplementarity in an important new way. Wordsworth mentions that sensation not only *"called* the mind / Into itself" (emphasis added) but "all her reflex powers / Wrapp'd in a still dream forgetfulness." This state approximates a kind of death, from which the self is later called back to life again by "those beauteous forms" of hill and trees (that is, by sensation):

> I lived without the knowledge that I lived
> Then by those beauteous forms brought back again
> To lose myself again as if my life
> Did ebb & flow with a strange mystery.

This fluctuating movement posits the self as an outside, along with "sensation," "life," hill and trees, discovered in the process of moving back from the inside. As Wordsworth is "by those beauteous forms brought back again" and realizes that "I lived without the knowledge that I lived," he returns to consciousness of the outward to discover the self is there too, on the outside (and alive) in relation to the mode of inner, indeterminate being in which he has unknowingly lived. What usually constitutes the self—impressions, sensations, the visitations of images from without, the exercise of reflex powers—is presented here as the outside of an inside in the same way as the changeful language on the countenance of the aged hills articulates the play of "thoughts" inside the self.

Yet Wordsworth goes an important step further here. If the "life" of which he is conscious at the beginning of the fragment is indeed the One Life, then he discovers that this life flows through himself too when he realizes that he continued to live when he was "without the knowledge that [he] lived." His own mysteriously ebbing and flowing "life" is continuous with the "life" of which he is pleasantly conscious. Wordsworth thus incorporates the One Life into the configuration, yet presents it not as a conjectural, extraneous metaphysic but as an immanent play of movement flowing through and determining outside and inside alike. He has now found the One Life to be posited as an integral part of the epistemological configuration, a configuration, he discovers, that includes the self too.

If we turn to the Christabel Notebook, we find these Alfoxden discoveries developed in significant new ways. Although of uncertain date, the fragments of philosophic blank verse in the Christabel Notebook display a unity of concern and approach that suggests they were written after their Alfoxden counterparts.[28] All presume the presence of the One Life unifying nature, sometimes implying it by default as Wordsworth recognizes the absence of an expected fellowship. But all correlate the "life" of nature with the "life" of the perceiving self, as if drawing on the fragment, just discussed, on 21[v] of the Alfoxden Notebook.

One Christabel fragment in particular appears quite emphatically to build upon this latter fragment. Developing the notion of the mind's flux outwards toward nature, and investigating further the role of sensation, this fragment explicitly acclaims the senses as, in effect, "reflex powers" in their own right:

> There is creation in the eye,
> Nor less in all the other senses; powers
> They are that colour, model, and combine
> The things perceived with such an absolute
> Essential energy that we may say
> That those most godlike faculties of ours
> At one and the same moment are the mind
> And the mind's minister.

(PW, 5: 343)

Geoffrey Hartman has pointed out that these lines cast in poetic form a programmatic philosophical theory that might originally have been written in prose—and might originally have been Coleridge's.[29] Here Wordsworth compounds a mind out of the senses: the "godlike faculties" of sense *"are* the mind" (emphasis added). Yet what leads him to claim this is something more than the senses' capacity to convey "a pleasant consciousness of life" (although such a capacity is implicit). Rather, it is their power to *give* "life," to "create" by giving determinate form to the otherwise indeterminate. The Alfoxden fragment on 21[v] prefigures this by making sensation both the mediator of external nature to the self and the arbiter of the mysterious "ebb & flow" of consciousness. Now, in this Christabel fragment, Wordsworth develops this notion by arguing that the senses are powers "that colour, model, and combine / The things perceived with . . . an absolute / Essential energy." By doing so, moreover, he establishes the self as equal in "power" to nature. The "absolute / Essential energy" of its senses parallels nature's "power," for the senses "Colour, model, and combine / The things perceived" just as nature gave "movement . . . multitude . . . order & relation" before.

This new emphasis in the Christabel Notebook on the senses and their affective power stabilizes the play between inside and outside by showing that two opposite movements can occur simultaneously or serially, and overlap.

Nature's influx can meet, and blend or clash with, the mind's own flux into
outside nature. Another Christabel fragment describes a seamless blending:

> Oh 'tis a joy divine on summer days
> When not a breeze is stirring, not a cloud,
> To sit within some solitary wood,
> Far in some lonely wood, and hear no sound
> Which the heart does not make, or else so fit[s]
> To its own temper that in external things
> No longer seem internal difference
> All melts away, and things that are without
> Live in our minds as in their native home.
>
> (*PW*, 5: 343)

Flux overlaps with influx, a configuration that Timothy Bahti has usefully
characterized as at once "both/and" and "neither/nor," which composes, as he
formulates it, "both/neither."[30] Both inside and outside appear outside and inside at once, while also appearing to be exclusively neither one nor the other.

Yet the result of this melting away of difference is not unity or fusion; no
terium quid is created. Rather, it is no more than coincidence, an overlapping
that erases boundaries, closes the gap between self and nature, and cancels the
displacement of mind from its minister. Gap and displacement continue, however, as fluctuating possibilities, ready to be uncovered once again if mind
should separate from its minister or "external things" display "internal difference"—that is, according as sensation calls the mind into or out of itself. What
this both/neither achieves is a temporary "still dream forgetfulness" of the indeterminate or inarticulate in the self—and in nature as well. At such moments all
is "pleasant consciousness of life" without any sense of displacement from the
immediacy of the senses. *The Prelude* presents a particularly paradigmatic instance of this:

> Oft in those moments such a holy calm
> Did overspread my soul that I forgot
> The agency of sight, and what I saw
> Appeared like something in myself—a dream,
> A prospect in my mind.[31]

Influx is coextensive with flux; together they create an evenly balanced supplementarity that rests on a "still dream forgetfulness" of all that is indeterminate
in self or nature.

Displacement occurs as the self suddenly becomes self-conscious, and
reflects that the ear has "coloured" and "modeled" the sound it hears—and as it
simultaneously reflects that the sound is also a "what" beyond the "how" of the
ear's determination of it.[32] Such a realization is perhaps only precariously held

in abeyance, but it unerringly reasserts the "activity" that is "deadly bane" to "wise passiveness." It relegates the objects perceived in the trance to the realm of the outside once more, at a remove from the inside, the self, whose immediate object is now its own "agency."

The trance thus precariously relies on a "still dream forgetfulness" that becomes in the Christabel fragments a kind of death:

> [L]ong I stood and looked,
> But when my thoughts began to fail, I turned
> Towards a grove, a spot which well I knew,
> For oftentimes its sympathies had fallen
> Like a refreshing dew upon my heart;
> I stretched myself beneath the shade
> And soon the stirring and inquisitive mind
> Was laid asleep; the godlike senses gave
> Short impulses of life that seemed to tell
> Of our existence, and then passed away.
>
> (*PW*, 5: 344)

It seems that the trance must exact this death as the necessary condition of its efficacy, for what is suppressed in this "still dream forgetfulness" clearly poses an epistemological threat not only to the trance or "wise passiveness" but even to the One Life as well.

However, in posing the situation in this way Wordsworth shows that the both/neither of the trance eventually yields to a categorical (and problematic) either/or. Valorizing the trance and the One Life it communicates as the most privileged form of experience, Wordsworth now appears ready to discredit the self because it all too easily inhibits its own accesses of sublimity, or unintentionally terminates them when they do occur—a self that, after the trance, resumes its "best activity" and more "habitual" mode of sensory existence. A passage in MS. RV of the two-part *Prelude* sharply defines this dichotomy:

> By such communion was I early taught
> That what we see of forms and images
> Which float along our minds and what we feel
> Of active or recognizable thought
> Prospectiveness, intelligence or will
> Not only is not worthy to be deemed
> Our being, to be prized as what we are
> But is the very littleness of life
> Such consciousnesses seemed but accidents
> Relapses from the one interior life
> Which is in all things, from that unity
> In which all beings live with God, are lost
> In god and nature, in one mighty whole

As indistinguishable as the cloudless east
At noon is from the cloudless west, when all
The hemisphere is one cerulean blue.[33]

From the point of view of the major poetry from 1798 onward, especially *The Prelude* of 1805, we can see that this divided attitude, more often featuring in less acute form as ambivalence about the self that is a "Relapse" from the trance, provides much of the motivating force behind Wordsworth's philosophical speculations. In particular, this ambivalence expresses an anxiety about teleology: Wordsworth wonders whether the self removed from the trance in time and place (or only by the epistemological barrier of "best activity") is not ipso facto shut off from the sources of its strength. The teleological problem of means and ends, which Wordsworth addresses at length in *The Prelude,* grows out of, and keeps returning to, this either/or—to what is, in the first instance, an *epistemological* problem.

The either/or that Wordsworth presents in these Christabel fragments is offered as the precondition and the residue of a both/neither, the trance itself in which inside and outside overlap. Both/neither logically implies as well the presence of a possible both/and, a possibility disclosed, in fact, in the notion of supplementarity delineated in a few Alfoxden fragments. Either/or, both/and, both/neither describe a certain play of movement which is primarily epistemological and yet which carries distinct metaphysical consequences. It is a fluctuating movement whose "ebb & flow" appears to follow no fixed pattern, insofar as either/or may result in both/and and both/and revert to either/or. Moreover, this movement traces the "argument" of the Notebooks taken as a whole. As we have seen, Wordsworth proceeds in these Notebooks by surmising more complex positions from (apparently) simple ones. Beginning with the notion of influx and its capacity to shape the self and imbue it with content and "life," he later surmises the presence and effects of a countermovement, the flux of mind outward onto nature. If the two movements supplement each other in the form of a both/and in the Alfoxden Notebook, they become less compatible and fall back into the antithesis of an either/or in those Christabel fragments that imply that the "absolute / Essential energy" of the senses is also the source of distortion and inhibition. The play between the determinate and the indeterminate displays the same structure and movement. In essence an either/or, the determinate and the indeterminate transform into a both/and when Wordsworth recuperates the indeterminate as an unknown mode of determinacy. Both/and culminates, of course, in the concept of the One Life. But an all-encompassing unity of this kind is not to be achieved without negotiating the play between inside and outside, determinate and indeterminate. In other words, both/and continues to imply, and dissolves back into, the either/or out of which it evolves. It continues to rely on the presence of differences, which, as a "what," enable as well as delimit the "how" of the One Life. The both/neither character-izing the trance marks a midway point in the return movement toward either/or. Retaining the all-encompassing sense of both/and, it nevertheless acknowledges the inhibiting presence of the "what" outside the configuration, the self "Wrapp'd in a still dream forgetfulness" and the indeterminate which for the moment appears all determinacy.

Either/or, both/and, both/neither posit a simple duality which augurs an obscure sense of possible unity but which it can never quite attain; yet equally, this duality never completely collapses into the categorical dualism of absolute difference and nonrelation. Outside and inside, determinate and indeterminate compose the ontology of this universe; and if the boundary line between one state and another keeps shifting, and if one pair of terms comprises a continuum, the whole that may be fashioned from the parts (the One Life) can only be conjectured in surmise, for some "what" always falls outside the configuration and circumscribes its scope. Some horizon encloses the expanse of vision; the One Life itself, or nature's language, will seem to proceed from phenomena which at bottom do not surrender themselves to human canons of determinacy. Usually Wordsworth will then either surmise that "There is a mind" even in the "forms inanimate" of nature, or reason that the self is blind to, and on the outside of, the all-pervading "life" around it.

These two alternatives posit one side or the other of the either/or, together adding up to both/and. The Christabel arguments about the flux of the mind suggest that the One Life may be a projection, a fiction; in contrast, if hill and trees and all of "inanimate" nature do indeed exude One Life which includes the self as well, then it appears that the self (alive and not alive, and not content to feel as nature feels) is the only block to its realization.

Yet by allying this self, in the Christabel fragments, with the inarticulate and the indeterminate as together composing a "what" outside the domain of the trance, a "what" which not only borders on or delimits the trance but is capable of thwarting or inhibiting it and bringing it to a close, Wordsworth posits the potential for errancy at the same time he posits the One Life. For the One Life, as we have seen in these fragments, is not posited *without* this "what" by which it is delimited. Whether simply an indeterminate outside or the self of flux and distortion, this "what" creates the possibility of error because the One Life, the trance, determinacy and articulateness are all dependent on it, are all given *with* it and *by* it, even if it is temporarily suppressed in a "still dream forgetfulness." Indeterminate and inarticulate in relation to the determinacy and articulateness displayed by the One Life in the trance, this "what," like the play of nature's sounds eluding the conceptual grasp of the hearer, constitutes the ground from which the One Life is experienced. If the self is "Wrapp'd in a still dream forgetfulness," or if the inanimate must be imbued with mind, then the indeter-minate becomes the epistemological criterion of the determinate. The self can never finally establish whether the One Life is a fiction resting on an unrecuperable indeterminacy, or a mode of being that a skeptical self—benighted up to this moment—has finally come to know.

Errancy is thus originally epistemological, but it evolves into the kind of teleological errancy featuring in *The Prelude* insofar as the dissolution of both/ and or both/neither into either/or separates self from nature. Conversely, when "Trances of thought and mountings of the mind" (*Prel,* 1. 20) befall the self, the disjunction of either/or begins to augur once again the tantalizing resolution of both/and. And if, as already mentioned, the sequential movement from one state to the next is not fixed, and if these fragments as individual texts move backwards and forwards in precisely this fluctuating fashion (for Wordsworth supplements influx with flux only to reassert influx), then the self "Wrapp'd in a still dream forgetfulness" and emerging as a "Relapse" from the trance can prove to be not the inhibiting or distorting force, inimical to the trance, that Wordsworth originally presumed it to be. In fact, the fragment about the "god-like faculties" of sense and their "absolute / Essential energy" goes on to make this point:

> In many a walk
> At evening or by moonlight, or reclined
> At midday upon beds of forest moss,
> Have we to Nature and her impulses
> Of our whole being made free gift, and when
> Our trance had left us, oft have we, by aid
> Of the impressions which it left behind,
> Looked inward on ourselves, and learned, perhaps,
> Something of what we are. Nor in those hours
> Did we destroy
> The original impression of delight,
> But by such retrospect it was recalled
> To yet a second and a second life,
> While in this excitation of the mind
> A vivid pulse of sentiment and thought
> Beat palpably within us, and all shades
> Of consciousness were ours.
>
> (*PW,* 5: 343–44)

This "Relapse" self, dead to itself during the trance, awakes not to terminate but to renew the "life" imparted during the trance. It seems Wordsworth expects erosion and extinction to be the norm, given how he marvels at retention here. Recalling the central passage from "In Storm and Tempest," these lines show in a somewhat different way that the memory is a life-giving power and the source of the continuing life of the self.

Amounting to a both/and in Wordsworth's fluctuating epistemological progression in the Notebooks, this discovery, this reclamation of the "Relapse" self, only serves, however, to compound the ambivalence of Wordsworth's differing valuations of the self in 1798. The alternation between either/or and both/and expresses an epistemological tension which in the terms Wordsworth offers in the Notebooks is clearly not to be resolved—just as, equally, we may surmise that these experimental fragments have not fully articulated it. In *The Pedlar* and *The Prelude* this tension will prompt further discovery and a more capable understanding of self and nature. But it is already evident in these Notebooks that if either/or, influx, the self-as-passive, and the One Life articulate an empiricist epistemology and the pantheistic metaphysics necessary to complete it, then both/and (and both/neither), supplementarity, the mind's flux, and above all the constitutive role of the indeterminate and the inarticulate have laid the foundations for the transcendentalism of Wordsworth's maturity.

2

Reading the Book of Nature and Surmising the Self:
The Pedlar

Wordsworth's decision to expand his character sketch of the narrator of "the story of Margaret"[1] into a full biography of some 350 lines that he entitles *The Pedlar* reflects the magnitude of the "self-discovery" that the Alfoxden and Christabel Notebooks record. *The Pedlar,* inserted in an addendum to MS. B of *The Ruined Cottage* (January-March 1798) and later offset as an autonomous poem in MS. D (February-November 1799),[2] delineates the self that might ideally be surmised from the evidence of the Notebooks. From their isolated insights and recollections Wordsworth formulates here a programmatic account of the self and its development. As before, he regards the "trance" as the primary formative experience, arguing that the vivid memory of it fosters the growth of faculties, the self's "skill to draw" power from nature. But as before, too, Wordsworth's predominant emphasis on retention and development gives space to a countertendency enforcing erosion and dislocation. From the start, Wordsworth is worried about the "wasting power / In all things which . . . /Might tend to wean" (159–61) the self from nature's "sweet influence" (159). And what proves to be "deadly bane" to "wise passiveness" is the self's own "best activity": "abstracted thought" (195) on the one hand, or the overwhelming intensity of "Accumulated feelings" (186), "the fever of [the] heart" (203) on the other. The self can interfere with the trance, qualifying the vision of the One Life, which this poem otherwise so confidently avows.

In *The Pedlar,* epistemology *is* biography, for even the Pedlar's wanderings of later life derive from these original instances of epistemological errancy. Yet, as before, wise passiveness and a disruptive "best activity" express conflicting philosophical positions. Arguing even more forcefully here the self's Lockean receptivity to nature, Wordsworth alternately counters that by stressing the self's "creative sensibility." If Wordsworth thereby seems to implement an incipient transcendentalism to compensate for the shortcomings of empiricist theories, he if anything widens the gap he is trying to close. "How" and "what" split farther apart, even in the very attempt to coordinate them. As a result, perception frequently begins and ends in uncertainty—as surmise—the self thereby also seeming less certainly articulated. As a result, too, Wordsworth successively revises his theory of nature in the course of the poem, as if to synthesize in a temporarily stable form the antithetical implications of the active/ passive either/or he pursues here. In the end, Wordsworth closes the dialectic by affirming one side of the either/or over the other, but letting that side appropriate the powers of the other (resulting in a slanted version of both/neither). That is, he reaffirms, in closing, the "power of [the Pedlar's] eye" (52) to see meaning and truth—a resolution that subsumes an incipient transcendental theory of the constitutive powers of mind under emphatically empiricist theories of external nature and the visual sense. Glimpsing the mind's autonomy from nature in this poem (an intuition whose full force will not be felt until 1804 in the climactic moments of *The Prelude*), Wordsworth all the more intently compounds a mind from senses that give full report of nature.

Before Wordsworth begins to narrate the formative trances of the Pedlar's childhood, he mentions an experience—reading—which at first seems to be of an entirely different order from communion with nature and potentially inimical to it:

> I loved to hear him talk of former days
> And tell how when a child, ere yet of age
> To be a shepherd, he had learned to read
> His bible in a school that stood alone,
> Sole building on a mountain's dreary edge,
> Far from the sight of city spire, or sound
> Of Minster Clock.
>
> (13–19)

Learning to read, and learning to read the bible, constitute an integral part in the processes of acculturation and socialization; they equip the boy with cultural skills, with religion and morality, thereby readying him for adult life in the human social community. "City spire" and "Minster Clock" invoke the idea of such a community, the civilized urban world in which culture, religion and morality find expression in various forms of social behavior. In contrast, Wordsworth's emphasis on rural solitude and isolation underscores the remoteness of this bleak, desolate landscape from the social activity cities afford. Yet at the same time, Wordsworth implies that the solitary and the isolated tacitly depend on the existence of the social and the civilized. The practice of religion is ideally a communal activity, sustained by the presence of fellow believers; and the activity of reading, though solitary in itself, relies on the ideal existence of a community of other readers (and writers), who, if "Far from . . . sight . . . or sound" of each other (and the boy), are sustained by the unifying medium of the written word. The contrast Wordsworth draws here between city and country is really that between culture and nature. The boy learns cultural skills which do not seem immediately applicable to nature, and which seem incongruous in context of nature; but it becomes evident, as the passage continues, that the cultural is indeed applicable to the natural, for the same criteria shape the boy's experience of both. In reading the bible (insofar as reading is a solitary activity) and in perceiving nature, the boy is deprived of the sustaining presence of others:

> From that bleak tenement
> He many an evening to his distant home
> In solitude returning saw the hills
> Grow larger in the darkness, all alone
> Beheld the stars come out above his head,
> And travelled through the wood, no comrade near,
> To whom he might confess the things he saw.

(19–25)

A "comrade near" might corroborate "the things he saw," if he were to see them too—just as other readers could confirm the meaning of what the boy learns to read in the bible. In fact, the similarity between the two situations intimates that they both pose essentially the same problems: How can one be sure of what one reads or perceives? How can one know that it really exists, or happened? and, above all, How is one to interpret it? The absence of a comrade leaves the certainty of perception in question. Did the boy really see "the hills / Grow larger in the darkness," or did he only think that that was what he saw? Solitude and isolation, as the conditions of perception both here and throughout the poem, mean that perception shades indistinguishably into imagination and surmise. In a comparable fashion, reading the bible involves surmising a variety of imaginative possibilities—historical, metaphysical, or personal—for which little evidence is present to the senses beyond the words on the page. Reading is equally a mode of perception, therefore, engaging the same kind of interpretive activity as does perception of nature. By juxtaposing the two kinds of perceiving, the two kinds of "reading," Wordsworth suggests their consonance, if not continuity (which he will develop in the course of *The Pedlar*)—even if in this incidental anecdote from the beginning of the poem they seem entirely unrelated.

Perception is the basis of the self's development in *The Pedlar*. This schoolboy primarily "learns" the processes and appearances of nature from repeated acts of perception:

>So the foundations of his mind were laid.
>In such communion, not from terror free,
>While yet a child and long before his time,
>He had perceived the presence and the power
>Of greatness, and deep feelings had impressed
>Great objects on his mind with portraiture
>And colour so distinct that on his mind
>They lay like substances, and almost seemed
>To haunt the bodily sense. He had received
>A precious gift, for as he grew in years
>With these impressions would he still compare
>All his ideal stores, his shapes and forms,
>And being still unsatisfied with aught
>Of dimmer character, he thence attained
>An *active* power to fasten images
>Upon his brain, and on their pictured lines
>Intensely brooded, even till they acquired
>The liveliness of dreams.

>   (26–43)

Reflecting on his sense impressions, the boy learns to exercise his faculty of judgment; he learns to discriminate amongst his impressions. Moreover, in the process, he "learn[s] something of what" memory, desire, imagination and the will "are": in exercising the "comparing power of the mind," he recalls earlier impressions from the memory, and learning of a desire for more "lively" impressions (as Locke would call them) he discovers the *"active* power" of the imagination to deliver them. Retention directly contributes to development, to *"active* power."

These self-assured cognitive acts conclude, however, in epistemological uncertainty. As the boy steadily concentrates on the "Great objects" lying "like substances" on his mind, he increasingly commutes them to a state of ideality. They appear to "haunt the bodily sense" like ghosts; they become the ideal standard to which he unfavorably compares "All his ideal stores, his shapes and forms," which, if also "impressions" of natural objects originally, are now as abstract and ideal as geometrical figures.[3] As the boy intensely broods on the "pictured lines" of the "images" he has fastened "Upon his brain," they acquire "The liveliness of dreams." Their very vividness begins to undercut their reality—a reality, however, which is already ideal (in that it is an "ideal store") and made even more ideal by the act of intense brooding (just as the hills grew larger in the darkness as the boy looked at them). Perception, then, evolves into surmise. Yet perception in this passage also *begins* in surmise. It is "deep feelings" which set these mental operations in motion—that is, something not objective but subjective—while the "Great objects" these feelings impress are but the vehicles for something suggestively indeterminate and no more than ambiguously objective: "the presence and the power / Of greatness." The uncertain margins of perception encroach on the self-assurance at the center.

Philosophically, one could say that Wordsworth traps the self in the veil of perception, that overpowering sensations and feelings cannot be definitively traced to precise causes in the objective world. Less extremely, one could say that Wordsworth exemplifies here the gap between self and nature, that distance and difference are givens of experience, conditions that inevitably implicate perception in surmise. As the poem will show, the self's sense of its proximity to nature, or of its continuity or identity with it, is revealed to be a surmise that temporarily suspends the self's more habitual consciousness of its own separateness. Such is the case in the ensuing conclusion to this passage, where perception actually issues into an explicit, formal surmise:[4]

> In the after day
> Of boyhood, many an hour in caves forlorn
> And in the hollow depths of naked crags
> He sate, and even in their fixed lineaments,
> Or from the power of a peculiar eye,
> Or by predominance of thought oppressed,
> Even in their fixed and steady lineaments
> He traced an ebbing and a flowing mind,
> Expression ever varying.
>
> (48–57)

Wordsworth's affirmation of "what" is usurped by a questioning consciousness of "how." Although "what" itself becomes a surmise in proportion as Wordsworth surmises "how," the act of surmising unhinges "how" from "what," dividing the perceiver from the perceived, even though postulating their continuity (by postulating that the perceived may be an effect of perception). The "ebbing and . . . flowing mind" that the boy traces in the "fixed lineaments" of the "naked crags" may be his own, in which case it is a projection of "creative feeling" or oppressing "thought." But it could also be nature's mind, or the One Mind, which the "power of [his] peculiar eye" enables him to trace. Any one or even all three explanations could be correct.

But if epistemology usurps metaphysics and throws it into question, the result is not subordination of one to the other, but an almost contradictory affirmation of both/and. This usurping questioning of agency first suggests that epistemology determines metaphysics, that "feeling" or "thought" has projected the mind onto the crags. Yet the very irresolution of the surmise allows metaphysics to reassert itself. Wordsworth ends by emphatically restating the original metaphysical proposition: *whatever* the agency of perception, the boy "traced an ebbing and a flowing mind, / Expression ever varying" in the "fixed and steady lineaments of the crags."

Jonathan Wordsworth is surely right when he observes of a similar instance at the conclusion of the poem that "Wordsworth's questioning of the basis of his belief has simply been a means, or had the effect, of emphasizing the belief itself."[5] Certainly this is the result here. Nevertheless, the question of agency is a major issue that insistently surfaces in *The Pedlar* and increasingly renders the poem's metaphysics problematic.[6] It transforms even the most confident claims into surmise—not necessarily because the claims themselves are unsupportable, but because the epistemological means of mediating them are finally uncertain. In the passage above, the three "Or" surmises seem at once exclusive of each other and yet compatible; and if the latter, we still feel that agency has not yet been exhaustively determined. There continues to be room for a remainder, unaccounted for, which makes the forms of epistemological determination specified so far seem tentative and provisional.

Indeed, the very certainty of epistemology, the precise specification of an agent, often entails in *The Pedlar* the exclusion or suppression of other less-certain kinds of agency. Clearly the self's creative power constitutes a less-certain form of agency, and, as in this example, it often refuses to be excluded but irrupts to give an "active" account potentially usurping the "passive" one. By the end of the poem, Wordsworth accords the self's creative power its proper place, but in his descriptions of trances before that point he cites only passive sense perception as the epistemological means of mediation. To be sure, these "passive" explanations inevitably rely on the unacknowledged workings of the self's "active," creative power, but Wordsworth's suppression of its presence overburdens the epistemology of "passiveness," and pushes the certainty of perception toward the uncertainty of surmise.

We can see these effects in the series of trances that constitute the major, formative events of the Pedlar's biography in the central section of the poem. Wordsworth may increasingly allow room for the self's activity—"intense conceptions" (87), powers and habits are always the precondition allowing wise passiveness to occur—but that activity is always commuted to the object as an effect of its own immanent intention. Direct influx, proceeding exactly according to the Lockean paradigm, thus carries that active power and presence from the object to the self. But the structure of supplementarity operative here causes chiastic switches that unsettle subject and object alike. Both become more indeterminate as they change roles or places. While Wordsworth, in the course of the poem, therefore seeks to develop a more accommodating epistemological theory of sign, meaning and reading, of the self and its powers, he also steadily revises his theory of nature. The result is an argument that moves to and fro, as Wordsworth counters the implications of one moment or stage of development by stressing the different effects of a later moment or stage.

In the first of these important trances Wordsworth shows the boy, who has been

> prepared
> By his intense conceptions to receive
> Deeply the lesson deep of love, which he
> Whom Nature, by whatever means, has taught
> To feel intensely, cannot but receive,

(81–91)

receiving precisely this lesson:

> Ere his ninth year he had been sent abroad
> To tend his father's sheep: such was his task
> Henceforward till the later day of youth.
> Oh then what soul was his, when on the tops
> Of the high mountains he beheld the sun
> Rise up and bathe the world in light. He looked,
> The ocean and the earth beneath him lay
> In gladness and deep joy. The clouds were touched,
> And in their silent faces did he read
> Unutterable love. Sound needed none,
> Nor any voice of joy: his spirit drank
> The spectacle. Sensation, soul and form
> All melted into him. They swallowed up
> His animal being. In them did he live,
> And by them did he live. They were his life.
> In such access of mind, in such high hour
> Of visitation from the living God,
> He did not feel the God, he felt his works.
> Thought was not: in enjoyment it expired.
> Such hour by prayer or praise was unprofaned;
> He neither prayed, nor offered thanks or praise;
> His mind was a thanksgiving to the power
> That made him. It was blessedness and love.

(92–114)

Influx creates a continuity between nature and the self, for the feelings of "gladness . . . deep joy" and "love" flow into the self to form its being. In positing this continuity, Wordsworth closes the gap, as far as he can, between self and nature. He firmly discounts anything that might detract from continuity: thought, offering thanks or praise to God, even consciousness of God (the boy is rapt in feeling God's "works," rather than God). The result is that the self becomes what it beholds—or rather, it becomes the feelings it "beholds": "His mind was a thanksgiving to the power / That made him. It was blessedness and love."

Wordsworth figures this reciprocity with nature as epistemological redundancy. As the self mirrors what it beholds, response becomes a reflex reiterating the stimulus received. This form of redundancy is anticipated by the actual verbal redundancy of receiving *"Deeply* the lesson *deep* of love" (emphasis added). Whether verbal or epistemological,[7] in figuring the experience of the trance redundancy expresses the closest approximation to unity that Wordsworth's poetry records. Yet in closing the distance between self and nature, it does not cancel the difference. Difference remains, and is the hinge of the supplementarity between self and nature. Referring to the "Sensation, soul and form" of the natural scene Wordsworth declares that "In them did he live, / And by them did he live. They were his life." Nature supplements the self by providing the life that the self appropriates as its own. Yet if continuity and proximity are suggested here, the prepositions "in" and "by" affirm an overlapping rather than identification.

Passive reception of the usurping influx, however, depends quite explicitly on the self's prior activity, so that the supplementarity achieved appears to be as much the result of the mind's own flux as of nature's influx. Usurpation occurs as a result of the self's intentional acts: the boy "beheld," "looked" and "read"—responses which grow steadily more active and purposeful. At this stage the outward scene is itself passive; yet as the boy's intentional activity culminates in "drinking" the spectacle, the spectacle itself, while passively melting into him, becomes active: it swallows him up. This switching between active and passive, as Wordsworth describes the "how" of the usurping act, creates a corresponding indeterminacy of "what." Both the self and the spectacle suddenly seem unfixed, as the outside flows into the inside. The boy's "spirit" drinks, while his "animal being" is "swallowed up." Correlatively, the scene has already become increasingly subjective and indeterminate in being described as "Sensation, soul and form / All melt[ing] into him."

These interchanges simultaneously generate a new concept of nature. Beginning the poem with the Alfoxden nature of power, shapes and forms, Wordsworth instills into that an ebbing and a flowing mind, only now to aggrandize that mind into God himself. For behind the declaration that "Sensation, soul and form / All melted into him. . . . In them did he live, / And by them did he live. They were his life" are St. Paul's words that in God "we live, and move, and have our being."[8] Although its primary function in Wordsworth's text is epistemological, the biblical allusion still carries its religious import. Wordsworth's claim thus tends to adequate perception of nature with perception of God—perhaps prompting the retraction that during this "visitation from the living God" the boy "did not feel the God, he felt the works." In the trance immediately following this one, this kind of adequation is treated more explicitly. God's "works" now become a "writing." Wordsworth therefore revises his theory of nature once again, as he makes nature into God's Book:

> A Shepherd on the lonely mountain-tops
> Such intercourse was his, and in this sort

Was his existence oftentimes possessed.
Oh *then* how beautiful, how bright, appeared
The written promise. He had early learned
To reverence the volume which displays
The mystery, the life which cannot die,
But in the mountains did he FEEL his faith,
There did he see the writing. All things there
Breathed immortality, revolving life,
And greatness still revolving, infinite.
There littleness was not, the least of things
Seemed infinite, and there his spirit shaped
Her prospects, nor did he *believe*—he saw.
What wonder if his being thus became
Sublime and comprehensive.

(115–30)

Working according to the kind of supplementarity we have seen so far, nature as text has written down the boy's "thoughts," his "faith": "There did he see the writing." Faith finds confirmation through sight: "nor did he *believe*—he saw." The Lockean paradigm is again dominant, and, as in the preceding instances, it converts thoughts or meaning into sensible, visible objects that can simply be seen and read. The "promise" therefore appears not only figuratively but literally "beautiful" and "bright." (Likewise, "prospects" are as much external as internal, exactly as in the Alfoxden Notebook.) The bible's promise of "the life which cannot die" becomes here a visible activity in nature: "All things there / Breathed immortality, revolving life, / And greatness still revolving, infinite." The Newtonian connotations of "revolving," "greatness" and "infinite" suggest, moreover, that "the power of a peculiar eye" enables the boy to perceive the supersensible as well. This boy can *see* "greatness still revolving" almost as if he were an astronomer gazing through a telescope at a planet revolving on its axis. And as if gazing through a microscope, he can almost see infinity in a grain of sand: "There littleness was not, the least of things / Seemed infinite."

Seeing underscores feeling in this passage. Wordsworth's capitalization of the verb "FEEL" should alert us to the fact that more activity is involved in both seeing and feeling than the Lockean paradigm implies. Although nature is the more active, the boy who witnesses it has not been, nor is, by contrast, passive. Feeling his faith in the mountains, seeing there what he believes, relies on reading, and in particular on having read the bible, on having "early learned / To reverence the volume which displays / The mystery, the life which cannot die," the "promise" of eternal life originally learned when he attended the school "that stood alone, / Sole building on a mountain's dreary edge." Promise and mystery—that is, the contents of the scriptures—have become supreme "intense conceptions" in the boy's mind; they have become "ideal stores" which now

actively mediate the natural scene before him. They transfigure "aught of dimmer character" on the mountainside into holy script.[9]

The text in the mind comes to (eternal) life in nature. The "written promise"
becomes actualized as the boy looks. It is incarnated in "All things" breathing
"immortality." What is actively entertained in the mind, and is ideal in character—text, conceptions, "thought," promise—is correlated with, and even appears to produce, an activity in external nature. One expects that Wordsworth
would openly recognize here the self's active imposition of its conceptions on
external nature, thereby giving it life, and that he would accordingly revise his
epistemological and metaphysical theories along transcendental lines. But the
unquestioned dominance of the Lockean model of direct influx prevents any
such theoretical adjustments. If anything, Wordsworth ascribes all activity even
more emphatically to the object. Here, the text is active, the reader passive;
meaning lives in (is literally lived *by*) the text and not in the reader, who must
surmise that the meaning, with its individual promise of eternal life, is applicable to himself.

And yet, as Wordsworth moves to narrate more of the Pedlar's biography,
and moves away from describing specific moments of visionary perception, he
strenuously taxes the Lockean paradigm by broaching the topic that "writing"
and "reading" have implicitly introduced: books. Wordsworth mentions the
books the youth reads as if to show how they corroborate the Book of Nature:
they confirm and elaborate its truths by duplicating and disseminating them.
But in supplementing nature and its meanings, books exacerbate the underlying
tensions between epistemology and metaphysics, setting "how" and "what" even
more at odds. If other objects besides nature hold the same meaning, then in
what way does meaning reside in an object? If it seems incarnate in natural
objects, can it do anything other than "lodge" in a manufactured object like a
book? And if nature is in some way a "writing" that the self reads just like a
book, is meaning anything more than the self's arbitrary imposition? As we can
see from the next section of the poem on books, the implications of the textual
model undermine the Lockean conception of direct influx.

For the Pedlar, then, nature as God's Book gives way to reading books in
nature: "Among the hills / He gazed upon that mighty orb of Song, / The divine
Milton" (144–46). Among the hills too, he "gazed upon" books of geometry and
mathematics. "And thus employed he many a time o'erlooked / The listless
hours when in the hollow vale, / Hollow and green, he lay on the green turf /
In lonesome idleness" (154–57). The statement "There did he see the writing"
now becomes literally true. Having traced a holy writing in nature, the Pedlar
now traces a human writing in books. Yet the substitution of books for God's
Book amounts to a fall. The books substituting for the Book of Nature attempt
to represent (if not recover) the Book (Milton) or nature (geometry, mathematics). The human and belated forms of writing stand in for another higher and

earlier form of writing. The sacred, apocalyptic history recorded in the bible, incarnate in nature, has yielded to geometrical and mathematical truth in books, which the self must inscribe (or reinscribe) in nature.

However, as Wordsworth physically interposes books into the natural scene he does more than separate nature from Book: he separates nature from the self. In fact, Wordsworth's mention of the site of reading only serves to "throw" nature "to a finer distance" from the self.[10] Reading books while lying on the green turf in the hollow vale may indicate proximity to nature—just as reading books may be intended to be continuous with reading nature: "What could he do?" Wordsworth asks, and immediately replies, "Nature was at his heart," as if reading books were the appropriate way of honoring nature-as-Book. But reading books necessarily blocks nature from view as the reader concentrates on the print on the page, thereby removing nature from proximity to "his heart—just as the sense the Pedlar reads in the book substitutes for, represents, a sense which was immediately present formerly in nature. This fall into separation poses a danger that seemed far from probable until this point in the poem: the erasure of nature, or its superfluousness, as books substitute for it. Wordsworth mentions in a parenthesis that seems unrelated to his argument that the value of books of geometry and mathematics is "especially perceived where nature droops / And feeling is suppressed" (151–52). We can easily see that reading books may cause nature to droop and feeling to be suppressed—and evoke the very listlessness and idleness that it is supposed to answer.

By keeping the self away from nature, books open up the possibility of errancy, as Wordsworth now explicitly recognizes: "and he perceived, / Though yet he knew not how, a wasting power / In all things which from her sweet influence / Might tend to wean him" (158–61). Books themselves might tend to wean the youth from nature by leading to a "truth" separated from nature altogether. The youth is aware of this danger:

> Yet not the less he found
> In cold elation, and the lifelessness
> Of truth by oversubtlety dislodged
> From grandeur and from love, an idle toy,
> The dullest of all toys.

> (176–80)

But this danger is the inescapable corollary of separating books, self and nature, for insofar as books substitute for nature, they separate meaning from nature. Meaning now becomes something the self *applies* to nature—and which it derives from books. The spirit and the letter must be consciously brought together, whereas formerly they composed one undifferentiated whole:

> Therefore with her hues,
> Her forms, and with the spirit of her forms,
> He clothed the nakedness of austere truth.
> While yet he lingered in the elements
> Of science, and among her simplest laws,
> His triangles they were the stars of heaven,
> The silent stars; his altitudes the crag
> Which is the eagle's birth-place, or some peak
> Familiar with forgotten years which shews
> Inscribed, as with the silence of the thought,
> Upon its bleak and visionary sides
> The history of many a winter storm,
> Or obscure records of the path of fire.
>
> (161–73)

The self imposes meaning by annexing nature to geometrical truth already in the mind. By inscribing (or reinscribing) truth in this way, the self strives to guard against the errancy of "cold elation," "lifelessness" and "oversubtlety." Wordsworth tries to fit again a "dislodged" truth onto nature—or rather to fit nature onto this truth, since he clothes its "nakedness" with nature's hues and forms.

Despite the youth's geometrical fieldwork, however, Wordsworth still keeps meaning and medium apart by conceding that truth transcends its object. Indeed, nature is expressly valued not for its intrinsic properties as a phenomenal medium but for the "grandeur" and "love" it exhibits—that is, again, for qualities that transcend the medium in which they too "lodge." In valuing nature, Wordsworth transvalues it, promoting a notion of "truth," of intelligible content, that leads in a direction away from its medium. To the degree that truth is transferable from book to nature, from medium to medium, it is dissociable from a medium altogether:

> He saw in truth
> A holy spirit and a breathing soul;
> He reverenced her and trembled at her look,
> When with a moral beauty in her face
> She led him through the worlds.
>
> (180–84)

Such a statement argues an almost apocalyptic severance of truth from medium. Even if "the worlds" through which truth leads the Pedlar include most prominently the phenomenal world of nature, they more pointedly invoke realms that are metaphysical, supernatural. If anything, "truth" resembles God in this passage: she is "A holy spirit" (like one of the persons of the trinity), at whose "look" the Pedlar, like Moses or any other biblical figure who has seen God, "tremble[s]."[12]

In this middle portion *The Pedlar*, books explicitly expose an epistemological breach between meaning and medium, truth and medium. Meaning or truth is transcendent, displaced, floating free, supposedly located in books yet more properly belonging in nature, and is in either case a secondary record of a previous immanent presence. As the youth matures, this epistemological dislocation translates directly into errancy. The riot of meanings in the self fails to harmonize with nature:

> But now, before his twentieth year was passed,
> Accumulated feelings pressed his heart
> With an encreasing weight; he was o'erpowered
> By nature, and his spirit was on fire
> With restless thoughts. His eye became disturbed,
> And many a time he wished the winds might rage
> When they were silent. Far more fondly now
> Than in his earlier season did he love
> Tempestuous nights, the uproar and the sounds
> That live in darkness. From his intellect,
> And from the stillness of abstracted thought,
> He sought repose in vain. I have heard him say
> That at this time he scanned the laws of light
> Amid the roar of torrents, where they send
> From hollow clefts up to the clearer air
> A cloud of mist, which in the shining sun
> Varies its rainbow hues. But vainly thus,
> And vainly by all other means he strove
> To mitigate the fever of his heart.

(185–203)

If thought leads to the dangerous extreme of "cold elation," then feeling poses a threat equally serious. Feeling surges toward its own "elation," fueled by thoughts that have become "restless." "Thought" quite explicitly contributes to feeling here: the "Accumulated" meanings of former trances have produced "intense conceptions" which make the youth "unsatisfied with aught / Of dimmer character." But when nature reacts with sufficient turbulence to satisfy his "disturbed" eye, the youth is not gratified, as we might expect, but counters by calling upon thought to subdue the riot of feeling. The accumulation of feelings has put the youth in excess of nature. In fact, feelings, memories, conceptions, abstract "truth" have all combined to produce a self that is "disturbed" and out of balance with nature.

In trying to further the Lockean paradigm by having more objects produce more meanings, Wordsworth thus seems to end up destroying it. Influx has given way to a free dispersal of meaning in which the object functions as no more than a contingent, arbitrary vehicle. Meaning now flows as much to this object as from it, the flux itself even generating an excess of unattached meaning. With a transcendental solution to meaning's transcendence as yet out of the question, Wordsworth's only recourse is to restore the Lockean paradigm by aggressively affirming the object's originary force.

The trance that Wordsworth next describes (and that is the climactic one of the entire poem) more than capably restores balance by presenting a nature whose abundant activity easily outweighs the self's disturbance. The self finds itself contained by a nature that now—of its own accord—expresses a meaning, a truth, exceeding any that self or books can offer. By this means, Wordsworth counters the unavoidable tendency toward transcendence and dislocation with a comprehensive vision of the immanence he so desires:

> From Nature and her overflowing soul
> He had received so much that all his thoughts
> Were steeped in feeling. He was only then
> Contented when with bliss ineffable
> He felt the sentiment of being spread
> O'er all that moves, and all that seemeth still,
> O'er all which, lost beyond the reach of thought
> And human knowledge, to the human eye
> Invisible, yet liveth to the heart;
> O'er all that leaps, and runs, and shouts, and sings,
> Or beats the gladsome air; o'er all that glides
> Beneath the wave, yea, in the wave itself,
> And mighty depths of waters. Wonder not
> If such his transports were; for in all things
> He saw one life, and felt that it was joy.
> One song they sang, and it was audible,
> Most audible then when the fleshly ear,
> O'ercome by grosser prelude of that strain,
> Forgot its functions, and slept undisturbed.

(204–22)

This trance easily subsumes and surpasses all the other visionary moments presented in the poem. Wordsworth invokes all creation here—both the visible and the invisible, the static and the moving, the animate and the inanimate, "All things" as well as "the least of things" of lines 115–30. Indeed, "greatness" and infinitude are encompassed too, when "All which [is] lost beyond the reach of thought / And human knowledge, to the human eye / Invisible" is nonetheless brought within range of what the heart can feel.

By insisting on this inclusion of the transcendent among the "works" of God to which the youth responds, Wordsworth ideally puts the foregoing discourse on books, as well as the question of errancy, into perspective. Book-learning, abstract truth, thought itself are all exhaustively contained in and by this trance as it extends beyond their conceivable limits. Correlatively, nature announces a meaning of its own exceeding all meanings that the self can apply to it: the One Life, joy, the one song. Surpassing the promise of immortality which "All things" breathe in the mountains—the One Life, joy, the one song imply not only breath, life and movement but self-consciousness as well. The "sentiment of being" that the youth feels "spread" over all creation amounts to creation's consciousness of its own existence. "Sentiment" suggests a register somewhere between sensation and feeling and is therefore the appropriate term to apply to a nature partly composed of "forms inanimate." Indeed, the sentiment of being now imbues the sunrise spectacle mentioned earlier with sensation of its own. Nature itself feels; the "works" feel. In their magnitude and all-pervasiveness, nature's sensations and feelings easily surpass the youth's, and so quiet the fever of his heart into contentment.

The one song all nature sings is a song of "joy" in "being," and if also a song of praise and thanksgiving to God then it is sung to a God who does not stand beyond and above nature but is immanent in it. A passage in MS. RV directly following Wordsworth's incorporation of this trance into book 2 of *The Prelude* (but rejected from other manuscript drafts) elaborates the implicit pantheism here. Wordsworth mentions "the one interior life / Which is in all things . . . that unity / In which all beings live with god, are lost / In god & nature in one mighty whole."[13] These lines again echo the words of St. Paul, but they stress, more pointedly than does the earlier trance, that the "works" are synonymous with God. Such a doctrine is more radical than any *The Pedlar* espouses, but it explicates the tendency that insistently informs Wordsworth's presentation of nature in the poem. The intelligible principle animating nature, and consistently regarded as transcending it, is finally made immanent in it. The mind in the crags gave earnest of it, but equally suggested the transcendent God of the trance at sunrise. Nature as God's Book approximates the identification of the phenomenal and the intelligible by presenting nature as a living writing; but it is a text that *represents* a transcendent presence rather than presents the presence itself. It is not until this trance elaborating the one life that we are finally given a vision in which the intelligible is fully immanent in the phenomenal, a vision that achieves as close a presentation of presence as Wordsworth can give.

Meaning, then, does not now "lodge" in the nature the Pedlar beholds, feels and hears, but is made incarnate in it. In this respect, the One Life, the one song, usurps nature-as-book, for a living voice usurps a living writing. The "voice of joy" (102), mentioned as not needed in the earlier trance at sunrise, here intrudes of its own accord as the one song of joy. Nature in all her forms inanimate, which Wordsworth celebrates in the Alfoxden Notebook, clearly proves that it has power to hold articulate language. And the song proves far more immediate and expressive than writing or even speech.

Once again, then, Wordsworth has revised his conception of nature. It is now a nature of articulate sound to which the youth responds; and although sight plays a major role in his trance, the youth does not so much see as feel and hear.

In fact, the result of seeing is feeling and hearing (as will be the case again on Mount Snowdon). Yet these successive revisions, like the successive restatements of epistemological agency, follow an ever more insistent dialectical pattern. Wordsworth stresses wise passiveness only to admit the self's creative contributions to experience, but this admission prompts him to emphasize nature's influxes all the more—until, after pushing each side of the either/or to the limit, he reaches the stage at which self and nature are so out of step that only an example of absolute immanence can call back a self whose self-vexing activity has left it epistemologically alienated from the outside world. The resolution toward which this dialectical to and fro leads is one in which Wordsworth stresses the One Life as forcefully as ever but now makes room for the self's creative activity. But given the way the youth's trance-experience of the sentiment of being follows from a preceding condition of restlessness and "fever" and relies on a still-dream forgetfulness of best activity when it occurs (in fact, it is because "His eye became disturbed" that the "ear . . . slept undisturbed" during the trance), then Wordsworth sides with the self's active agency more than with nature's life and power. To be sure, the sentiment of being, the One Life and the one song of joy compose an impressive array of metaphysical effects, but even in this trance the self's epistemological agency qualifies their autonomy. In the final thirty-six-line section of the poem the same thing happens even more pointedly. Wordsworth begins by presenting an almost contradictory both/and (both the One Life and yet the self's activity too) but then dwells entirely on the self and its interpretive powers. As we have seen in the course of the poem, conceptions, ideal stores, accumulated feelings, active powers, apprehensive power and thought have all combined to produce a self that knows how to read and interpret with discrimination and precision. The self becomes sole arbiter of nature's meanings—of sounds, shapes and forms that Wordsworth insists are as instinct with the One Life as ever:

> Though he was untaught,
> In the dead lore of schools undisciplined,
> Why should he grieve? He was a chosen son.
> He yet retained an ear which deeply felt
> The voice of Nature in the obscure wind,
> The sounding mountain, and the running stream.
> From deep analogies by thought supplied,
> Or consciousnesses not to be subdued,
> To every natural form, rock, fruit, and flower,
> Even the loose stones that cover the highway,
> He gave a moral life; he saw them feel,
> Or linked them to some feeling. In all shapes
> He found a secret and mysterious soul,
> A fragrance and a Spirit of strange meaning.
> Though poor in outward shew, he was most rich:

He had a world about him—'twas his own,
He made it—for it only lived to him,
And to the God who looked into his mind.

(324–41)

As in the surmise of a mind in the crags earlier in the poem, Wordsworth gives two opposite explanations: the youth "saw" the loose stones that cover the highway "feel," "Or linked them to some feeling." Despite nature's apparent autonomous activity, Wordsworth concentrates more on the self's creative projections. The result, however, is not a new transcendental theory, but a peculiarly empiricist form of solipsism. Wordsworth continues this passage with the lines: "Such sympathies would often bear him far / In outward gesture, and in visible look. / Beyond the common seeming of mankind" (342–45). What saves the self and the private world it has "made" from a Berkeleyan "abyss of idealism" is "the God who looked into his mind."[14] This God can confirm the "meaning" that the Pedlar finds "In all shapes" because he sees it too. Yet Wordsworth is doing no more than enlisting God's corroboration; he is not invoking God as author of nature or creator of its meanings. God, then, fulfills the function of the comrade whom the boy lacked at the beginning of the poem—someone to whom he might confess the things he saw to see if they are true.

God-the-comrade, partner in seeing the loose stones feel, implicitly shares some of his divine attributes with the Pedlar. In this passage the Pedlar takes on God's functions of giving life and establishing meaning insofar as he gives a "moral life" "To every natural form" and finds "In all shapes / . . . a secret and mysterious soul, / A fragrance and a Spirit of strange meaning." Furthermore, just as the eye of God has power to look into his mind, so the Pedlar's eye has similar powers of penetration:

[H]e had an eye which evermore
Looked deep into the shades of difference
As they lie hid in all exterior forms,
Near or remote, minute or vast; an eye
Which from a stone, a tree, a withered leaf,
To the broad ocean and the azure heavens
Spangled with kindred multitudes of stars,
Could find no surface where its power might sleep;
Which spake perpetual logic to his soul,
And by an unrelentingly agency
Did bind his feelings even as in a chain.

(346–56)

Earlier, as he had felt the sentiment of being spread over all that moves and all that seemeth still, the Pedlar resembled the God of Genesis scanning his creation to see if it was good. Here again the Pedlar scans the broad ocean and the azure heavens, but with the sole purpose of determining meaning. Finding no surface where its power might sleep, the eye "spake perpetual logic to his soul." The secret and mysterious soul, the fragrance and the Spirit of strange meaning residing in all shapes, are unerringly elicited by the eye's power, and fixed in enduring relation as the eye speaks its "perpetual logic."

With an eye as magisterial and authoritative as God's, the Pedlar becomes a double of God in much the same way as books doubled nature earlier. As before, supplementation means appropriation, substitution, and once again a disruption of influx—in short, a revised theory of nature in light of a revised epistemology. In finding meaning in all shapes, the self once again regards "Exterior forms," and "surfaces" as a writing. But not quite. This is not God's Book of Nature inscribed with a holy, living writing; and even though nature has a voice at the beginning of the concluding sequence, it is not nature as a living utterance that commands the self's attention now. Rather, the signs the self reads are ones that it has itself inscribed. What is remarkable about this is that the eye usurps its own act of inscription: the eye *"spake* perpetual logic to his soul" (emphasis added). Seeing signs is usurped by speaking them—exactly as writing was usurped by song earlier in the poem. Moreover, the "logic" that the eye speaks not only combines the various ideas of "meanings," "truth," "thought" and "conceptions" that have played such an important role in the poem, as well as the notions of order and structure integral to the idea of "writing," but in being "perpetual" also appropriates the eternal and immortal qualities of the divine writing in nature. The eye in speaking perpetual logic, therefore, takes over the activity originally exhibited either by nature itself or by God in nature: that of writing or uttering thought, truth or meaning. The voice which formerly spoke in nature now speaks in the eye. And since articulate utterance, whether speech or song, is the most palpable representation of originary presence to be found in Wordsworth's poetry, the logic the eye speaks presents itself as ipso facto true.

Opening the poem's concluding sequence with a both/and, Wordsworth resolves it, then, by transposing it into an either/or in which he finally conflates one side into the other. The self's eye arrogates the object's powers, leaving the object a simple outside of surfaces, shapes and forms displaying only "shades of difference" to be "looked" at or "into." Once again it may seem that Wordsworth has reached a transcendental landing-place, since it is the self's epistemological activity that organizes this barely differentiated manifold of sense impressions into coherent meaning and truth. But once again Wordsworth refuses to depart from empiricist explanations. Kant's undifferentiated manifold remains instead Berkeley's visual field of light and colors covering Locke's external world of shapes, extension, resemblance and difference. And if the eye's perpetual logic anticipates Kant's a priori categories of the understanding and their constitutive role in experience, Wordsworth nonetheless conceptual-izes the eye's functioning in strictly empiricist terms: the eye not only colors models and combines the things perceived with an absolute essential energy but reads out loud their movement, multitude, order and relation, thereby establish-ing meaning and truth. Moreover, the result of visual activity is a strict Lockean-Hartleyan necessitarianism: the eye speaking perpetual logic to his soul "by an unrelenting agency / Did bind his feelings even as in a chain." The direct influx that with Locke proceeds from outside to inside is here commuted entirely inside as an effect of the eye's power—an influx flowing from the eye to deeper inside the self, where it carries certain necessary effects.

Wordsworth shows how a wise (socialized) self derives from the eye's epistemological power in the biographical narrative before the concluding sec-tion of the poem. There he says that the Pedlar had an eye

> which, under brows
> Of hoary grey, had meanings which it brought
> From years of youth, which, like a being made
> Of many beings, he had wondrous skill
> To blend with meanings of the years to come,
> Human, or such as lie beyond the grave.
>
> (306–11)

Meanings firmly lodge, therefore, in the eye, and if Wordsworth shows us here how the spirit shapes her prospects, then he literalizes those prospects as first of all the property of the eye. Prospects are shaped in and by the eye, for the eye not only "had meanings which it brought / From years of youth" but *has* "meanings of the years to come, / Human, or such as lie beyond the grave." Transcendent visionary power is finally made fully immanent in the eye. Yet the incipient transcendentalism of the eye's constitutive power takes the form of an empiricist visual faculty.

As Wordsworth moves back and forth in *The Pedlar* affirming now nature and now the self as the active, creative force, he offers successive theories of nature but a developing theory of the self. Nature alternates between being a collection of sights and sounds, a language, God's Book of Nature and a pantheistic presence permeated by the One Life. By comparison, the self is increasingly defined by its epistemological activity: passive receptivity blends with active powers, fostering retention and growth and leading to a mature adult who is increasingly presented as an efficient and accurate reader-interpreter of nature and an authoritative arbiter of meanings.

To be sure, various rifts have emerged along the way, as self and nature get out of step or epistemology and metaphysics prove irreconcilable. While we might be able to see how a Kantian transcendentalism could resolve some of the problems, Wordsworth's answer is simply to close the gaps by wilfully reaffirming those problematic empiricist theories. In "Tintern Abbey," as we will see next, these rifts prove not so negotiable, and transcendentalism all but comes forth from the inconsistencies of empiricism and pantheism. But in the other philosophical poetry of these early years—that is, the two-part *Prelude* of 1798–99 and, one may add, the first 167 lines of book 3 of *The Prelude,* which conclude books 1 and 2 (as the two-part *Prelude* becomes)—no significant philosophical developments occur to surpass the ones we have already encountered. Wordsworth expatiates more fully on the self's activity, but epistemologically his autobiographical discourse does not add anything that is not already present in *The Pedlar*'s biography. In fact, we can judge the theoretical parity between the two works in the way climactic passages from *The Pedlar* are transferred to *The Prelude* and put in similarly prominent positions: the One Life–one song sequence goes into the conclusion of book 2: the sequence on "loose stones on the highway" and "the power of a peculiar eye" constitute the peroration of the first part of book 3 (concluding "The glory of [Wordsworth's] youth" [*Prel,* 3. 171] prior to his going to Cambridge); while furthermore the passage entitled "Fragment" in the Alfoxden Notebook occupies an important place also in book 2. But in "Tintern Abbey," Wordsworth's first sustained exercise in autobiography, present perception of nature (as seemingly straightforward as similar moments in the Notebooks) suddenly opens irresolvable philosophical problems as Wordsworth tries to apply to himself all the theories that he has worked out on the Pedlar.

3

"Uncertain Notice":
Seclusion and Impression in "Tintern Abbey"

Written in July 1798, "Tintern Abbey" differs from the poetry discussed so far in that a keen sense of absence and loss now informs the self's interaction with nature. Wordsworth approaches nature from the other side of a gap, and thereby throws the confident claims of *The Pedlar* into question. As in Cambridge in book 3 of *The Prelude,* it is a self that has lived "thro' such change entire / And this first absence from those shapes sublime / wherewith [he] had been conversant" (3. 101–3) that approaches nature now, a self for whom the gap of "Five years . . . five summers, with the length / Of five long winters" (1–2), mentioned at the start of the poem, has meant the near loss of nature itself.

Wordsworth claims, of course, that "thro' such change entire / And this . . . absence" the self has survived intact. Though propless for five years the building has stood thanks to nature's original influxes and the "powers and habits" which they fostered, and which still survive. But if habit is to be vindicated in "Tintern Abbey," it must first be put to the test. It is not unquestioningly asserted as a medium of continuity, but subjected to a searching examination to see if it can carry that continuity. Continuity becomes the central issue in "Tintern Abbey": continuity of nature, of experience, of the self and of meaning—and continuity via another person too. And Wordsworth puts continuity and habit to the test by reducing them to their radical, fundamental form: repetition. Nowhere in his poetry does he present such a paradigm of repetition itself as an event to be examined from every angle for all that it authorizes and initiates. By doing so, moreover, Wordsworth tries to establish certain teleological conclusions. Habit and continuity, if vindicated by this event of repetition, will in turn confirm, so Wordsworth hopes, nature's benevolent intent and the ongoing, purposive course of his life.

The gap of five years and the absence from the physical scene constitute the conditions themselves upon which habit, continuity and teleological intentions must all be predicated. For though originally deriving from or linked to nature, they have all flourished during the gap and in the absence—such that

Wordsworth sets out to verify them by juxtaposing them to their source via this act of repetition, by comparing effects to causes. These acts of repetition and return differentiate "Tintern Abbey" from the other poetry of 1798, for the self presented in this poem is determined by gap and absence to a greater extent than is the case throughout of the larger part of *The Prelude*. Not until book 7 (and from that point on) do such conditions become so definitive.

The Notebook fragments and *The Pedlar* have largely shown how this divorce has come about. Powers and habits themselves and various accumulated thoughts and feelings have interposed to separate self from nature. But exactly as in *The Pedlar* these circumstances translate into biographical errancy: Wordsworth quite simply "quit [these] hills" and "wandered far," learning "The still, sad music of humanity" (91) in "towns and cities" (35) during the intervening five years. Recent historicist studies have opened up this gap to show how biography and history shape the poem and motivate Wordsworth's acts of repetition and return.[1] Wordsworth consciously admits his life and times into the poem, however, only insofar as they contribute to a besetting dislocation. He presents towns and cities and his experiences there as a clear antagonist to nature, an inimical counterpresence that is never very far in the background. Despite its actual biographical origin, the basic given of the poem is a wide breach between subject and object—a breach that Wordsworth conceptualizes and seeks to close epistemologically.

Wordsworth's project in "Tintern Abbey," then, is to establish connections. Philosophically, this translates into an even more radical examination of Lockean influx. The dominant concept, traced through many permutations, is "impression" (Wordsworth uses the verb "impress" at lines 6 and 126); and he tracks its movements both farther back and farther forward than in *The Pedlar* or Notebook fragments. Following the Hartleyan associationist theory so favored by Coleridge at this time, Wordsworth draws the connections between sensations, physiology, mood and moral behavior; but he also refers impressions to their origin in the One Life, "A motion and a spirit, that impels / All thinking things, all objects of all thought, / And rolls through all things" (100–102). The origin and end of impression's tendency turn out to be, to use a phrase from the poem slightly out of context, a "more deep seclusion" (7). Impression and seclusion function as each other's opposite: they entail, begin, urge, lead to, thwart and end each other. Each is the outside margin of, and marginalizes, the other. Moreover, the movement of impression, whether from or to seclusion, is steadily idealizing: the boy of "glad animal movements" (74), for example, matures into a man whose most "serene and blessed mood" is to have "the breath of [his] corporeal frame / And even the motion of [his] human blood / Almost suspended" in order to "become a living soul" and "see into the life of things" (41–49). As Wordsworth traces the path of impressions, he shows how, in becoming successively refined, they epistemologically lead to an idealist metaphysics. Quite clearly, one form this metaphysics takes is pantheism, but insofar as pantheism is essentially the systematic corollary of impressions that are themselves motions that roll through things, the metaphysics is really an empiricist idealism that defines phenomena according as they are presented in sensation. The numerous subjective epithets Wordsworth uses throughout the poem to describe nature and his experiences substitute, as Marjorie Levinson points out, qualitative, affective definitions for quantitative, denotative ones.[2] And yet not quite. Wordsworth refuses a thoroughgoing subjective idealism, and at several key moments exploits the ambiguity of subject-object relations. For the idealizing course of impressions and the deep seclusions they bring within range of intuition traverse and circumscribe a transcendental ground. By crossing gaps and forging connections Wordsworth uncovers that ground in a way that anticipates and more than half realizes an authentic transcendental idealism.

The scene Wordsworth surveys a few miles above Tintern Abbey expresses the harmonious unity of the picturesque. As the popularity of Gilpin's *Observations on the River Wye, and Several Parts of South Wales, &c* suggests,[3] Tintern Abbey and the Wye Valley had become, by Wordsworth's time, a recognized attraction for tourists eager to experience the pleasures of landscape. The pleasure Wordsworth's scene affords is that of a pervading sense of quietness and seclusion. But the pleasurable sensations Wordsworth feels are not only passively received but actively created by the yoking together of disparates. The picturesque is quite explicitly the product of composition:

> Five years have past; five summers with the length
> Of five long winters! and again I hear
> These waters, rolling from their mountain-springs
> With a soft inland murmur.—Once again
> Do I behold these steep and lofty cliffs,
> That on a wild secluded scene impress
> Thoughts of more deep seclusion; and connect
> The landscape with the quiet of the sky.

(1–8)

Congruent with the Lockean idiom of *The Pedlar*, these lines deploy the same epistemological strategy of morticing and annexing the mental to the material. "Thoughts" are "impress[ed]" on the scene in the same way that characters are stamped on a waxen tablet (a metaphorical analogue for the mind in Locke's epistemology). The result is an all-pervading sense of seclusion and quietness as "Thoughts of more deep seclusion" are "impress[ed]" by the cliffs "on a wild secluded scene," and as "The landscape" is "connected" with "the quiet of the sky."

Yet exactly as in comparable moments in *The Pedlar*—especially the surmise in which the boy traces an ebbing and flowing mind in the crags—the question of agency is problematic. While "cliffs" are the subject of the verb "impress," the syntax of the sentence and its punctuation allow for doubt in the case of "connect." The subject could be "I" rather than "cliffs." The syntactical ambiguity is important because of the epistemological ambiguity it creates. It would be easy, but reductive, to say that Wordsworth projects his own agency here, because it would not only separate self and landscape, consigning each to its appropriate sphere and functions, but undermine the authority of the outward object. What is important is not that Wordsworth half creates the sense of seclusion and quietness but that he perceives the outward scene itself as creating it.

The "Thoughts of more deep seclusion" are ambiguous too. Does Wordsworth mean that the "Thoughts" derive from the "more deep seclusion" of the human mind? Or does he mean "Thoughts" *about* a deeper seclusion— that is, the notion that the steep and lofty cliffs make the secluded scene look even more secluded? Many statements in the poem corroborate the first interpretation: the deep seclusion of the mind "'mid the din / Of towns and cities" (25–26) in the second verse paragraph, and, in the fifth verse paragraph, the "gleams of half-extinguished thought" (58), the secluded thoughts that this second visit to the banks of the Wye recalls from obscurity in the memory. The second interpretation, however, finds support from the immediate context: the "waters, rolling from their mountain-springs / With a soft inland murmur" convey the idea of physical and geographical "more deep seclusion." Yet, as in the surmise from *The Pedlar* with its three "or" explanations, the two interpretations are not mutually exclusive. And the result in either case is finally the same. The "Thoughts" the cliffs impress on the scene seem no longer to be the perceiver's, while they do not yet altogether seem to be the cliffs' either. Subject-object interaction is epistemologically ambiguous. Furthermore, the effect of "Thoughts" on the object is a transcendentalization of the object: the physically secluded scene conducts beyond itself to a more deep seclusion that is indifferently physical and mental (as if the one is a metaphor for the other). In looking at the object, Wordsworth sees something more than, and different from, the object. Perceiving seclusion turns into imagining a more deep seclusion.

This movement of perception beyond and away from the object given becomes even more evident in the ensuing lines of the opening verse paragraph. As a result, the mood of harmonious unity gives way, in the last few lines, to something quite different. Wordsworth views

> These plots of cottage-ground, these orchard tufts,
> Which at this season, with their unripe fruits,
> Are clad in one green hue, and lose themselves

> 'Mid groves and copses. Once again I see
> These hedge-rows, hardly hedge-rows, little lines
> Of sportive wood run wild: these pastoral farms,
> Green to the very door; and wreaths of smoke
> Sent up, in silence, from among the trees!
> With some uncertain notice, as might seem
> Of vagrant dwellers in the houseless woods,
> Or of some Hermit's cave, where by his fire
> The Hermit sits alone.
>
> (9–22)

The landscape blends the natural and the human, the wild and the cultivated. If the description presents a harmonious unity, as the overriding "one
green hue" implies, it is really a *concordia discors* in which the discordant rather
than the concordant strikes the final and rather ominous note. There is a playful
tension between the natural and the human, between the wild and the cultivated,
as the word "sportive" indicates—a tension that seems evenly balanced (at least
to line 17), even if wild nature slightly has the upper hand over domesticated
nature. Yet this easy continuity takes on a different character in lines 17 through
22. Wordsworth moves from surveying a semidomesticated nature to a wilder
nature where the only traces of human presence are the "wreaths of smoke /
Sent up, in silence, from among the trees! / With some uncertain notice," which
he interprets as evidence of "vagrant dwellers in the houseless woods, / Or of
some Hermit's cave, where by his fire / The Hermit sits alone." As Richard
Onorato says, "the 'vagrant dwellers' are wishfully imagined by Wordsworth
to be living in Nature, and living no doubt in the contentment that Wordsworth
associated with Nature, rather than the actual destitution one associates with
itinerant vagrancy."[4] The reference to vagrancy (a condition always associated
with destitution in some of the companion poems to "Tintern Abbey" in *Lyrical
Ballads*) in fact qualifies the idea of contentment and undermines the harmony
of the scene as a whole. For even if the fires are not those of vagrants but of
charcoal-burners—since charcoal burning to provide fuel for the ironworks at
Tintern was a major cottage industry in the Wye Valley—then Wordsworth
partially admits in one way or another the contemporary economic and social
realities of his time into his picturesque landscape. If the fires are those of
vagrants, then readers would make the connection to Tintern Abbey itself, a
notorious "dwelling-place of beggars and the wretchedly poor," as Mary Moorman says; if they are those of charcoal-burners, then he tacitly registers the
encroachment of industrialization on this famed, national beauty spot.[5] The
Hermit, we can probably assume, is poetic license, a fiction meant to restore the
idyll that the mention of vagrancy may have jarred. But even here the accent is
finally dissonant. The Hermit sits "alone"—a word that usually means in
Wordsworth's poetry the solitude of isolation (as is the case later in the poem)

rather than an exultant solitariness. The final cadence of the word, coming at the end of the half line, the sentence and the verse paragraph, only accentuates the sense of melancholy and abandonment that *"houseless* woods" (emphasis added) carries for the vagrants (a likely paradigm for them is the "Poor naked wretches" of *King Lear,* whose "houseless heads" find no shelter against the storm).[6] These half-repressed references and intrusive connotations significantly disturb the harmony of the opening scene, pushing the compositional unity towards discordant disequilibrium.

Unlike similar scenes described in the present tense in the Notebooks, this scene is not innocently presented for its own sake as if to see what truths or principles about nature or the self may come to light. Rather, given the five-year gap and the anxious longing Wordsworth brings to the moment, the scene is pressed to serve as proof of beliefs Wordsworth already has in mind, to revalidate principles he has formulated away from the scene and as a result of it and which he now wishes to see demonstrated once again. If nature autonomously behaves now in the same way as it did five years before, then Wordsworth can proceed on the assumption that his notions are correct. And the behavior he wishes to see and does see is precisely these acts of impression and connection—not only the pervasive sense of quietness and seclusion but the interpenetration of wild and domesticated, natural and human, as well.

The Lockean concept of impression ideally traces a cause-effect line from external objects to the mind—impressions themselves constituting the raw materials of all our knowledge as we combine and modify them into ideas. Wordsworth gives a straightforward example of this in his record of sights and sounds: the "one green hue," the waters' "soft inland murmur," for example. But he also plays variations on this basic pattern in a way that not only broadens its scope and complicates its functioning but orients it in a transcendental direction. He dwells at some length (given the proportions of this twenty-two-line description) on the "orchard-tufts" that "lose themselves / 'Mid groves and copses," and the hedge-rows, which he revisionistically defines in three stages: "Once again I see / These hedge-rows, hardly hedge-rows, little lines / Of sportive wood run wild." In both details, there obtains an interplay between retention and erosion as nature partially reclaims what human hands have fashioned. But the values of the binarism are unclear, as is the question of which side is which. Normally, Lockean impression proceeds from the natural object to the human subject, where the unknowable powers of mind govern retention and erosion ("there seems to be a constant decay of all our *Ideas,* even of those which are struck deepest, and in Minds the most retentive," says Locke).[7] In these descriptions, however, Wordsworth both follows and reverses the order as he not only makes retention and erosion external actions but makes both nature and the human alternately (though not so equally) impress and erode. This implicit reversal of the Lockean model is startlingly explicit in his first use of it, where the cliffs impress thought on the scene. Usually an object impresses something on a subject that the latter turns into a thought; here, one object impresses a thought on another object. But in its implicit metonymic and metaleptical maneuvers, Wordsworth's figure starts changing empiricist epistemology into transcendental. Metaleptically, he has substituted the cliffs as causative agent of his own act of impression (itself a reversal of the usual Lockean model), when they are really an effect of it: they too are as much determined by his thoughts of seclusion as is the "wild secluded scene." And in spatially connecting the landscape with the quiet of the sky (if the cliffs are the subject of the verb "connect"), they also function as a metonymy for the seclusion, enhancing it in the same way as a frame enhances a picture. Yet as Wordsworth substitutes effects for causes while still letting it be obvious which is effect and which is cause, he essentially enacts the Kantian epistemological schema. The Kantian a priori categories of the understanding (such as quantity or relation) are projected outwards onto the object allowing that object to be experienced and known, although to ordinary common sense (and to Lockean theory) the object alone appears to be the cause of our knowledge of it. For Kant, then, as for Wordsworth here, the object, "caused" by the subject's categories and therefore an effect of them, presents itself as the cause of the effects that the subject registers. Moreover, insofar as Wordsworth adds a frame to the picture while successfully blurring certain boundaries between inside and outside (nature, for example, impresses thoughts and erodes and retains, just like the mind), he encompasses a ground that is potentially transcendental because the activity by which it is known is constitutive. Impression and connection, retention and erosion play out across a surface that recedes into a simultaneously infiltrating more deep seclusion. Here and throughout the poem, these actions constitute nature and self alike, suggesting a both/neither in which each can be the mirror and measure of the other but in which each is marginalized by the other. With boundaries so uncertain, with more deep seclusion as much in the center of the picture as beyond the edges of the frame, and with the frame itself eroding under the pressure of impressions, Wordsworth on the one hand puts all faith in the scientific certainty of those impressions but on the other submits them to the "wasting power" of erosion, as it were, in order to uncover those more deep seclusions.

One consistent evidence of this is the way perception always strains towards a more deep seclusion. The wreaths of smoke, for instance, literally arise from a more deep seclusion. The "some uncertain notice" they give of human presence in the woods is really an ambiguous sign, although Wordsworth takes it as certain "notice" of a seclusion that only becomes ambivalent. Wordsworth surmises that smoke indicates vagrant dwellers or a Hermit—a more deep seclusion than he can bring within reach of certain knowledge. The certainties Wordsworth associates with the sign (homelessness, vagrancy) outweigh the uncertainty of the sign itself. This disequilibrium constitutes a true displacement, for what is actually visible and knowable is displaced in favor of what is not visible or knowable.

Such a tendency to displace attention from what is immediately in view towards another location which is not in view and which is then made the center of a concentration of meanings becomes, in fact, a dominant pattern in the poem, and culminates in Wordsworth's turn to Dorothy in the final verse paragraph. Such a pattern is also discernible in the title of the poem: "Lines Composed a Few Miles Above Tintern Abbey, On Revisiting the Banks of the Wye During a Tour, July 13, 1798." Tintern Abbey itself, of course, constitutes no part of the scene that Wordsworth surveys, for it is the landscape farther upstream, a few miles "above" the Abbey, that he describes, a landscape rapidly cut off (secluded) by the winding narrow gorge of the Wye itself. Tintern Abbey, then, is technically a fortuitous reference point both in the title and on the map.[8] But as a more deep seclusion it functions in precisely the same way as the vagrant dwellers and the Hermit. Indeed vagrant dwellers and Hermit serve as metonymies for the Abbey, as surrogate markers of its distant presence a few miles downstream. For if the Abbey is thought of as the "dwelling-place of beggars and the wretchedly poor," as Moorman mentions, then these vagrants dwelling in the houseless woods upstream would represent the Abbey's overflow population, and indicate the extensive infiltration this far away of one aspect of the Abbey's identity: ruination, destitution, desolation—contingent fates suffered alike by the Abbey building and the vagrants who are its metonymies (the Church's institutions of charity have also failed, as Levinson points out).[9] Equally, the Hermit expresses the other aspect of the Abbey's identity: religious devotion, quiet, repose and seclusion. Proceeding beyond the limits that perception reaches as he moves in thought from smoke to vagrants and Hermit (and by extension to the Abbey and the meanings it enshrines), Wordsworth makes seclusion a function of impression—and one that literalizes, in both place and persons, impression's interplay of retention and erosion. Curiously (and an encouraging sign for Wordsworth's connective project in this poem) the various seclusions seem as much the landscape's impressions as his own.

Returning to the scene after an absence of five years, Wordsworth turns his attention from what is immediately in view to what he cannot see. He compares the present with the past, nature with "towns and cities," and the cause with its effects. As he reviews the influence of this scene on his life during the intervening time, he explicitly theorizes it in terms of Lockean impression—or rather Lockean-Hartleyan associationism, since he argues a direct evolution from original sense impression to final moral effect:

> These beauteous forms,
> Through a long absence, have not been to me
> As is a landscape to a blind man's eye:
> But oft, in lonely rooms, and 'mid the din
> Of towns and cities, I have owed to them
> In hours of weariness, sensations sweet,
> Felt in the blood, and felt along the heart;
> And passing into my purer mind,
> With tranquil restoration:—feelings too
> Of unremembered pleasure: such, perhaps,
> As have no slight or trivial influence
> On that best portion of a good man's life,
> His little, nameless, unremembered, acts
> Of kindness and of love.

(22–35)

Following the mechanistic psychological model (here physiologically conceived, after Hartley), Wordsworth marks the passage of "sensations sweet" in the blood, along the heart, and into the "purer mind." Besides naming the conscious influences and their results, he also correlates unconscious influences with unconscious results: "unremembered pleasure" may "perhaps" have influenced "little, nameless, unremembered, acts / Of kindness and of love." The scientism and certainty of all this, one feels, is meant to be proof enough, the physiology lending support to the psychological. But these impressions undergo strange transformation in their passage: they become steadily idealized, even transcendentalized,[10] and indeed seem to begin as well as end in transcendental space. For just as Wordsworth has been secluded from the original scene during the five-year gap, so too, in a sense, has the landscape. Committed to memory as "beauteous forms," it has been transported from its original location to dwell in Wordsworth's mind "in lonely rooms, and 'mid the din / Of towns and cities." Seclusion nests inside seclusion nests inside seclusion—much as smoke, vagrants, Hermit and Abbey composed another nest of seclusions. If the Hartleyan psychology substantializes the impressions emerging from this origin it carries them to an end in an even more deep seclusion:

> Nor less, I trust,
> To them [the beauteous forms] I may have owed another gift,
> Of aspect more sublime; that blessed mood,
> In which the burthen of the mystery,
> In which the heavy and the weary weight
> Of all this unintelligible world,
> Is lightened:—that serene and blessed mood,
> In which the affections gently lead us on,—
> Until, the breath of this corporeal frame
> And even the motion of our human blood
> Almost suspended, we are laid asleep

> In body, and become a living soul:
> While with an eye made quiet by the power
> Of harmony, and the deep power of joy,
> We see into the life of things.

(35–49)

In the movement to this still dream forgetfulness in which Wordsworth lived without the knowledge that he lived while seeing into the life of things, impressions get steadily refined. As suggested by the references to "burthen" and "weary weight" and (in the following verse paragraph) to times "when the fretful stir / Unprofitable, and the fever of the world / Have hung upon the beatings of [his] heart" (52–54), the action of impression consists in the freeing of a lighter ideal content from a corporeal weight that perplexes and retards. Impression itself, however, is the very lifeblood circulating through the system. Remarkably, within twenty-six lines Wordsworth refers three times to the heart and the circulation of the blood, thereby gaining a large measure of scientific assurance by representing impressions as immanent with autonomous life. The life in impressions may seem to pass out of the blood when breath and circulation almost cease as "we are laid asleep / In body, and become a living soul," but if so, it then passes into "things" to become the "life" into which "We see." Here again impressions issue into deep seclusion: the ultimate effect of the landscape seen five years earlier has been the self's power of visionary trancelike insight into a pantheistic One Life.

But a similar kind of dislocation happens here as at the origin, when beauteous forms found themselves in rooms in towns and cities. For this trancelike insight into the life of things is not explicitly linked to landscape vision. While the sublime gift originally derived from landscape vision, it does not recur specifically in its presence. In addition, the "things" into whose life "We see" are not specified as being either natural or nonnatural. Even more important is the fact that metaphysical insight occurs almost by accident, as "the affections gently lead us on." It is not the goal of impression's tendency so much as its fortuitous effect. The scientism of his physiological analysis notwithstanding, the connections Wordsworth forges precariously support the burthen of this mystery. He may rest his case on the necessitarianism of Lockean-Hartleyan associationism, as if the power of his peculiar eye, when he first saw the Wye Valley, had bound his feelings as in a chain. But the links of the chain are proving to be contingent rather than necessary.

The problem of causal linkage and what kind of proof can be drawn from a less-than-certain linkage openly emerges in the critical outburst that constitutes the third verse paragraph of the poem:

> If this
> Be but a vain belief, yet, oh! how oft—
> In darkness and amid the many shapes
> Of joyless daylight: when the fretful stir
> Unprofitable, and the fever of the world,
> Have hung upon the beatings of my heart—
> How oft, in spirit, have I turned to thee,
> O sylvan Wye! thou wanderer thro' the woods,
> How often has my spirit turned to thee!
>
> (49–57)

This is proof by passionate assertion—that is, proof by habit; but however unassailable as evidence, habit can amount to no proof of necessary connection at all. Wordsworth can adduce only contingent juxtaposition, contiguity in time and space: a certain feeling has habitually triggered a certain response. As if conceding that his argument is unconvincing as he proceeds to defend it, he labels it "a vain belief." But a note of defensiveness has been increasingly audible in his discourse on habit in the previous verse paragraph, as the initial boldness of his claims gave way to caution. From "I have owed," Wordsworth moved to "perhaps" and then to "Nor less, I trust . . . I may have owed."[11]

The crisis here, then, is that Wordsworth's argument is in danger of being completely undone by the very evidence that is supposed to demonstrate it. The subtle, far-reaching causal chain of the second and third verse paragraphs has been articulated in the five-year gap, so that Wordsworth finds himself marginalized by the powers and habits that, deriving from nature in the first place, now seem to block the gap between himself and nature. Return to the site and repetition of the original event would ideally reactivate the cause of the long series of effects and thereby unblock the gap and reconnect self to nature. Such a hope motivates Wordsworth's turn from passionate assertion to the present moment of perception. But fears of erosion—that established habits exert their own wasting power over the original impulses that the self wishes to retain—as well as an unavoidable recognition of the self's disconnection from nature, pervade Wordsworth's efforts to reconnect himself with the outward scene:

> And now, with gleams of half-extinguished thought,
> With many recognitions dim and faint,
> And somewhat of a sad perplexity,
> The picture of the mind revives again:
> While here I stand, not only with the sense
> Of present pleasure, but with pleasing thoughts
> That in this moment there is life and food
> For future years. And so I dare to hope,
> Though changed, no doubt, from what I was when first
> I came among these hills.
>
> (56–67)

In general, Wordsworth coordinates his present perception of the scene with his memory of it; the place looks much as he remembers it and, feeling the same kind of "pleasure" as he did when first there, he "dare[s] to hope" "That in this moment there is life and food / For future years," just as there was in the first moment five years earlier. Yet Wordsworth's inherently epistemological account shows the experience to be more complicated. Memories do not altogether gibe with present perception; in fact, memories and present perception jostle one another, each half creating the other. While memory of the first experience of this landscape and the desire for repetition situate the present moment, this moment in turn orders the memory. Memory cannot quite emerge from its deep seclusion to make a full impression. The picture of the mind may revive again with many recognitions, but they are dim and faint, while the gleams of half-extinguished thought that accompany the revival seem to show not only thought's spirited resistance to semiextinction but its quiescent sufferance of it. Does present perception half extinguish thought, or is thought (of the past, in the memory) already near death and brought back to a glowing half-life by present perception? That Wordsworth's phrasing allows these opposite interpretations suggests how much his epistemology plays the line between erosion and retention, seclusion and impression.

Moreover, what precisely is "The picture of the mind"? I have thus far taken it to mean the picture in the mind, the visual image of the place that Wordsworth committed to memory when first there. But it could also mean the picture of how his mind was, of who he was, either during the five-year period spent in towns and cities (the more likely interpretation, given the subject of the previous two verse paragraphs) or five years earlier when he first came to the place (the less likely interpretation if we take seriously his claim fifteen lines later: "I cannot paint / What then I was?" [75–76], he says, following that, of course, with a fairly detailed self-portrait). The point is, however, that the ambiguity of the preposition "of" generates a double reference that conflates outer and inner. By the first interpretation the phrase points to the landscape, by the second to the self. The one, of course, functions as sign of the other, as its measure and supplement (as in the poetry we have examined). But if both overlap and conflate, thanks to "of," they do so in an inner mental space that seeks to correlate itself with the external field of vision. To some extent Wordsworth thus seems to be striving after a Kantian both/and of transcendental idealism and empirical realism, whereby mental categories make real for experience an external world that objectively exists. What prevents that resolution and still keeps his conceptualization empiricist is his temporalizing of the two activities: he takes categories formed some time ago and imposes them on the present. Kant avoids this truth to a temporal order by consigning these categories to an inner, atemporal transcendental domain, where they come into play automatically and unconsciously.[12]

Truth to the temporal order of experience is always a fundamental principle in Wordsworth's poetry, and in this case it exposes discontinuities and the wishfulness of imputed connections. Even as he dares to hope about the future on the basis of the present and the past, Wordsworth cannot but register the difference of the present from the past and the inexorable effects of change. The simple aesthetic response of five years earlier, for example, when nature was "all in all" to him and "had no need of a remoter charm / By thought supplied" (75, 81–82), has been replaced by a response which emphatically does call upon a remoter charm by thought supplied, since gap and absence now define the self:

> For I have learned
> To look on nature, not as in the hour
> Of thoughtless youth; but hearing oftentimes
> The still, sad music of humanity,
> Nor harsh nor grating, though of ample power
> To chasten and subdue.
>
> (88–93)

Thrown into a "strenuous calculation of gain and loss," as Geoffrey Hartman calls it,[13] Wordsworth locks himself into a cycle of repetition as if thereby to stabilize the flux. Describing his "present pleasure" and the "other gifts [that] / Have followed" in "recompense" for "such loss" (86–88), he recounts a habitual experience of visionary insight that resembles the trancelike insight discussed in the second verse paragraph. And insofar as he is rehearsing for a second time the gifts that followed from the 1793 visit, Wordsworth is repeating himself:

> And I have felt
> A presence that disturbs me with the joy
> Of elevated thoughts: a sense sublime
> Of something far more deeply interfused,
> Whose dwelling is the light of setting suns,
> And the round ocean and the living air,
> And the blue sky, and in the mind of man:
> A motion and a spirit, that impels
> All thinking things, all objects of all thought,
> And rolls through all things.
>
> (93–102)

In this strenuous calculation, the "something far more deeply interfused" outweighs the pleasures interfused on the surface only, when nature was "all in all" for the youth. Yet in echoing the pantheistic passage of the second verse paragraph, these lines nonetheless go an important step further. Here Wordsworth not only sees into the life of things but names the life he sees: registering it first as a simple if shadowy epistemological working—a "sense sublime / Of something far more deeply interfused"—he gives it determinate metaphysical form as "A motion and a spirit, that impels / All thinking things, all objects of all thought, / And rolls through all things."

As he does so, Wordsworth presses the transcendental tendencies of his empiricist philosophy even further. An index of this is the way he not only sustains an explicitly empiricist vocabulary (thinking things, objects of thought) but uses it at the limit.[14] Something far more deeply interfused corresponds precisely with the more deep seclusion of the first verse paragraph (the latter is on the surface, of course, but by its own action aims at the deeper level of this interfusion). And as the deepest of seclusions, the something interfused names both an action and an effect that simultaneously inscribe a transcendental domain. All physical space and mental space become the permeable province of this "motion and a spirit"; they are grounded in and by this transcendental "something." Yet the "something" itself is known by and as its action and effect: interfused and interfusing, it "dwells" in all phenomena, is a "motion and a spirit" (a doublet for a single identity) and "impels" and "rolls through" things. In short, Wordsworth has reached that transcendental point at which seclusion, impression and connection are indifferently one and the same. As a motion and a spirit impelling and rolling through things, this something is completely identified by its Lockean behavior of impression. Yet given as more deeply interfused, this something is a seclusion that has been already impressed, already connected. As such, Wordsworth proceeds to the originary limit, at which the interplay of active and passive, inside and outside, cause and effect, is indeterminable. In analyzing in these ways what is undecidably action and state (and in invoking it as an atemporal event), Wordsworth essentially gives us a transcendental idealism—as is more evident from the sweeping grandeur of the transcendent realm he poetically invokes in lines 95–99 ("Whose dwelling is the light of setting suns," etc.). But in figuring that transcendentalism as almost palpable, sensory motions and shapes, Wordsworth keeps it still within an empiricist physique.

Despite the major gain in philosophical insight that this passage secures, it does not counteract Wordsworth's impending sense of loss. The self, in the present, is still at a remove from the desired connections, despite the rhetoric of interfusion. To be sure, nature, its workings and meanings have generally become internalized (and transcendentalized) in passing "into [the] purer mind." But this outcome does not bring Wordsworth any closer to nature in the present or really prove his argument, especially since this passage forms part of a debate on present self versus past and falls into repeating the argumentative gist of the second verse paragraph. If anything, in fact, this passage actually separates the present self from nature even further. For this self comes close to transcending the need for nature altogether, since it is a "presence," a "motion and a spirit" rather than nature's surfaces and phenomenal particulars that preoccupy it now.

In fact, if this motion and a spirit "impels . . . and rolls through all things," then the precise phenomena triggering insight of this elevated kind are irrelevant—provided that they do "disturb [him] with the joy of elevated thoughts." Wordsworth has conceded as much in ascribing these trancelike insights to the province of the five-year absence. Then, if anything, the heavy and the weary weight or the still, sad music of humanity was the necessary, immediate condition of insight—replacing, in a sense, the landscape itself as the occasion, even if landscape continues to be necessary as the original sufficient condition.

Here again, as in the second verse paragraph and really throughout the poem, the cause remains dislocated from its effects and is even supplanted by its effects. In returning to this landscape and repeating his earlier acts of perception Wordsworth may at first be trying to see whether the same cause will produce the same effects; but given the course of his argument in the poem, it now seems that he is trying to see whether effects can even find a cause. Secluded in the realm of effects and changed by them into a different person from what he was five years earlier, Wordsworth can only problematically locate a cause in a landscape that has itself "changed, no doubt, from what [it] was" (66). Were he able to get back to a cause, then, it would not be the same one. Powers and habits have shut him into a deep seclusion on the margins, locking him into a cycle of repetition in which the rehearsal of effects now serves to honor causes as a distant, generalized origin:

> Therefore am I still
> A lover of the meadows and the woods,
> And mountains; and of all that we behold
> From this green earth; of all the mighty world
> Of eye, and ear,—both what they half create,
> And what perceive; well pleased to recognise
> In nature and the language of the sense,
> The anchor of my purest thoughts, the nurse,
> The guide, the guardian of my heart, and soul
> Of all my moral being.

(102–11)

The ostensible logic here is that Wordsworth continues to love nature because it is the major and most obvious indicator of this "motion and a spirit," of "something far more deeply interfused." But he is forcing his argument. In concluding "Therefore am I still / A lover of the meadows and the woods," he all but admits that we would not expect him to continue so. Moreover, his way of honoring "nature and the language of the sense" tends to distance them as origin and keep them problematic as causes. Being "well pleased to recognise" implies a conversant facility for some time with the role of nature and the senses that relegates them as causes to the past. Yet given the problem of connections,

Wordsworth does not state the causal link so categorically. Nature and the language of the sense are presented as supplementary, and even secondary, to an identity that could have originated elsewhere: they anchor, guide, guard, and are the soul of, a "being" that is separable from the outward impressions on it. Wordsworth thus preserves the sense of margin, dislocation, epistemological gap, even as he negotiates boundaries by overtly half transcendentalizing his epistemological theory: he expressly recognizes here that "eye" and "ear" "half create" what they "perceive." If Wordsworth crosses the gap by half creating, he also thereby concedes the self's seclusion.

Locked by these various seclusions into a cycle of repetition, Wordsworth finds that restating more strongly the gist of the second verse paragraph has only accentuated his predicament. Nature, the causal objects of his desire, the security of the knowledge, powers and habits with which he is "well pleased" all seem either all the more unreachable or suddenly at risk. His misgivings break through the argument as he makes the transition to the next and final verse paragraph:

> Nor perchance,
> If I were not thus taught should I the more
> Suffer my genial spirits to decay:
> For thou art with me here upon the banks
> Of this fair river; thou my dearest Friend,
> My dear, dear Friend; and in thy voice I catch
> The language of my former heart, and read
> My former pleasures in the shooting lights
> Of thy wild eyes. Oh! yet a little while
> May I behold in thee what I was once,
> My dear, dear Sister! and this prayer I make,
> Knowing that Nature never did betray
> The heart that loved her.

(111–23)

The various forms of seclusion, then, have caused his "genial spirits to decay" to some extent by this point—just as "Nature," his nurse, guide and guardian, now looks as if it could "betray" him in the future. Fear of these possibilities, as well as the urgent desire to break out of the various seclusions and dislocations and affirm true and lasting connections, motivates Wordsworth's turn to his sister Dorothy. She answers his problems by being a third-party mediator who synthetically resolves the unending antithesis of self and nature. For to Wordsworth, she is both himself and nature.

Wordsworth puts Dorothy in the position of his former self, and sees in her a record of his former self. The "wild ecstasies" (138) she is experiencing on the banks of the Wye precisely resemble his own five years earlier, and, like his, will mature in due course "Into a sober pleasure" (139). Half imagining for her the same kind of misery that he witnessed or felt in towns and cities ("If solitude, or fear, or pain, or grief, / Should be thy portion" [143–44]), he nevertheless projects for her a seamless development towards an ideal point of integrated selfhood that surpasses his own present state (and possible future state): "in after years," he prays, "thy mind / Shall be a mansion for all lovely forms, / Thy memory be as a dwelling-place / For all sweet sounds and harmonies" (136–42). As a double of himself, Dorothy thus not only maintains the past from erosion (his past self and all his arguments about the past and its efficacy) but secures the continuity of an even better future (he imagines her as an ideal, more perfect version of himself, and also as continuous with her present and his former selves). In mirroring him, Dorothy demonstrates, by autonomously repeating, his arguments about self and nature, which up to this point lacked sufficient outward proof. But in differing from him and surpassing him, Dorothy further dispels the potential solipsism by objectively realizing his desire: a continuous connection to nature in the future that will be so deep as to amount to an interfusion, for nature's forms, sounds and harmonies are to "dwell" in the mansion of the mind.

But besides accommodating nature, Dorothy also *is* nature for Wordsworth. After hailing nature as anchor, nurse, guide, guardian and soul, he appeals to Dorothy to take on precisely these tutelary functions in the future. Moreover, she essentially replaces the landscape—not only as record of his former self but as object of his view, as it is she whom he now surveys. Yet Wordsworth also puts Dorothy to work here in other ways that progressively articulate her synthetic resolution of self and nature as a transcendental ground.

First, Wordsworth half identifies Dorothy with some aspects, whether acknowledged or suppressed, of the opening scene. In hoping that nature will "so inform / [Her] mind . . . , and so feed [her] / With lofty thoughts" (125–28) as to fortify her against all forms of "sad perplexity" that humanity can inflict and that he has felt, he imputes to her the "cheerful faith" (133) and the resilience that must equally be imputed to the Hermit and the vagrant dwellers in the woods if they are to thrive and remain part of the pastoral harmony described at the beginning of the poem. Like the Hermit, Dorothy may also experience "solitude"—while, like the vagrants, she may also experience "fear, or pain, or grief." Dorothy partially becomes a metonymy for these people as Wordsworth transfers their psychological present to her possible future, actually admitting into consciousness via this third-party detour what is unnameable in its first, more deeply interfused presence. But more noticeably and perhaps more importantly, Wordsworth pictures Dorothy as exposed to the elements in the same way as these people are; he envisions nature, as it were, raining down on her own "houseless head":

> Therefore let the moon
> Shine on thee in thy solitary walk;
> And let the misty mountain-winds be free
> To blow against thee.
>
> (134–37)

The results of such exposure, however, will not be an enduring "houselessness" but a strong, stable house. When the props are removed the building will stand, for by then

> thy mind
> Shall be a mansion for all lovely forms,
> Thy memory be as a dwelling-place
> For all sweet sounds and harmonies.
>
> (139–42)

Surpassing Wordsworth's own mind (which, during the five years spent in towns and cities, constituted little more than a temporary lodging for "These beauteous forms"), Dorothy's mind, like the mind of God, will become a "mansion" for all nature, for it will contain *"all* lovely forms, . . . *all* sweet sounds and harmonies" (emphasis added). But as a strong, stable mansion, her mind also resembles the House of the Lord secluded in the landscape, Tintern Abbey itself.[15] For just as she becomes a metonymy for vagrant dwellers and Hermit, so does she also personify the object of which they are the metonymies. She comes to symbolize all that the Abbey itself symbolizes: the continuity of "faith" through solitude and desolation (to which the Abbey, though propless, still stands dedicated).

Retaining these various strengths against the wasting powers of human life and natural elements, Dorothy is therefore defined by impression and seclusion in such a way as to become the site of connection itself, the repository of all the poem's values, the ground on which all the strategies, actions and principles of the poem interfuse. Nature makes its impression on her, as Wordsworth can clearly tell from "the shooting lights / Of [her] wild eyes" (118–19)—and so does he in shaping her in his own image. The result is a safe seclusion in which he and nature can dwell forever:

> Nor, perchance—
> If I should be where I no more can hear
> Thy voice, nor catch from thy wild eyes these gleams
> Of past existence—wilt thou then forget
> That on the banks of this delightful stream
> We stood together; and that I, so long
> A worshipper of Nature, hither came
> Unwearied in that service; rather say

With warmer love—oh! with far deeper zeal
Of holier love. Nor wilt thou then forget,
That after many wanderings, many years
Of absence, these steep woods and lofty cliffs,
And this green pastoral landscape, were to me
More dear, both for themselves and for thy sake!

(146-59)

Dorothy will not only emit gleams of his past existence but remember his present self and all the circumstances pertaining to the present moment. Selves, absence and nature are all committed to her charge for her safekeeping—a deep seclusion that in turn makes its impression on Wordsworth. While Wordsworth believes she sees and feels his faith now, he imagines her as being able to revive the picture of his mind without any loss of vividness at some future date. He thus feels himself constituted by her reciprocal power of impression. Like himself and yet different, identified with nature and yet human, Dorothy is situated as the midway ground on which the various binarisms—self and nature, past and future, presence and absence, impression and seclusion—coexist and are reconciled. With the imbrications so thick at this point, Dorothy becomes an explicitly *transcendental* ground because she is both inside and outside, both self and nature and yet neither one exclusively, a both/neither in whom the epistemological barriers separating Wordsworth from his object are obviated by her functional subsumption of time and place (Wordsworth commutes everything to her for her to constitute). If Wordsworth earlier regarded nature as ground when reaching its deep seclusions or discovered his own mind to function in a similar way, Dorothy's mind surpasses both because it subsumes both. Because of its constitutive function and especially because of its simultaneous inner and outer situation, her mind is therefore a true transcendental ground—and the philosophical position Wordsworth has unknowingly reached, a true transcendental idealism. True to his empiricism at this time, however, he figures that transcendentalism in wholly sensory form: the ground is not recognized or seen as such; instead, it is known only by the building standing on it.

In the Notebook fragments, *The Pedlar* and "Tintern Abbey" we can see Wordsworth consciously working with the standard empiricist epistemology and metaphysics of his time. Obviously excited by the theories of personal identity and development, nature and perception that philosophy has to offer, he puts them to poetic use in such a way that anomalies rapidly come to light. The major difficulty he encounters (the inadequacies of a passive theory of mind and an active theory of nature) pushes him away from Lockean theory towards incipiently Kantian positions. As he openly starts theorizing about the powers of mind and how it "half create[s]" as well as passively "perceive[s]" (or rather half creates *when* it perceives), Wordsworth opposes Locke on precisely the same grounds and in precisely the same way as Kant does. And as an active theory of mind correspondingly challenges an active theory of nature, Wordsworth also starts exploring the notion of a transcendental ground as he seeks to determine who or what constitutes what or whom. Moving steadily towards such insights in the Notebooks and *The Pedlar,* he articulates them more fully in "Tintern Abbey," as we have seen. Although a belief in a pantheistic One Life in nature (and behind that a more standard, orthodox faith in God) is a major empowering force in this poetry (and in the two-part *Prelude* of 1798–99), it is broached in such a way that the question of epistemological agency provides as much of the interest as the metaphysics itself. There obtains throughout this poetry a productive theoretical traffic, then, between nature and mind and one that Wordsworth cannot resolve or let come to rest. While mind and its activity successively rise in importance here and throughout the next few years (in the 1805 *Prelude* especially), Wordsworth is not prepared to commit himself to one party at the expense of the other—and not prepared, furthermore, to side with one philosophy to the exclusion of another. As he deconstructs empiricism in this poetry, he unconsciously and only half constructs transcendentalism. The tension between the two tendencies works to best effect in the philosophical ambiguity of such frequently used words as "form," "image," "shape," "outline." They name realities that can be inner or outer or both. The mean that such words strike is at some point precarious. As he reexamines the interrelations of mind and nature and revises his philosophical theories, he posits the reality of such words differently. In the process he writes his way into transcendentalism proper, giving a different image and outline to the shapes and forms of mind and nature.

4

Concluding *The Prelude:*
Wordsworth's Transcendentalism in 1804

We move from the empiricist-pantheist poetry of 1798 to the transcendental poetry of 1804. We can make this large a leap because, as already suggested, the work Wordsworth does on *The Prelude* during the intervening years does not alter so much as extend his earlier philosophical insights. With several important passages from the Alfoxden Notebook and *The Pedlar* transferred almost verbatim to *The Prelude*—with the Discharged Soldier episode, more-over, which was first drafted in the Alfoxden Notebook, becoming the conclusion of book 4, and with book 5 amplifying the argument on books already given in *The Pedlar*—it is not hard to see that the philosophical foundations laid in 1798 prove particularly strong and enduring. The anticipations of transcendentalism we have noticed so far remain largely just that—anticipations. It is not until the spring of 1804 that Wordsworth fulfills those anticipations and breaks into new transcendental territory.

The transcendental poetry I wish to examine includes the "Immortality" Ode (begun in 1802 but concluded in March 1804) and three climactic sequences from *The Prelude* all written in March or early April 1804: the linking passage between the two "spots of time" narratives in book 11 (11. 316–45), the Climbing of Snowdon in book 13 (13. 1–116), and Crossing the Alps in book 6 (6. 488–572).[1]

Wordsworth himself canonizes these texts. In *Poems* (1815), in which he organizes his poems according to poetic form, the dominant mental faculty they engage or the period of life to which they refer, the Ode stands outside the series, coming last in the volume after "Old Age" and "Epitaphs," as if its statement were consummate and final, as if it were the last word. The *Prelude* texts are also equally climactic. All are presented as unexpected sublime revelations: as part of the "spots of time" conclusion for the five-book *Prelude* (about which more below), the linking passage contributes to its closing theoretical statement, while the Alps and Snowdon sequences are positioned at the middle and end of the 1805 autobiographical epic, as if only by crossing the divide could Wordsworth reach the final summit. In one way or another, then, these texts conclude the poem; they contain the last word *The Prelude* has to say on self and nature. This poetry of 1804 thus carries all the authority of ultimate truth, as if imparting Wordsworth's consummate visionary insight into the self's origins and tendency, a destiny passing from immortality through nature to its home in infinitude. It is no wonder, then, that the transcendental vision of 1804 should be seen as Wordsworth's greatest and lasting achievement.

I wish in this chapter to return this poetry to its philosophical context, which will make the transcendental landing-places Wordsworth reaches less absolute and more tentative. For this poetry is integral to the state of *The Prelude* in early 1804 and the issues Wordsworth is wrestling with. By examining this context, by attending to the filiations among these texts, we can best assess their philosophical achievement and see how Wordsworth's transcendentalism follows on from and relates to his empiricism.

Though technically independent of *The Prelude,* the "Immortality" Ode is linked to it in several important ways. In general, the poem glosses some of its central themes: childhood, the relation of past to present, the relation of self to nature and the dwindling of imaginative power, the loss of the "visionary gleam" (56), as Wordsworth calls it (themes which are nearly all central to "Tintern Abbey," of course). A less direct but more explicitly philosophical link is traceable via the Ode's role as a rejoinder to Coleridge's "Dejection: An Ode," a poem that openly announces transcendental positions and has a profound impact on *The Prelude* too. In the three *Prelude* passages Wordsworth deploys Coleridge's theories in "Dejection," openly espousing his argument and closely echoing his language in the linking passage between the two "spots of time." (In fact, Wordsworth emerges as in closer agreement with Coleridge in *The Prelude* than in the Ode.) In a less apparent but still significant way, the Ode invokes certain topographical features similar to those of the *Prelude* passages.

Topographically, of course, the Snowdon and Alps sequences are quite close: whether metaphorically or literally, Wordsworth finds himself in the mist in a mountainous terrain only to have blindness lead to sudden revelation. If this landscape, also half descried in the linking passage between the "spots of time," is thus common to all, it suggests how much these texts reflect and refract one another, for they were all written within a few weeks of one another.

Wordsworth completed the Ode (stanzas 5–11) in early March 1804. At the same time, of course, he was bringing the five-book *Prelude* to completion. Books 1–3 of this work corresponded closely with books 1–3 of the 1805 *Prelude,* and book 4 comprised the majority of both the later books 4 and 5; but book 5 essentially comprised what became in 1805 book 13, lines 1–65 and 70–165, and book 11, lines 123–388. That is, it began with the Climbing of Snowdon, and then (with the lines about "The perfect image of a mighty Mind" [13. 69] not yet written) discussed the "analogy betwixt / The mind of man and nature" (1850 *Prel,* 623), then proceeded to "Imagination, How Impaired and Restored" (as Wordsworth puts it in the title of book 11 in 1805), offering causes for imagination's impairment in a general way and finally moving to its restoration through the good offices of nature, Wordsworth's loved ones and the "spots of time" sequence. Wordsworth composed the Snowdon sequence, Jonathan Wordsworth writes, "within days, weeks at most, of composing stanzas V-XI of the *Intimations Ode";*[2] and the same is true of the linking passage between the two "spots of time," which amplifies the theoretical context of these episodes and echoes both the Snowdon climb and the Ode.

But around 10 March 1804, Wordsworth abruptly abandoned this five-book work, and decided to expand it into a longer poem. Jonathan Wordsworth explains that

> two factors seem especially to have influenced Wordsworth's decision to work towards a longer poem: dissatisfaction at having left out important biographical material and unwillingness to make a further attempt on the central philosophical section of *The Recluse*. The five-book *Prelude* had stayed within a chronological framework but skipped two years between the summers of 1789 and '91 in order to reach the climactic imaginative experience of the Ascent of Snowdon. In beginning his last book, Wordsworth had shown his unease—

> > Once (but I must premise that several years
> > Are overleaped to reach this incident). . . .

But besides the issue of omitted "biographical material," an important problem that also emerged was that "the five-book *Prelude* had made a not altogether convincing attempt to portray 'Imagination Impaired': the lines in question lack credibility because of their failure to relate the faltering of imaginative power to the external events, social and political, which had in fact been its cause." To redress these omissions Wordsworth began immediately writing about his 1790 vacation in France and Switzerland (book 6 was well underway by the end of March) and by early June he had most likely written "a version of Book IX and the first half of X" dealing with his "Residence in France." Wordsworth composed the sequence describing his crossing of the Alps probably in late March—"within days, weeks at most, of composing" the Snowdon sequence.[3]

What we can infer, then, from the state of *The Prelude* in the spring of 1804 is that the recognition that disrupts an otherwise coherent and completed text is a real anxiety about the kinds of dislocation we have been considering in Wordsworth's poetry of 1798. However one might paint in the human features of this dislocation—as political, historical, psychological —Wordsworth evidently portrays it as epistemological in ultimately regarding it as a question of imagination's impairment and restoration, of alienation from nature and the failure of response and finally their correction.[4] We can gauge the importance of the problem not only from the fact that Wordsworth chose to expand *The*

Prelude in the way he did but from the order of the final book of the five-book *Prelude*. The Snowdon climb with Wordsworth's "meditation" (13. 66) on the interaction between mind and nature, a near-two-hundred-line sequence that is climactic and authoritative (in draft form in MS. W as well as in book 13 of 1805), cedes to an equally long sequence documenting the failure of this imaginative interaction, a sequence that would seem to call into question everything that has just been affirmed. Just as in *The Pedlar,* where sublime scenes and climactic visions nonetheless conduct to the youth's disturbance, so Wordsworth gives way here to the unavoidable either/or of antithetical argument.

The movement is important because it is paradigmatic of the course of Wordsworth's transcendental argument in 1804. If we put the passages in likely order of composition we can see that they swing back and forth in affirming and then doubting, fearing loss but then registering joy, as one claim counters another and one landing-place gives way to another. The Ode, presumably at the start of this sequence, records the loss of light (though finding another kind of radiance to compensate for the loss), but the light burns steadily in the linking passage between the two "spots of time" (though in the final lines added in 1805 it gutters and is all but extinguished); on Snowdon the light shines forth strong again, whereas in the Alps it goes out with a flash only to flare forth right away in the apostrophe to Imagination and then take on apocalyptic coloring in Gondo Gorge. If we read the texts in compositional sequence we can watch this changing chiaroscuro play across a landscape that also changes. Although Wordsworth finally elevates Snowdon above the Alps in the completed 1805 text (the lines on "The perfect image of a mighty Mind," added some time in late 1804 or early 1805, cap his developing argument in these passages about the relation between mind and nature), we can better trace the philosophical tensions that are my concern here if we follow the unfolding plot of the compositional sequence.[5] I begin here with the Ode, then discuss in order the linking passage between the "spots of time" narratives, the Climbing of Snowdon in its MS. W version, Crossing the Alps, and finally the lines on "The perfect image of a mighty Mind" to see how they redirect the Snowdon scene and its interpretation (and answer the Alpine sequence). By reading in this order we will see how strong a hold empiricism maintains on Wordsworth's mind, even as he forges with complete conviction into transcendental territory. But first we should consider the transcendentalism and its provenance.

I mentioned earlier that Coleridge would have kept Wordsworth informed about his own changing philosophical beliefs. Although he never put down his "notes for the Recluse" as Wordsworth begged of him in early March, he would assuredly have grounded Wordsworth in the rudiments of German transcendentalism during the previous three years. Wordsworth evidently learned the elements of the critical philosophy very well, as his increasing emphasis in the course of *The Prelude* on the imagination and the power and beauty of the mind clearly shows. His understanding of the critical philosophy takes shape, however, in the poetic dialogue with Coleridge, in the exchange of odes. In March 1802, Wordsworth wrote the first four stanzas of the "Immortality" Ode, ending with questions that seemed unanswerable then:

> Whither is fled the visionary gleam?
> Where is it now, the glory and the dream?
>
> (56–57)

The change in outward nature, the loss of "celestial light" (4), seems so far a problem of the object. Coleridge replied a week later in the first draft of "Dejection: An Ode" (his verse letter of April 4, 1802, to Sara Hutchinson), making the failure of nature wholly the problem of the subject—and a problem of the failure of imagination:

> I may not hope from outward forms to win
> The passion and the life, whose fountains are within.
>
> O Lady! we receive but what we give,
> And in our life alone does nature live:
> Ours is her wedding garment, ours her shroud!
>   And would we aught behold, of higher worth,
> Than that inanimate cold world allowed
> To the poor loveless ever-anxious crowd
>   Ah! from the soul itself must issue forth
> A light, a glory, a fair luminous cloud
>   Enveloping the Earth—
> And from the soul itself must there be sent
>   A sweet and potent voice, of its own birth,
> Of all sweet sounds the life and element!
>
> (45–58)

Behind Coleridge's complaint we can glimpse the theories that he summarizes so succinctly in *Biographia Literaria:* quoting Leibniz's axiom that "There is nothing in the mind that was not before in the senses, except the mind itself," he adds that "We learn all things indeed by *occasion* of experience; but the very facts so learnt force us inward on the antecedents, that must be pre-supposed in order to render experience itself possible" (Coleridge's emphasis).[6] Coleridge dramatizes that movement inward on the antecedents in "Dejection." The "fountains . . . within," the "light" and "voice" all point to something prior in the self—structure, categories and acts—that allows the outside world to become real, to be known and enjoyed. Coleridge expresses these presupposed antecedents as a giving and receiving, a giving first from which a receiving follows.

Although his claim that nature is dead unless we give it life sounds more radical a doctrine than Wordsworth would countenance, Wordsworth at least comes to agree with Coleridge (two years later) that the transaction between self and nature consists in giving and receiving. In the linking passage between the "spots of time," he concedes: "but this I feel, / That from thyself it is that thou must give, / Else never canst receive" (11. 332–34). He comes to see, then, following Coleridge, that the problem of the subject is at bottom the reason for nature's diminution. This transcendental doctrine explains events on Snowdon and in the Alps too. But its contractual reciprocity is only half perceived in the "Immortality" Ode.

The "Presumptive Evidence" of the "Immortality" Ode

In answering Coleridge yet in glossing the concerns preoccupying Wordsworth in *The Prelude,* "Ode: Intimations of Immortality from Recollections of Early Childhood" prefigures the problems that interrupt the course of *Prelude* composition in March 1804. The poem announces the crisis that the later *Prelude* itself, from book 5 on, will seek to answer. In a more general and less biographical form than in *The Prelude,* Wordsworth explores the full import of the self's dislocation from meanings that formerly had seemed immediate (in the Alfoxden Notebook, for example, if already less so in *The Pedlar* and "Tintern Abbey"). In fact, in fully acknowledging, in the course of the Ode, that dislocation is the epistemological given, the sole premise of all present and future experience, Wordsworth learns what constitutes the self's humanity, which if emerging as a less than abundant recompense for the lost light of earlier immediacy nonetheless binds self to nature by implicating both in the epistemological problematics of meaning.

In the Ode, Wordsworth squarely confronts the problem of meaning, regarding it first of all as a problem of the object:

> There was a time when meadow, grove, and stream
> The earth, and every common sight,
>   To me did seem
>   Apparelled in celestial light,
> The glory and the freshness of a dream.
> It is not now as it hath been of yore;—
>   Turn wheresoe'er I may,
>   By night or day,
> The things which I have seen I now can see no more.

(1–9)

What is at issue, it seems, is "outness" in the Coleridgean sense.[7] The object itself seems diminished, for Wordsworth can *"see"* (emphasis added) but not "feel" the beauty of the world:

> The Rainbow comes and goes,
> And lovely is the Rose,
> The Moon doth with delight
> Look round her when the heavens are bare,
> Waters on a starry night
> Are beautiful and fair;
> The sunshine is a glorious birth
> But yet I know, where'er I go,
> That there hath past away a glory from the earth.
>
> (10–18)

While eclipse of the former glory of outness becomes with Coleridge the occasion for surmise about whether the subject or the object bestows the "light" of life, with Wordsworth it promotes surmise about that "light" itself as the antecedent which must be presupposed in order to render the dualism of subject and object possible. Bypassing Coleridge's concern with priority, with either/or, Wordsworth proceeds directly to both/and, where the underlying problem is really that of vision itself, the problem simultaneously determining subject and object alike. As a result, the problem of the object is also the problem of the subject—as becomes evident in stanza 3 when Wordsworth recognizes that his own "thought of grief" (22) wrongs the season. But the interdependence of "outness" and "in-ness" registers most forcefully in stanza 4, where the subject usurps itself with a perception of the object which, while redounding to intrinsic characteristics of the object, yields a cognitive content that is subjective:

> —But there's a Tree, of many, one,
> A single Field which I have looked upon,
> Both of them speak of something that is gone:
> The Pansy at my feet
> Doth the same tale repeat:
> Whither is fled the visionary gleam?
> Where is it now, the glory and the dream?
>
> (51–57)

What the self can "see" or "see no more" when "look[ing] upon" outward sights prompts Wordsworth to do more than question the duality of perceiver and perceived; it causes him to speculate about "The excellence, pure spirit, and best power / Both of the object seen, and eye that sees" (*Prel* 13. 378–79). Surveying outward sights and pondering inward meaning, Wordsworth speculates about the light itself which makes vision—and the "perception" of meaning—possible.[8] Focusing in the Ode on the visible and the invisible, Wordsworth surmises the optics of "celestial light," from which he then commensurately determines the power of a peculiar eye.

All that the self beheld in early childhood respired, so it seemed, with unproblematic inward meaning. Wordsworth figures meaning—and, more deeply, the sense of meaningfulness itself—as a simple radiant light. Whether passively perceiving or actively creating meaning, the self sees a light; and the phenomenon allows that this light may emanate not only from the subject or the object (or both) but also from another independent source: an invisible transcendental source such as God. As a figure, celestial light bespeaks some form of presence, whether conceived of as an original unproblematic immediacy or, in mediated form, as a particular disposition of meaningfulness. To explain that former sense of presence and its loss now, Wordsworth rears the structure of a figural metaphysics on the epistemological base of seeing outward sights.

Stanzas 5–8 of the Ode delineate this celestial metaphysics, and from it Wordsworth surmises different explanations for the loss of light. His surmise of the origin is at once a surmise of tendency—not only because tendency is the immediate occasion of surmise ("Whither is fled the visionary gleam?") but also because the closest approximation to the origin Wordsworth can reach is at best already a tending away from it. If God is "our home" (65) and the ultimate source of celestial light, the most that Wordsworth can surmise is "behold[ing] the light, and whence it flows" (69),[9] a figure which entrenches distance—and an epistemological breach—even as it aspires after proximity to presence.

The Ode, by any account, is the epitome of surmise, but in the central stanzas we can see surmise reach its period. Wordsworth strives to reach the origin itself, where he finds that dislocation, in whatever form, is the closest he can get to presence. Any figure he surmises is necessarily an "exterior semblance" which "doth belie" (109) some inward, and perhaps ineffable, meaning.[10] Even the child, who at his "being's height" (123) is a "Seer blest" (115), an "Eye among the blind" (112), can do no more than repeat the act of beholding something whose inward meaning is undisclosed and no doubt divergent from its "exterior semblance" representing it. The child "read[s] the eternal deep, / Haunted for ever by the eternal mind" (113–14). However fluid a form of writing, "the eternal deep" appears "formed" if not "fixed" in its meaning in comparison with those meanings forever forming in the "eternal mind" which wrote the deep.[11] That the child is "Haunted" by this "mind" suggests that he senses a continuing and differing play of intentions from those inscribed in the deep—a possible variance which turns what he sees and understands into an "exterior semblance" of unfathomable inward meaning.

At the origin, the child beholds and reads: he *tends,* therefore, by pursuing meanings and intentions which are not his own and which he can never truly fix but which he appropriates and shapes into a particular form as he interprets the fluid text of eternity. At the origin is dislocation, which necessarily generates tendency. And because all the child knows of the origin is a semblance, and because his vantage point is always that of dislocation, the tendency he pursues can look like (and probably is) error, as if he is "blindly with [his] blessedness at strife" (126). As stanzas 7 and 8 insist, tendency is not only inevitable but apparently arbitrary, and even wilful too.

These middle stanzas of the Ode (5–8) present Wordsworth's "best conjectures" (*Prel,* 2. 238) of how celestial light was lost, a metaphysics of loss in which tendency plays an active part. But while Wordsworth must presuppose an antecedent metaphysical tendency because it cannot be remembered, he nevertheless projects into "the time of unrememberable being" the actual tendency of loss that he *does* remember.[12] The original memory that he can locate is at best a memory of loss—a memory of celestial light vanishing:[13]

> O joy! that in our embers
> Is something that doth live,
> That nature yet remembers
> What was so fugitive!

(130–33)

From this vantage point, memory thus corroborates the "presumptive evidence" of surmise; it produces our faintly glowing "embers" as proof of our vanished celestial "blaze" (*Prel,* 8. 630)—and as the only "index" yet remaining of the "utmost" we once knew (and can now recall only as a "thought" in surmise).[14] Yet this memory, in substantiating surmise, further entrenches the breach: Wordsworth recollects that dislocation and wayward tendency obtained at the earliest time of *rememberable* being as well:

> Not for these I raise
> The song of thanks and praise;
> But for those obstinate questionings
> Of sense and outward things,
> Fallings from us, vanishings;
> Blank misgivings of a Creature
> Moving about in worlds not realised,
> High instincts before which our mortal Nature
> Did tremble like a guilty Thing surprised:
> But for those first affections,
> Those shadowy recollections,
> Which, be they what they may,
> Are yet the fountain light of all our day,
> Are yet a master light of all our seeing.

(140–53)

The immortal child's beholding and reading fathers the mortal child's obstinate questioning. Verifying the antecedents which hitherto could only be presupposed, Wordsworth affirms that tendencies do indeed trespass from their proper path as mortality assumes the bequest of immortality: "those obstinate questionings of sense / And outward things" trace a reading which translates "fallings from us" into an inevitable "inner falling-off" (*Prel,* 4. 270). But if tendency is ipso facto errancy, it is because "obstinacy" is a priori, conditioned by the dislocation subsisting at both the mortal and the immortal origins, as the middle stanzas of the Ode have shown. Beholding, reading, obstinately questioning, moving about and trembling—the self strives "with such earnest pains" (124) to determine its own location, to take its bearings from the fading light. In the process, the self expresses and discovers vital facets of its own identity.

In fact, Wordsworth's surmise of the origin, of the passage from "Immortality" to "mortal Nature," amounts, as it were, to a Kantian deduction of personal identity. Fugitive light, dislocation and obstinate tendency compose the schematic a priori of this self—a self which from the first moment of phenomenal experience is, as Wordsworth postulated in a discarded passage in MS. RV of the two-part *Prelude,* a "Relapse from the one interior life." Waking from "a sleep and a forgetting," the self is left alone (more radically than is the boy in book 2 of *The Prelude* when the props of his affections are removed) with only a dim and undetermined sense of not-yet-known modes of being on the one hand, and a dimmer and less-determined sense of barely remembered modes of being on the other. Having surmised the antecedents, Wordsworth is able to characterize the self at the very moment at which the nonsensible engages with the sensible, the transcendental with the empirical. His theory therefore posits both the metaphysical and epistemological structure of the self: both the "light" and the "seeing."

Dislocation, then, determines identity; it shapes "our mortal Nature." Unable in time to "keep / [Its immortal] heritage" (111–12), the self inherits instead "that strong frame of sense in which we dwell."[15] Through a process of action and reaction, the self tests the strength of this new inheritance while at the same time registering the vanishing of celestial light. Action and reaction thus express affect—the effect on the self both of the "sense" that impinges and of the light that is eroded. Such affect in turn fathers "our first *affections*" (emphasis added). Beholding, reading, obstinately questioning, feeling misgivings and guilty tremblings, the self begins to experience how these "affections" constitute "the human heart" (201); it learns how dislocation, which keeps us forever beholding, reading and obstinately questioning, is the author of "our mortal Nature" and is the base on which our humanity is reared. "[T]hose first affections, / Those shadowy recollections," Wordsworth claims, "Are yet the fountain light of all our day, / Are yet a master light of all our seeing." He takes them as evidence of the self's continuity, which the "something that doth live" in "our embers" confirms. Memory, even if only of a forgetting, thus offers itself not only as the ground of identity but as the premise of an intimation of immortality, an intimation which surmise can renew repeatedly:[16]

> Hence in a season of calm weather
> Though inland far we be,
> Our Souls have sight of that immortal sea
> Which brought us hither,
> Can in a moment travel thither,
> And see the Children sport upon the shore,
> And hear the mighty waters rolling evermore.
>
> (162–68)

But however much this intimation appears to affirm continuity and thereby redeem loss, it does not restore exactly what had been lost. It is not the past which it brings into view but the present: not the immortal past of Wordsworth's *own* preexistence but the immortal present of others' preexistence coextensive with his own phenomenal present now. If anything, in fact, the vision affirms temporal discreteness rather than continuity, a permanent dislocation which puts the self's past immortality forever out of reach.

The very attempt to trace continuity ends up affirming discontinuity, dislocation. In fact, it intimates the self's historicity, its finitude, its mortality. In the stanzas that follow, Wordsworth in effect "bend[s] to the law of death as applying to our own particular case."[17] Yet correlatively, he finds incontrovertible evidence of continuity in the very dislocation forcing him "to admit the notion of death as a state applicable to [his] own being."[18] Because dislocation is the condition of "our mortal Nature," our humanity, it therefore constitutes a form of continuity itself, the foundation on which everything since has been reared. This Wordsworth implicitly acknowledges as he returns from "thought"—from memory and surmise—to the sunshine and joy of the May morning:

> Then sing, ye Birds, sing, sing a joyous song!
> And let the young Lambs bound
> As to the tabor's sound!
> We in thought will join your throng,
> Ye that pipe and ye that play,
> Ye that through your hearts to-day
> Feel the gladness of the May!
> What though the radiance which was once so bright
> Be now for ever taken from my sight,
> Though nothing can bring back the hour
> Of splendour in the grass, of glory in the flower;
> We will grieve not, rather find
> Strength in what remains behind;
> In the primal sympathy

> Which having been must ever be;
> In the soothing thoughts that spring
> Out of human suffering;
> In the faith that looks through death,
> In years that bring the philosophic mind.
>
> (169–87)

Because of dislocation, Wordsworth realizes that he can join the "throng" only "in thought." The creatures' present joy is his past joy; what they experience now he experienced in the past. Yet for such loss, he argues, there is recompense. In fact, he is almost truculent about it ("What though . . ."). For through his *own* heart he feels a kind of gladness which dislocation alone has made possible: the precarious, difficult gladness of a *human* heart, won with effort over the succession of days bound each to each in recompense for the loss of light and all its attendant joys. In stanza 10 of the Ode, Wordsworth turns to face his own humanity; he accepts a human identity, whose intrinsic difference from celestial light derives from the original premise of dislocation.

Wordsworth finds continuity, then, in dislocation itself, in the series of actions and reactions whereby the self responds to the fugitive light, or substitutes for it some human tendency—its own human "affections" by which means it works its way toward finding "Strength in what remains behind." Human affections fill the place left by celestial light, and as compensatory substitutions they therefore become *human* "semblances" of that light. "[P]rimal sympathy" is the "mortal" version of proximity to presence, a giving and receiving of the same light in the state of dislocation. And while "the soothing thoughts that spring / Out of human suffering" betray the painful cost of dislocation, "the faith that looks through death" and "the philosophic mind" reveal a new, emerging *human* radiance, which reapproximates celestial light by illuminating the way toward a possible future immortality.

Yet in affirming an autonomous human identity, Wordsworth nonetheless understands how this human "heritage" is entailed on the human self. As he immediately surmises in the opening lines of stanza 11, dislocation, fostering autonomy, now threatens to "sever" (189) the self from nature, just as it originally severed the self from celestial light. As the antecedent of "severance," dislocation is originally the law of life, the author of "our mortal Nature," but now it has conducted to "the law of death" which, in the opening lines of stanza 11, Wordsworth implicitly accepts as "applying to our own particular case":

> And O, ye Fountains, Meadows, Hills, and Groves,
> Forebode not any severing of our loves!
> Yet in my heart of hearts I feel your might;
> I only have relinquished one delight
> To live beneath your more habitual sway.

> I love the Brooks which down their channels fret,
> Even more than when I tripped lightly as they;
> The innocent brightness of a new-born Day
> Is lovely yet.

(188–96)

Given that "the radiance which was once so bright / Be now for ever taken from [his] sight," Wordsworth therefore takes nature to be all the more meaningful—precisely because it is the best "semblance" of that former radiance. Compensatory substitution of this order guides Wordsworth's turn to nature in every line of the final stanza. Released from the "might" of "Immortality," its former "Master" (120), the self has since "live[d] beneath [the] more habitual sway" of nature, whose "might" he feels in his "heart of hearts." Yet Wordsworth earnestly hopes that nature, unlike celestial light, will prove to be "A Presence which is not to be put by" (121). For just like the embers in *our* nature which recollect the fugitive light, nature's semblances continue to resemble—even if they dissemble—celestial light. Dislocation turns all to semblance, but nature affords presumptive evidence of celestial substance behind the semblance in that the light of nature has continued to shine and is forever renewed: "The innocent brightness of a new-born Day / Is lovely yet."

Even if the brooding Day is not Immortality's, and even if resemblances fade into a dissembling "shadowiness" like that celebrated in stanza 9 as daylight yields to darkening clouds, Wordsworth nonetheless proclaims a "sympathy" between two sets of "semblances" which he hopes "will ever be." Nature's semblances sympathize with human semblances also substituting for the vanished light. Both born of a "primal" dislocation, natural semblance and human semblance sympathize with and resemble one another:

> The Clouds that gather round the setting sun
> Do take a sober colouring from an eye
> That hath kept watch o'er man's mortality;
> Another race hath been, and other palms are won.

(197–200)

This "eye" may be conditioned to a darker end of the celestial spectrum than the "Eye" of the immortal "Seer blest," but it surpasses that "Eye" in possessing the peculiar power of "colouring" the objects of its perception. "The Clouds . . . take a sober colouring" from this eye because it is through the medium of the mortal that the self perceives, and this, like Kant's transcendental categories of the mind, determines the object's appearance. Sympathetic to this eye, furthermore, is another eye—the setting sun—which, as the eye of heaven, has also "kept watch" over man's mortal race while running its own race over earth and ocean. Resembling the sun, of course, is "The Soul that rises with us, our life's

Star" (59). Each is a semblance of the other; but both are semblances of celestial light. As such, then, they are bound each to each as semblances of semblances, doomed to dissemble the radiance they would simulate. This metaphysic registers as an optical effect and as epistemological fact in that the "sober colouring," the product "Both of the object seen, and the eye that sees," shades the light and substitutes for it a "shadowiness" whose distinction is its opacity, its substantive *objectivity,* rather than its translucence, however flawed, as a semblance. If to behold the light of nature is to look through a glass darkly at the dim refraction of celestial light, it is also to "look upon" nature as the mirror of man—to see in a mortal nature the reflection of *"our* mortal Nature" (emphasis added). Nature thus becomes all the more meaningful not only because, like the human self, it offers semblances of the fugitive light but also because it shares in sympathy with this self the dislocation of a "mortal" object existing at a remove from the light.

In the final two stanzas of the Ode, Wordsworth takes earnest pains to embrace our mortal human nature. But in the Ode's final lines themselves, he bears witness to an inward meaning which "our mortal Nature" could alone respire—a meaning which is not a mere semblance, a dim reflection, of celestial light but one which, originating in our mortal nature, and from its vantage point of dislocation, reflects on celestial light itself. Wordsworth now appreciates that "Another race hath been, and other palms are won." Having lost the eternal life of preexistence, he has gained instead the mortal life of "affections" and "loves"—the specifically human "Strength" of *feeling,* which enables the self to mourn the loss of celestial light in the first place and now to fear the severing of mortal loves, the loss of the human and of nature in death itself. The setting sun forebodes, of course, the setting of "our life's Star." And such a death, according to the astronomical calculations of stanza 5, should foretell its future rising in celestial realms "elsewhere" (60). But at the end of his Ode, Wordsworth raises the song of thanks and praise less for the prospects of a joyful reunion with celestial light than once again and even more strongly for human obstinacy, which now makes mortal shadowiness preferable to the light of a possible immortality in the future. For the incorruptible crown awaiting the runner of life's race in heaven,[19] Wordsworth would gladly substitute "other palms," the "coronal" (40) of mortal humanity itself;

> Thanks to the human heart by which we live,
> Thanks to its tenderness, its joys, and fears,
> To me the meanest flower that blows can give
> Thoughts that do often lie too deep for tears.
>
> (201–4)

If Wordsworth does redeem loss in the "Immortality" Ode, then it is by dint of bravely championing our mortal nature in lieu of celestial light. The thought of death makes life all the dearer—and in particular "the human heart by which we live." As an emblem of life's worth, an "index" (though the least significant) to the "utmost," "the meanest flower that blows" would be lost in death's "severing of our loves," so that it is both nature and human nature that Wordsworth mourns for. Yet the prospect of the light of sense going out sparks a blinding flash of inward meaning: this flower "can give / Thoughts that do often lie too deep for tears." The final line, arresting in its impenetrable obscurity, suggests the overwhelming presence of the "utmost" (but ineffable) meaning: the sorrow of death, perhaps, too deep for tears, or possibly the sublime faith in a future immortality too deep, in its way, for tears of joy.[20] In any event, the line bears witness to the mystery of immanence rather than the transcendence which the Ode overtly celebrates. The meanest flower that blows is to Wordsworth a frail shrine of mortal meanings, certainly a mere "Label" but also a sure "index" of our mortal Nature's utmost meaningfulness. Wordsworth looks upon this flower as if it were an epitaph, as if it were growing on the site of mortality itself, which is indeed "the place of thought," the mortal soil in which human thoughts lie buried too deep to find relief in any form of human expression.[21] If the sober coloring of the final line of the Ode looks like "the darkness of the grave" (118), it is a darkness visible equally as blinding as the celestial light. The sense of presence, of utmost meaning, which celestial light bespeaks in earlier stanzas of the Ode, is now "a state applicable" to this rival figure, which conveys an utmost meaningfulness equally indeterminable but which, unlike celestial light, presumes the whole human heart as antecedent and origin: "its tenderness, its joys, and fears," and, one might add, its forebodings, its loves, its faith, strength and misgivings. Resisting the self's commutation to the celestial soil of immortality, Wordsworth decides to defend the mortal soil of the human heart. And the meanest flower that blows, by giving "Thoughts . . . too deep for tears," shows how well entrenched is the human heart in that soil, as if the human were entirely immanent in nature itself.

The human heart, the flower, and "Thoughts . . . too deep for tears" argue the interdependence of subject and object. Self and nature are bound each to each by the dislocation which threatens loss and yet which, by that very act, makes mortal meaning possible. At the end of the Ode, Wordsworth relinquishes the immortal in favor of the mortal; but he had to presuppose an antecedent immortality in order to win his way toward understanding how mortal tendencies, affections and meaning were made possible. Even if celestial light appears from this vantage point to be an optical illusion, its surmised presence, its loss, and now its absence have nonetheless fathered a waking reality:[22] the precarious natural piety of the human heart, which cherishes and is upheld by the visible—and also by the invisible whose semblance the visible has become.

I have offered this reading of the Ode because the poem gives a careful deduction of transcendentalism (just as "Tintern Abbey" aims at as close a logical argument). The Ode does not present discrete lyrical moments offset by explanatory hypotheses as, say, *The Pedlar* does, but beginning in the most general way in experience it analyzes the antecedents that must be presupposed in order to render this experience possible. The more obvious and celebrated aspect of the poem is the transcendental vision of stanza 5, the immortal realm of preexistence and proximity to God. But as Wordsworth affirms in his defense in the Isabella Fenwick note, he uses the Platonic notion as an enabling poetic idea.[23] It is also, really, a heuristic philosophical idea, for Wordsworth's strategy is to posit the transcendent in order to deduce the transcendental. Wordsworth's emphasis is not on God and immortality but on the nature of the self, its a priori activity, and its orientation in the phenomenal world. To this extent the poem is surprisingly Kantian. While Wordsworth intuits the noumenal being of the self and poetically figures the noumenal realm of God and immortality that he can really only indeterminately "think," his actual concern is with the mind's transcendental structure and operations.

Yet in a Fichtean way Wordsworth posits the self in relation to a not-self, and posits them together as a binarism defined by the same problematic of meanings. Nature and self both emerge as "semblances" dislocated from presence and therefore constituted by the system of representations that contains them. Wordsworth coordinates their activities as semblances, but the question of being remains: nature may work like the self, shaping and respiring with inward meaning in the same way the self does, but the enabling, persistent recognition in the Ode (both cornerstone and stumbling-block) is that nature is a different kind of being from the self. In proper transcendentalist fashion, Wordsworth confines himself to acts rather than beings, or, as Coleridge phrases it in *Biographia Literaria,* to knowing rather than being.[24] That is, his focus is the transcendental activity of knowing, not ontological identities and actual empirical origins. Even so, the question of being persists as a potentially disruptive (and potentially empiricist) issue. For if self and nature, by the end of the Ode's argument, become "semblances," what really are they semblances of? If the only answer Wordsworth gives is "celestial light," he has nonetheless reached an ontology of imitations whose originals are intrinsically figurative.

Envoi to the Ode

These issues are openly confronted in the Snowdon and Alps sequences, but some of them—the self's transcendental nature particularly—appear in the linking passage between the two "spots of time" in book 11. Although a brief landing-place between these two narratives, the passage is an important landing-place between the Ode and the later *Prelude* passages. Reiterating the Ode to a remarkable degree in both the movement of its thought and in the poignancy of its ending (in the 1805 version), and pursuing the same preoccupation with light and darkness, sight and seeing, the passage becomes an envoi to the Ode.

Writing in March 1804, and rereading his account of the first "spot of time," Wordsworth remembers a very different perception of the landscape in question. Originally, at about age six, Wordsworth noticed, while looking for the guide from whom the mist had separated him, and after stumbling across the site of a gibbet,

> A naked Pool that lay beneath the hills,
> The Beacon on the Summit, and more near,
> A Girl who bore a Pitcher on her head
> And seem'd with difficult steps to force her way
> Against the blowing wind.

(11. 305–8)

The "visionary dreariness" (11. 311) of this "ordinary sight" (11. 309) cedes to a radically different mood when Wordsworth revisits the spot many years later:

> When in a blessed season
> With those two dear Ones, to my heart so dear,
> When in the blessed time of early love,
> Long afterwards, I roam'd about
> In daily presence of this very scene,
> Upon the naked pool and dreary crags,
> And on the melancholy Beacon, fell
> The spirit of pleasure and youth's golden gleam;
> And think ye not with radiance more divine
> From these remembrances, and from the power
> They left behind? So feeling comes in aid
> Of feeling, and diversity of strength
> Attends us, if but once we have been strong.

(11. 316–28)

"The spirit of pleasure and youth's golden gleam" are an acceptable substitute for the Ode's lost "visionary gleam," for the luster they shed, magnified by the "radiance more divine / From these remembrances," approximates the celestial light which had formerly apparelled every common sight. Indeed, this new gleam illuminates the "visionary dreariness" formerly investing this "ordinary sight." For, as if revising the early stanzas of the Ode, Wordsworth insists that memory does not lose sight of memory but compounds memory, generating a "radiance" of considerable intensity and "power." This empirical discovery about the power and continuity of the self issues into a revelation of the self's transcendental form:

> Oh! mystery of Man, from what a depth
> Proceed thy honours! I am lost, but see
> In simple childhood something of the base
> On which thy greatness stands, but this I feel,
> That from thyself it is that thou must give,
> Else never canst receive. The days gone by
> Come back upon me from the dawn almost
> Of life: the hiding-places of my power
> Seem open; I approach, and then they close.
>
> (11. 329–37)

Awed by this vision of "greatness," the "mystery of Man," Wordsworth utters "I am lost," a phrase he repeats almost verbatim in the apostrophe to Imagination in book 6 and echoes obliquely on Snowdon in book 13. Whatever the shades of consciousness blended into the phrase (disorientation, confusion, amazement), being lost becomes the precondition for finding oneself: "I am lost, but see." The self may be lost, but seeing continues uninterrupted, as if it is ultimately the "eye" which possesses the peculiar power of constituting the "I" and determining its forward direction. Looking from "I" to "thou" and back again to "me," the eye sees its way toward appropriating the greatness of Man for the "I," for the self.

In doing so, however, Wordsworth empiricizes these transcendental revelations. The first effect of this is a tantalizing sense of the continuity and power of the empirical self. Wordsworth openly espouses Coleridge's give/receive doctrine here, but he inflects it differently, making the transaction confirm the subject's power (the object's power being originally bestowed on it by the subject). Wordsworth recognizes that the "greatness" of the self consists in its power to invest landscape with "visionary" meaning in the first place and then be susceptible to that affect (to memory) now. Commensurately, this "greatness" argues the self's continuity of identity, a positive ground in which the conscious "I" can find itself:

> The days gone by
> Come back upon me from the dawn almost
> Of life: the hiding-places of my power
> Seem open; I approach, and then they close.

For a moment, all is possibility in this vision. Wordsworth seems about to recapture all the fallings from him and vanishings which the Ode presented as irretrievable. But this enticing promise of full self-presence reverts to dislocation; and power slips away from the self. To a great extent the subject/object and active/passive dichotomies force this outcome, leaving Wordsworth in empirical self-consciousness at a remove from his transcendental goal. The subject/object split between I/thou and I/me and the active/passive play of "Come back"/"approach" and "open"/"close" lock the self in a spatialized either/or in which one side finally blocks out the other: being "lost" is the necessary antecedent to "hiding-places" opening, but in approaching those hiding-places to find out where power had been hidden (and lost from sight of the "I"), the self finds that its act of looking, its very consciousness of seeing, obscures the object seen. One side of the binarism blocks out the other.

In the lines added in the final text of May 1805, the closing of hiding-places leaves the self in as radical a state of dislocation as that described in the closing stanzas of the Ode. The self is left with only its (waning) power to "see":

> I see by glimpses now; when age comes on,
> May scarcely see at all, and I would give,
> While yet we may, as far as words can give,
> A substance and a life to what I feel:
> I would enshrine the spirit of the past
> For future restoration.

(11. 338–43)

Wordsworth speaks as if the severance he feared in the Ode has already happened, as if the sun has set and the light lost to darkness—circumstances making him strive all the more for connection and continuity. Yet instead of the triumphant claims about the "Visionary Power" of language that Wordsworth makes at the close of book 5 (5. 619)—and whose phrasing he echoes in the last lines of this passage—he dwells instead on the print wearing out (as Locke says), on the fading of memory and the loss of vision. Transcendental insight yields completely to a weakening empiricist faculty of sight.

"[W]hat I feel" depends on what I see. Yet quite clearly in this passage, as in the first "spot of time" (and in *The Pedlar* as well), to see is also to feel, precisely because what the self sees is its own light illuminating every common sight. What it sees is, as it were, its own feeling, which it has projected onto the landscape, thereby making an "ordinary sight" extraordinary. This passage surpasses the Ode inasmuch as Wordsworth accepts as fact what is no more than an intermittent possibility there: the light's origination in the self and not some possibly transcendental source. To this extent he successfully turns transcendental perspicacity into genuine empirical accomplishment. In this linking passage between the two "spots of time" he abundantly affirms the power of the self, its "strength" of feeling and of memory. Yet if these are a genuine recompense for the lost immediacy, the fugitive sense of presence briefly recuperated when hiding-places open, they also entrench the state of dislocation which ultimately threatens to sever the self from direct vision of any light at all.

Imagination and Its Resemblances on Mt. Snowdon

In the linking passage between the "spots of time" narratives Wordsworth glorifies the self but for the moment does not acknowledge nature. Although the physical scenes play a determining role in the "spots" narratives themselves, Wordsworth's intention is to show "that the mind / Is lord and master, and that outward sense / Is but the obedient servant of her will" (11. 271–73). As Wordsworth moves from passage to passage in this series of transcendental texts in early 1804, his argument swings to and fro, so that having celebrated the self he next turns to give nature its due. After being lost in wonder at the mystery of Man, he then finds himself awed by the mystery of nature as he recounts his climb of Mt. Snowdon. Theorizing how one mystery complements the other, Wordsworth reaffirms both/and and forestalls the severance looming in the two previous texts.

The vision Wordsworth experiences on the top of Mt. Snowdon comes as a dramatic revelation. Not only was there nothing in the night to suggest that such a surprise could occur ("a dripping mist / Low-hung and thick . . . cover'd all the sky"; 13. 10–11), but Wordsworth's own absorption in his "private thoughts" (13. 19) renders him relatively oblivious to events around him: "by myself / Was nothing either seen or heard the while / Which took me from my musings" (13. 20–22). He climbs "with forehead bent /Earthward, as if in opposition set / Against an enemy" (13. 29–31). But behavior of this kind is an ideal precondition for sudden revelation—for "usurpation," in fact, as Wordsworth calls it in the Alps (6. 533), where a similar sequence of events unfolds to even more startling effect. On Snowdon, what Wordsworth suddenly "sees" usurps both his musings and the appearance of the environment too:

> [A]t my feet the ground appear'd to brighten,
> And with a step or two seem'd brighter still;
> Nor had I time to ask the cause of this,
> For instantly a Light upon the turf
> Fell like a flash: I look'd about, and lo!
> The Moon stood naked in the Heavens, at height
> Immense above my head, and on the shore
> I found myself of a huge sea of mist,
> Which, meek and silent, rested at my feet.
>
> (13. 36–44)

Climbing in order "to see the sun / Rise from the top of Snowdon" (13. 4–5), Wordsworth finds the glorious birth he expected to see preempted by the splendid vision of a different celestial light—the moon, who looks round her now that the heavens are bare. In his surprise, Wordsworth implicitly voices his response in the "spots" passage ("I am lost") as he states, "Nor had I time to ask the cause of this." The "flash" of celestial light shows to him a "world" not visible before:

> A hundred hills their dusky backs upheaved
> All over this still Ocean, and beyond,
> Far, far beyond, the vapours shot themselves,
> In headlands, tongues, and promontory shapes,
> Into the Sea, the real Sea, that seem'd
> To dwindle, and give up its majesty,
> Usurp'd upon as far as sight could reach.
> Meanwhile, the Moon look'd down upon this shew
> In single glory, and we stood, the mist
> Touching our very feet; and from the shore
> At distance not the third part of a mile
> Was a blue chasm; a fracture in the vapour,
> A deep and gloomy breathing-place thro' which
> Mounted the roar of waters, torrents, streams
> Innumerable, roaring with one voice.
> The universal spectacle throughout
> Was shaped for admiration and delight,
> Grand in itself alone, but in that breach
> Through which the homeless voice of waters rose,
> That dark deep thoroughfare had Nature lodg'd
> The Soul, the Imagination of the whole.
>
> (13. 45–65)

Rivalling Gondo Gorge in the Alps sequence and the various sublime visions in *The Pedlar,* this scene from the top of Snowdon presses *all* nature into service: mountain, moon, the heavens, mist, the real sea, a hundred hills, chasm and the roaring voice of waters from innumerable streams and torrents. It is indeed a "universal spectacle," and the cooperation of all nature to stage these effects argues, so Wordsworth concludes, nature's active intention. The spectacle "throughout / Was shaped for admiration and delight"—intended to elicit a specific response, which even "the grossest minds," as Wordsworth asserts in his meditation following the vision, "cannot chuse but feel" (13. 83–84). "Grand in itself alone," the spectacle also displays design in the sense of pattern or arrangement—which is implemented in nature's own acts of self-usurpation: moon usurps mist, mist usurps sea, sound usurps light.

The question of design becomes the subject of Wordsworth's meditation "Upon the lonely Mountain when the scene / Had pass'd away" (13. 67–68). Wordsworth meditates on the production of design, the intentional process of shaping particulars into a patterned configuration. This is his explicit concern in the earliest version of the Snowdon episode in MS. W:

> My present aim
> Is to contemplate for a needful while
> (Passage which will conduct in season due
> Back to the tale which I have left behind)
> The diverse manner in which Nature works
> Oft times upon the outward face of things,
> I mean so moulds, exalts, endues, combines,
> Impregnates, separates, adds, takes away,
> And makes one object sway another so
> By unhabitual influence or abrupt,
> That even the grossest minds must see and hear
> And cannot chuse but feel.[25]

Although Wordsworth perhaps ascribes more actions to nature than are evident in the scene, he accurately summarizes its behavior. Nature has moulded the mist into an imitative landscape, adding and combining the materials as it endues them with form, taking away from the real sea and land beneath, but separating surface from surface and realm from realm as it makes the moon and homeless voice of waters exert their "sway."

The "manner in which Nature works" is in fact the same as that in which imagination works, as Wordsworth well perceives, and it is the revelation's objective demonstration of this which fills him with "admiration and delight" and motivates his meditation. The "power" which "Nature thus / Puts forth upon the senses," he proclaims,

> is in kind
> A brother of the very faculty
> Which higher minds bear with them as their own.
> These from their native selves can deal about
> Like transformations, to one life impart
> The functions of another, shift, create,
> Trafficking with immeasurable thoughts.
>
> (MS. W, 20–26)

This argument forms the core of Wordsworth's meditation in all the later versions, in the 1850 as well as the 1805 text, despite local revision of phrases or elaboration of particular ideas. Indeed, the 1805 text (MSS. A and B) stresses intention—as well as internal patterning—more emphatically than does MS. W: Nature "thrusts forth" (13. 86) rather than "Puts forth" its "Power" (now capitalized), while the resemblance between the activity of nature and the activity of mind is exhaustively formulated. "The Power . . . which Nature thus"

> Thrusts forth upon the senses, is the express
> Resemblance, in the fulness of its strength
> Made visible, a genuine Counterpart

> And Brother of the glorious Faculty
> Which higher minds bear with them as their own.

(13. 86–90)

This "Brother," this "genuine Counterpart," is an autonomous entity, so that the trafficking between mind and nature is a trafficking between design and design, intention and intention. Nature is already constituted with design and intention of its own—as is the human mind.

> They [i.e., higher minds] from their native selves can send abroad
> Like transformations, for themselves create
> A like existence, and when'er it is
> Created for them, catch it by an instinct

(13. 93–96)

In MS. W, Wordsworth names the parallelism (a reciprocity of give/receive) "this analogy betwixt / The mind of man and Nature" (MS. W, 27–28), which he then proceeds to illustrate with other "living pictures, to embody / This pleasing argument" (MS. W, 32–33). But, as the course of MS. W indicates, the "argument" itself is far more "pleasing" than the "pictures" meant to illustrate it; indeed, they "embody" nothing more—and if anything much less—than what the scene on Snowdon embodies already.[26] The "pleasing argument" breaks off; and when copied over in another section of MS. W, this time with the "analogies" cut, the argument breaks off yet again at precisely the same place:

> To this one scene which I from Snowdon's breast
> Beheld might more be added to set forth
> The manner in which oftener Nature works
> Herself upon the outward face of things
> As if with an imaginative power.

(1850 *Prel*, 623)

The phrase "As if with an imaginative power" perhaps betrays some indecision after all about nature's power. For while the concept of "analogy" specifies with certainty the nature of *relations,* it does not name the essences of the objects brought into relation. If nature's power works "As if" it were imagination, is it in fact imagination? In the 1805 text, Wordsworth confidently ascribes imagination to nature; it "lodges" in "That dark deep thoroughfare" "Through which the homeless voice of waters rose" (13. 63–64). Should this commit Wordsworth to changing his argument from "analogy" to identity?—to the distribution of the *same* productive power to both mind and nature, which could further imply that mind and nature are somehow the same?

These questions, one might say, rupture Wordsworth's meditation, for the manuscript drafts, in the spring of 1804, leave the issue unresolved. Not until the final draft of May 1805 (MS. A), written most likely either in late December 1804 or early 1805, does Wordsworth reach a conclusion.

The question of being intrudes into Wordsworth's meditation on the scene, for more than only his knowledge of objects is at issue or a description of activity without regard to the being of the objects performing the activity. Quite clearly, the "mystery" at which Wordsworth pauses to marvel is the autonomous materialization of mental operations in nature. And Wordsworth enhances the mystery by emphasizing the palpable phenomenality of nature. We are always aware that the activity is the work of rock, water, mist, night, moon and sound. If anything, Wordsworth focuses on nature at the expense of mind in the MS. W version of the meditation: he introduces "higher minds" as if to show that they also happen to do what nature does, as if they can serve as an added example to illustrate nature's workings. Indeed, it is only when he expatiates on "higher minds" at line 24 (that they too "can deal about / Like transformations," etc.) that we fully realize that nature's activity describes the self as well, that the inherently physical operations of moulding, enduing, separating, combining, adding and taking away are also epistemological operations that minds perform. But it is precisely here that the question of being surfaces. A monistic language that describes the same behavior in two different kinds of beings tends to collapse dualism into monism—as becomes evident when Wordsworth tries carefully to discriminate each side of the dualism and specify their relation: nature's imagination is not only the "express / Resemblance" and "genuine Counterpart" but "Brother of the glorious Faculty / Which higher minds bear with them as their own." The common parentage designates a close connection of being. Fraternal faculties imply fraternal minds in fraternal bodies. Even more, these brothers look like identical twins, whose relationship may be freely reciprocal but only because the human twin has decided to emulate his natural brother. As indicated in lines 24–26 of MS. W and more pointedly in their revision in MS. A quoted above (13. 93–96), higher minds imitate nature in returning "like transformations" or catching them when they are "created for them." Nature's imagination seems subtler and more creative than that of higher minds.

The question of analogy and resemblance thus becomes vexed by entailing the question of being, which in turn entails the question of priority. For on Snowdon who really resembles whom? Wordsworth makes nature be the express resemblance of mind only next to make mind resemble nature. It seems we have a both/and that threatens to revert to an either/or—a philosophical situation similar to that in several Alfoxden fragments. While Wordsworth does not deduce mind from nature or nature from mind here, the fraternal reciprocity repeats the same structure of supplementarity. Is the Snowdon sequence in MS.

W in early March 1804 closer, therefore, to the empiricism and pantheism of six years earlier than to the explicit transcendentalism of a few weeks later?

There is much in the MS. W version, apart from the inconclusiveness of the meditation, to suggest as much. In fact, there is little in the drafts to suggest transcendentalism at all. In dwelling on the autonomy of nature's own imagination, Wordsworth pointedly insists that it is *not* the projection of a Kantian a priori category. The reciprocity between mind and nature, furthermore, might seem to anticipate a Fichtean trafficking between self and not-self in which the self's infinite activity posits and is delimited by the corresponding infinite activity of the not-self. But again, Wordsworth's paramount emphasis on nature and its autonomy preempts this schema: not the self's workings but nature's workings are his sole interest in the draft version. It might seem, then, that Wordsworth is close to the pantheism of 1798 inasmuch as nature's imaginative workings seem essentially a quantitatively more intricate version of the mind in the crags in the Notebook. Yet the Snowdon sequence stops far short of pantheism: no One Life or sentiment of being pervades the scene, even if imagination, soul, intention and activity are made immanent in it.[27] What the meditation suggests most of all, really, is a tenacious empiricism. We cannot but recognize the forceful necessitarianism of Lockean-Hartleyan associationism when Wordsworth stresses that even the grossest minds must see and hear and cannot choose but feel nature's impressive activity. Moreover, the centerpiece of his meditation—on which he rests his case, and at which he rests, being unable to press further—is pure Lockean epistemology: adding, combining, separating, taking away, moulding, enduing and so on. If this is the language to describe imagination's functioning (as it is later in Wordsworth's Preface of 1815 and Coleridge's *Biographia Literaria*),[28] it is inherently and originally an empiricist language.

The consequences are that the Snowdon sequence in MS. W proves to be a provisional, unstable landing-place. No longer pantheism and not yet transcendentalism, it seems to be empiricism by default. But that empiricism partly foreshadows transcendentalism even if only in the way the Lockean language successfully straddles a both/and. Applying equally to nature and mind, this language implies a monistic metaphysics to embrace the dualism. We can see Wordsworth working on constructing just that in "some abortive 'try-out' passages" in MS. W (1850 *Prel,* 619).[29] As if moving away dialectically from nature after the meditation on the scene, Wordsworth now explores more fully the structure and activity of this self that can respond to nature so efficiently:

> But also such an one must have been used
> To feed his soul upon infinity
> To deal with whatsoe'er be dim or vast
> In his own nature [*blending*] in a form

> Of unity through truth-inspiring thoughts
> By one sensation, either be it that
> Of his own mind the power by which he thinks
> Or lastly the great feeling of the world,
> God and the immortality of life
> Beneath all being evermore to be.

(1850 *Prel*, 620)

This passage and others around it in the manuscript show Wordsworth groping towards the final, extended version of the meditation, including here ideas that will go into the passage on "The perfect image of a mighty Mind." But what is philosophically important is that Wordsworth expressly seeks to reconcile duality as unity. The monistic-dualistic Lockean epistemology produces here the "one sensation" that blends "in a form / Of unity" both consciousness of self and consciousness of the external world. Yet self and nature resemble one another here as Wordsworth chiastically transposes essentially the same predicates from one to the other. Self-consciousness is consciousness of "infinity" and "whatsoe'er be dim or vast" in one's own "nature" ("being" in 13. 73); correlatively, consciousness of nature is "the great feeling of the world / God and the immortality of life / Beneath all being evermore to be." The different consciousnesses contain virtually the same sense of infinity, vastness and depth, shading into unknowable "being" and ultimately God. Apparently, Wordsworth is starting to sketch in an incipient Fichtean metaphysics insofar as the dialectics of infinity, delimitation and activity define self and nature alike. But perhaps, more important, especially from the point of view of the transcendentalism of crossing the Alps and the later version of the Snowdon scene, is that Wordsworth openly refers to "being." He intuits here on the basis of epistemology a metaphysics that will accommodate ontology. In the MS. W meditation, by contrast, as the Lockean language materializes the mental in nature, it diverts epistemology from metaphysics and ontologizes it instead.

The Alps and the Power of a Peculiar Eye

The three-part sequence in book 6 describing Wordsworth's crossing the Alps—his disappointment at Simplon Pass after learning that he had unknowingly crossed the Alps (6. 488–524), the apostrophe to Imagination in the moment of writing as he suddenly sees what went wrong and how (6. 525–48), and then his descent into Gondo Gorge with its compensatory revelation of the sublime (6. 549–72)—resembles the Snowdon climb and meditation in that a similar mist-enshrouded mountainous landscape contributes to insight into the imagination and its workings. Snowdon is the forerunner of the Alps in anticipating the kinds of insights that suddenly assume apocalyptic proportions here. Indeed, since Geoffrey Hartman's magisterial interpretation of the sequence some twenty years ago, Crossing the Alps has been regarded as the summa of Wordsworth's transcendental vision and the summa of the Wordsworthian sublime.[30] Hartman argues that in writing about his Alpine crossing Wordsworth comes "face to face with his imagination" (39) and realizes the apocalyptic severance of self from nature. Wordsworth realizes that "Our destiny, our nature, and our home / Is with infinitude, and only there" (6. 538–39)—with imagination, that is, and not with nature. He realizes that "the mind cannot be satisfied with anything in nature, however sublime" (46). Despite this climactic revelation Wordsworth inevitably binds himself to nature once again largely because, as Hartman argues the Snowdon sequence proves, the "imagination and the light of nature are one" (60). On all other occasions except the apostrophe in book 6, nature is the medium of imagination's appearance—as it is again in Gondo Gorge, after the apostrophe, when Wordsworth, in Hartman's words, "sees not as in a glass, darkly, but face to face" (45).

I summarize Hartman's argument in brief at the outset in order to characterize Wordsworth's transcendentalism in Crossing the Alps and to suggest that the turn to nature is philosophically necessary to complete the system. The autonomy of the self, its independence from nature, the definition of its essence as infinite activity, as imaginative striving, its reliance on nature as the limitation of a not-self dialectically enabling full self-realization (that is, the failure of nature in Simplon Pass when Wordsworth realized he had crossed the Alps), but the positing of an external nature that is understood to be equally infinite and equally active once the self has realized these qualities of infinite activity for itself—all add up to a transcendentalism of a post-Kantian, distinctly Fichtean kind that Wordsworth seemingly, by turns, either suddenly discovers, consciously articulates or unknowingly dramatizes. Knowing what the transcendental contents of his vision are, we can better appreciate the transcendentalism of the process of vision and the drama of Wordsworth's argument, which are my focus here. That is, we can then see how the philosophical context of 1804 and the antecedent texts we have been examining prepare Wordsworth for this sudden breakthrough into transcendentalism and how this transcendentalism negotiates the vexing questions emerging in those texts.

On Tuesday, August 17, 1790, Wordsworth and his walking companion Robert Jones crossed Simplon Pass and unknowingly "cross'd the Alps" (6. 524). It seems, from Wordsworth's account of it, that they might have been hoping for a high, rugged divide (and hence their upward climb), not realizing that the plateau they had already crossed was the summit of Simplon Pass itself.[31] In any event, Wordsworth was disappointed to miss the sublime experience he had been eagerly anticipating. Bewildered, dejected, aware of being blind to the spiritual landmark on which he had set his sights, Wordsworth nonetheless discovered that his "dejection," his "deep and genuine sadness" (6. 491–92), was "dislodg'd (6. 551) when he entered Gondo Gorge, which, evoking in him the terror and awe of the sublime, granted a vision in abundant recompense for that missed before.

In the spring of 1804, Wordsworth remembers and "rereads" as he writes, as he did in the case of the "spots of time" episodes.[32] And as before, he faces a seemingly inexplicable breach between two radically different affective states: dejection, the failure of vision on the one hand, and sublime awe, the fullness of vision on the other. In book 6, the finality of the realization "that we had cross'd the Alps" (6. 524) triggers in the moment of writing in March 1804 sudden insight into the self, the apostrophe to Imagination and the soul's glory:

> Imagination! lifting up itself
> Before the eye and progress of my Song
> Like an unfather'd vapour; here that Power,
> In all the might of its endowments, came
> Athwart me; I was lost as in a cloud,
> Halted, without a struggle to break through.
> And now recovering, to my Soul I say
> I recognise thy glory; in such strength
> Of usurpation, in such visitings
> Of awful promise, when the light of sense
> Goes out in flashes that have shewn to us
> The invisible world, doth Greatness make abode,
> There harbours whether we be young or old.
> Our destiny, our nature, and our home
> Is with infinitude, and only there;
> With hope it is, hope that can never die,
> Effort, and expectation, and desire,
> And something evermore about to be.
> The mind beneath such banners militant
> Thinks not of spoils or trophies, nor of aught
> That may attest its prowess, blest in thoughts
> That are their own perfection and reward,
> Strong in itself, and in the access of joy
> Which hides it like the overflowing Nile.

> (6. 525–48)

These "rapturous, almost self-obscuring lines," as Geoffrey Hartman has called them (40), look before and after to explain the failure and then the return of vision, but they are equally if not more intent on describing, in its own terms, the usurpation in the present moment, whose very strength and immediacy suppress its referential relations to its initiating problematic. That problematic is figured in the first half of the epic simile that is the apostrophe's immediate antecedent in the manuscript drafts (and which Wordsworth subsequently transferred to book 8):[33]

> As when a traveller hath from open day
> With torches pass'd into some Vault of Earth,
> The Grotto of Antiparos, or the Den
> Of Yordas among Craven's mountain tracts;
> He looks and sees the Cavern spread and grow,
> Widening itself on all sides, sees, or thinks
> He sees, erelong, the roof above his head,
> Which instantly unsettles and recedes
> Substance and shadow, light and darkness, all
> Commingled, making up a Canopy
> Of Shapes and Forms and Tendencies to Shape
> That shift and vanish, change and interchange
> Like Spectres, ferment quiet and sublime;
> Which, after a short space, works less and less,
> Till every effort, every motion gone,
> The scene before him lies in perfect view,
> Exposed and lifeless, as a written book.

(8. 711–27)

This scene in many respects condenses the Snowdon scene. Inverting it by offering a "Canopy" overhead rather than a sea of mist "at [his] feet," Wordsworth takes its tendencies further than he could have envisaged earlier. In ending up with the scene in "perfect view, / Exposed and lifeless, as a written book," he pursues the imaginative activity on Snowdon to the limit. The ferment quiet and sublime of substance and shadow, shapes and forms and tendencies to shape, which unsettle and recede, shift and vanish, change and interchange, plays out the acts of moulding, enduing, adding, separating, combining and taking away to their ultimate conclusion in lifeless, empty immobility. The difference here, as these acts add up or count down to nothing, is that Wordsworth de-ontologizes epistemology: he knows that he has more than half-created what he "sees, or thinks / He sees." Such a recognition severs knowing from being, and reinstates the either/or of the self's agency rather than nature's activity. The sudden, immediate consequence is that Wordsworth recognizes imagination to be his own inner power—and a power that overtakes him now as if from the outside:

> Imagination! lifting up itself
> Before the eye and progress of my Song
> Like an unfather'd vapour; here that Power,
> In all the might of its endowments, came
> Athwart me; I was lost as in a cloud,
> Halted, without a struggle to break through.

The experience Wordsworth seeks to capture is an experience of self-presence that can be articulated only after the fact once the sensation has ebbed away into thought. The apostrophe lines constitute, as Mark Reed has said, a "frail shrine" for the spirit, which, like the linking passage between the "spots of time," give, "as far as words can give, / A substance and a life to what [Wordsworth just felt]."[34] As in that passage too, and as becomes evident from the Alpine sequence as a whole, the unspoken protocol of give/receive arranges Wordsworth's understanding of events: if disappointment at the failure of nature at the Pass is exposed as his own imaginative lifelessness, he now sees that imaginative life and self-fulfillment are the presupposed antecedents of giving and receiving. As a result, the hiding-place of the self's power opens, and the vision is so overpowering it prevents the self from approaching (rather, the vision approaches, overtakes, Wordsworth, and without any threat of the hiding-place closing). On Snowdon, Wordsworth was lost in the cloud but broke through to see the hiding-place of imagination in the fracture in the vapor; here, the "unfather'd vapour" is itself the figure for imagination and it wraps Wordsworth in blinding insight into power and its hiding-place.

As the light of sense goes out in flashes it shows to Wordsworth the invisible world. It reveals to him a transcendental domain, the ground of the self, in which he momentarily finds himself. Yet the apostrophe does not celebrate that invisible world so much as the liminal position from which it is glimpsed, as if this moment of self-presence is unsustainable and leaves the self at a remove from presence in the position of dislocation, from which it then "reads" the vision, organizing immediate intuitions into doctrinal formulations:

> [I]n such strength
> Of usurpation, in such visitings
> Of awful promise, when the light of sense
> Goes out in flashes that have shewn to us
> The invisible world, doth Greatness make abode,
> There harbours whether we be young or old.
> Our destiny, our nature, and our home
> Is with infinitude, and only there;
> With hope it is, hope that can never die,
> Effort, and expectation, and desire,
> And something evermore about to be.

We readily sense that Wordsworth has experienced directly the "infinitude" that is "our nature, and our home" (the 1850 version explicitly centers infinitude in the self: it is "our being's heart and home" [6. 604; 1850 *Prel,* 209]), but insofar as he simultaneously stresses "destiny" and the energetic mental activity through which we pursue our destiny (hope, effort, expectation, etc.), then we palpably sense Wordsworth's liminal stance and the relation of desire at a remove, which make self-presence, the "something evermore about to be," the something hoped for again because it briefly once was. The invisible world and the vision of infinitude figuratively name the transcendental ground, for Wordsworth is giving, as far as words can give, the contents of the noumenal self; he is describing the self as it is in itself. Yet knowing, as he does in the Ode, that one can only ever give a figure for the intrinsically unknowable, he raises the louder song of praise for what is the more knowable, the process of vision that unfolds on the threshold: the light of sense going out and its flashes, the visitings of awful promise, the usurpation itself. He thus celebrates the moment and method in which the empirical issues into the transcendental, epistemology into metaphysics. For all the apostrophe's extractable Fichtean doctrine of infinitude, activity and self-realization, the greater achievement here is Wordsworth's articulation of the "mystery" of process, a concern which is more nearly Kantian in this case than Fichtean. For Wordsworth gives the antecedent transcendental a priori that must be presupposed in order to render vision possible. In delineating the process of imagination's usurpation, he articulates a schematic a priori that is at once enabling structure and productive category. Infinitude, as the noumenal ground of the self that cannot be given as determinate content, thus becomes the *form* and condition of consciousness—while hope, effort, expectation, desire and the sense of something evermore about to be characterize the mind's intension towards its objects both empirically and transcendentally.

The "Greatness" that Wordsworth celebrates in "usurpation" and the "visitings / Of awful promise" is really the sense of "awful promise" itself, the epistemological activity in which the self suddenly intuits infinite possibility and meaningfulness before it actually reads what it sees and determines meaning. Wordsworth posits the antecedents of seeing and an antecedent seeing that are presupposed in the reading of vision. Seeing his own seeing and its power and infinite possibility, Wordsworth understands the power of a peculiar eye and the logic it can speak: for this eye can read the visible, the invisible and the visionary, and trace with hope, effort, expectation and desire the play of awful promise from something evermore about to be to something that actually is.

Wordsworth's transcendentalism is thus a transcendentalism of both form and content, and is, quite clearly, an eminent achievement. Yet Wordsworth does not stop here. He returns to his story—and turns to nature. If in turning to nature he binds himself again to nature, then he does so as a result of intuiting that self and nature are implicated in the same metaphysics. The Gondo Gorge sequence should be regarded as consequence and complement of the apostrophe to Imagination—all the more so since it constitutes a second usurpation and one that nature autonomously presents. In moving down into the Gorge, moreover, Wordsworth confronts the questions of being and resemblance temporarily suspended in the experience of self-presence described in the apostrophe:

> The dull and heavy slackening that ensued
> Upon those tidings by the Peasant given

Was soon dislodg'd; downwards we hurried fast,
And enter'd with the road which we had miss'd
Into a narrow chasm; the brook and road
Were fellow-travellers in this gloomy Pass,
And with them did we journey several hours
At a slow step. The immeasurable height
Of woods decaying, never to be decay'd,
The stationary blasts of water-falls,
And every where along the hollow rent
Winds thwarting winds, bewilder'd and forlorn,
The torrents shooting from the clear blue sky,
The rocks that mutter'd close upon our ears,
Black drizzling crags that spake by the way-side
As if a voice were in them, the sick sight
And giddy prospect of the raving stream,
The unfetter'd clouds, and region of the heavens,
Tumult and peace, the darkness and the light
Were all like workings of one mind, the features
Of the same face, blossoms upon one tree,
Characters of the great Apocalypse,
The types and symbols of Eternity,
Of first and last, and midst, and without end.

(6. 549–72)

The tumult and peace, darkness and light resemble the ferment of shapes and forms and tendencies to shape in the cavern; and as the possible "workings of one mind" they exemplify the same kind of imaginative activity of enduing, combining, separating, adding and taking away that Wordsworth observes on Snowdon. They are disparates organized with greater difficulty and sterner effort into a unitary design: features of the same face, blossoms upon one tree. Yet in seeing them as organized in this way, Wordsworth regards them as disposed according to the dialectics of immanence and transcendence that only problematically informed his theorizing about the materialization of the mental on Snowdon. As the workings of a transcendent mind, nature's features and activity in the Gorge appear to make "Eternity" immanent in phenomenal form: Wordsworth sees "first, and last, and midst, and without end" in the fixed and steady lineaments of the naked crags. Eternity and its predicates obviously correspond to the infinitude the self all but completely attains in the apostrophe—while nature's unremitting striving in the Gorge also reflects the energetic motions of hope, effort, expectation and desire, and something evermore about to be. The Gorge would seem to offer, then, a more complicated case of the mental made real in nature—or, better, the transcendental made empirical, the subjective objective. And if in this way Wordsworth incorporates being into the scheme, he is able to do so because he relates both self and nature to the same transcendental ground. The self's infinitude and infinite activity and nature's

Eternity and eternal striving reflect one another because both resemble and derive from an original infinitude, activity and Eternity: God himself. Self and nature resemble one another because both are types and symbols of something antecedent which they not only represent but half make immanent. Wordsworth's use of the term "symbols" makes all the difference here. Although governed by the cautious rubric of the simile ("were all like"), "symbols" claim a synecdochic continuity with what they symbolize: in this case, Eternity, ground, God. Being, therefore, tropes and substantializes mind; it not only resembles or represents it but is itself a part continuous with the whole.

Wordsworth intuits possible immanence, then, but concedes transcendence. The metaphysical success here is that, given the dualism of mind and nature, the only possible resolution that can be reached is via the detour of a third term, a common ground that comprehends both. Falling short of theology, this maneuver nevertheless makes the phenomenal a derivative of the noumenal, the transcendent: it is an appearance ("like"), an imitation, a resemblance, a type and, so Wordsworth claims, a symbol. The maneuver is philosophically honest in that it allows skepticism its place and admits the distinction between knowing and being while affirming the possibility of their resolution in a comprehensive, unifying system. But insofar as metaphysics still rests on the epistemology of imitative representation (despite the additional mediations of the symbol), Wordsworth potentially exposes transcendentalism to disruption. He tries to prevent that possibility by rethinking the question of resemblance in the revised version of the Snowdon meditation, to which he turns several months later when bringing the thirteen-book *Prelude* to completion.

"The Perfect Image of a Mighty Mind"

The new lines Wordsworth adds to the meditation dramatically alter the character of the Snowdon scene and its meaning:

> A meditation rose in me that night
> Upon the lonely Mountain when the scene
> Had pass'd away, and it appear'd to me
> The perfect image of a mighty Mind,
> Of one that feeds upon infinity,
> That is exalted by an underpresence,
> The sense of God, or whatsoe'er is dim
> Or vast in its own being.

(13. 66–73)

The "mighty Mind" functions essentially as a template that fits nature and the human mind alike. It is a transcendental schema whose signal advantage is its central position as a third term. It is an antecedent that is at once structure and activity, descriptively ordering the functioning of both mind and nature.[35] The mighty Mind completes the earlier Snowdon sequence by grounding its dualism in the transcendental monism that a third term can supply: before, nature and mind resembled one another, but now we can see that they did so because both really resemble the mighty Mind. Logically as well as aesthetically Wordsworth completes the scene by putting the mind into the picture and giving us the picture of the mind—whereas before he had included its workings and only some features of its face (its mouth or throat in the "breathing-place" in the vapor through which mounts the "voice of waters"; and possibly its eye in the moon looking down on this "shew"). And yet if Wordsworth puts the mind in, he also safely leaves it out. The scene is a "perfect image" of this mind and not the mind itself. He makes no causal claims about the relation of image to object.[36] For this mind has not caused its representation in nature; rather, nature has freely chosen, of its own accord, to stage this representation. More than before, then, Wordsworth now expressly observes and preserves the distinction between knowing and being, image and reality, mind and nature.

Yet for all its stabilizing, even-handed management of the mind/nature dualism, the introduction of the mighty Mind sets going a differential play of resemblances and types that ontologically unsettles the scene. For example, minds begin to split and proliferate in the meditation. Higher minds are a type of the mighty Mind and clearly Wordsworth's mind is of a type with higher minds (and therefore, at his being's height, it must resemble the mighty Mind); and all these minds are to be kept safely away from their unwanted, poorer cousins: grossest minds. Yet Wordsworth also half introduces still more minds: God informs the "underpresence" of the mighty Mind, while nature's usurpations and the features of its face resemble the workings of the "one mind" in the Alps. Evidently, the mighty Mind is the ideal type of mind in itself, an abstract, heuristic standard with which other minds can be compared. But once an ideal type has been made the founding principle of the system, it then turns everything else into a type. Nature may be primarily itself and also resemble higher minds, but it finally becomes the type of a type. Wordsworth essentially revises all nature as representation. Consequently, as analogies and resemblances proliferate, suggesting an unending allegorical reading of the scene,[37] the both/and disintegrates into an either/or dualism: either mind exceeds nature, and knowing exceeds being, because the scene fits so perfectly into all the mental categories that exhaustively contain it, or nature exceeds mind, and being exceeds knowing, because so many mental categories seem to fit the scene. One could keep hold of the both/and here by saying that the mutual accommodation implies the authenticity and autonomy of each side—a Kantian resolution that affirms both transcendental idealism and empirical realism. Yet Wordsworth's insistent analogizing skews the philosophical configuration. While the sheer number of resemblances and types Wordsworth adduces suggests that perhaps they might not fit after all (or that no one analogy fits convincingly), nature's seemingly pliant correspondence to them suggests that it has the autonomous power to determine the mental (to accept, revise or reject the categories imposed on it). In any event, Wordsworth enmeshes his transcendentalism in empiricism. In seeing nature as imitative representation, as a "perfect image," he revives the possibility of an empiricist epistemology while reopening the ontological problem of the relation of the original to the imitation; and in also seeing nature as autonomous object exceeding various mental categories, he presents it as extensive, unassimilable being. In other words, he no sooner consolidates his transcendentalism than he lays it open to Lockean materialism.

During the spring of 1804, as he expanded *The Prelude* from the five-book into the thirteen-book work it finally became by early 1805, Wordsworth wrote in closely connected sequence the texts that constitute the poem's climactic statements and propound his transcendental philosophy. If he sees into the mind's infinitude, its autonomy, its infinite activity, as well as glimpses in blinding flashes the transcendental realm of origin or ultimate home, his path to these visionary insights is dialectical and beset with persistent contradictions. As he moves to and fro affirming the independence of mind and then its reciprocity with nature, the deep-seated anxiety motivating his argument is really the misgiving uncovered in the "Immortality" Ode that the severance between mind and nature may be final. If anything, in the texts we have examined he increasingly, and reluctantly, concedes this possibility. His intensifying interest across this series of texts in semblances, resemblances, types and symbols, and finally "The perfect image" expresses his desire to forge connections that he knows cannot be established on any empirically verifiable causal basis. That is, he fears the severance has become absolute. Admittedly, in the apostrophe in the Alpine sequence Wordsworth recognizes as much, but he immediately counters that with a vision of nature's resemblance to a mind. Even the more intricate versions of reciprocity and resemblance in the revised Snowdon meditation threaten the same outcome: as both/and reverts to either/or, mind and nature each begin appearing as the other's ontological remainder, the outside of an inside.

The consequences, as Wordsworth moves further into *Prelude* composition in later 1804, is that the transcendentalism he has secured—which otherwise duly accommodates subject and object, their activity and interrelations in a unitary system—founders on the notions of being it has not yet accommodated and on the theory of representation it cannot accommodate. In both cases, the antagonist sooner or later comes forward in the garb of empiricism.

5

"What, and Whither, When and How": Diffusing Transcendentalism in Books 7 and 8 of *The Prelude*

We have been examining two series of closely interlinked texts, one from 1798 and the other from 1804, that explicitly treat philosophical problems. Whether the poetry has been descriptive, narrative, lyrical or autobiographical, Wordsworth has sustained via its mediations an intense engagement with philosophical issues; and in investigating those issues so scrupulously he has made various important discoveries. Clearly the several different landing-places, especially of the spring of 1804, can be made to support a well-defined philosophical position, provided we do not press for complete consistency but attend instead to broad outlines and general features. Yet however persuasive and well-founded any worldview, it is not something that can be constantly thought, maintained as a systematic whole, or continually reaffirmed. Rather, it will be pondered intermittently and in part and will often slip from thought for long stretches at a time precisely because it has become a belief, a dependable constant, that can be presumed upon and put to use again when necessary. And when reinvoked and put to use, it will probably be revised in some way or other. Such is the destiny of Wordsworth's transcendentalism during the course of 1804. As Wordsworth expands *The Prelude,* starts filling in the gaps, and generally immersing himself in the task of unfolding his autobiographical narrative, he inevitably takes his mind off the philosophical issues preoccupying him in March. Yet he also at times turns back to those issues in order to make his story follow on from and be consistent with the principles and theories he has developed.

Although the texts composed in the spring of 1804 become *The Prelude*'s climaxes and conclusion, it is impossible to know, as Jonathan Wordsworth points out, whether Wordsworth saw them in this light as he proceeded with composition.[1] Whether he did or not, their transcendentalism proves to be strong and lasting. Wordsworth allusively deploys their language, thinks along the same lines or theorizes in terms of the concepts they have provided in later books of *The Prelude*. I wish to discuss here two such books that illustrate this progression—and with some startling consequences: books 7 and 8.

Books 7 and 8 are a good case in point because, ostensibly, they are far removed from the "Immortality" Ode, Crossing the Alps and the Climbing of Snowdon. Book 7 deals with Wordsworth's "Residence in London." Chronologically, it focuses principally on February–May 1791 when Wordsworth lived there, but it also incorporates experiences from other times, especially his stay in September 1802 when Charles Lamb took him and Dorothy to Bartholomew Fair. Although the title announces the book's link to other *Prelude* books and their themes (book 3: "Residence at Cambridge"; books 9 and 10: "Residence in France"), the book itself is a satire on the city, its manners and morals, which advances the autobiographical story only insofar as Wordsworth tells us how he entertained himself in London. Book 8, "Retrospect: Love of Nature Leading to Love of Mankind," does not advance the story at all. As the title suggests, it takes us back to the beginning again and rehearses the story we have already been told, if from a more abstract, theoretical perspective. These books are so digressive, and Wordsworth can afford to be so expansive and free-ranging, because of the confidence and security the transcendental theories of earlier 1804 have given him. In books 7 and 8 these antecedents are presupposed, and Wordsworth relies on them as he discursively applies them to new topics and other times and places. Wordsworth thus seeks to consolidate his transcendental "system" by extending it to new territory and by making it the new vantage point from which to review familiar territory.

The links between books 7 and 8 and the texts of March 1804 will begin to become clear if we again consider compositional history and manuscript evidence. Book 8, the majority of which was drafted in MS. Y, is the work of October 1804; book 7 was written after it in November, and is contained in MS. X.[2] One link we have already noted is the cavern simile. Though originally part of the Alpine sequence in MS. WW, it was moved to book 8, expanded to twice its length to include the resurgence of shapes and forms and tendencies to shape on the cavern roof as the perceiver looked again, and made to refer to Wordsworth's response to London: disappointment and emptiness followed by renewed excitement. The mere transference suggests that Wordsworth's London experience may have something in common, then, with his experience at Simplon Pass and in Gondo Gorge. Another, perhaps more telling, link is the ten-line passage that concludes book 8:

> Thus were my thoughts attracted more and more
> By slow gradations towards human Kind
> And to the good and ill of human life;
> Nature had led me on, and now I seem'd
> To travel independent of her help,
> As if I had forgotten her; but no,
> My Fellow beings still were unto me

> Far less than she was, though the scale of love
> Were filling fast, 'twas light, as yet, compared
> With that in which her mighty objects lay.

(8. 860–69)

This passage was written in the spring and is part of MS. W. As Mark Reed observes, "it tends to confirm that the poet's concern with the subject of the development within himself of love of man relative to love of nature, the topic of book 8, was well defined in the spring."[3] Wordsworth seems to understand that it follows in consequence, as a corollary, of his transcendental insights of March. In MS. Y, in which Wordsworth develops this subject into the argument of book 8, there is a lengthy passage of some 230 lines that he excluded from the final draft but which shows several points of contact with the poetry of March. Giving here a condensed account of the individual's development that closely resembles that in *The Pedlar,* Wordsworth frequently echoes the language and ideas of the Ode and the *Prelude* passages: finding the earth apparalled in celestial light during childhood, the individual grows up to experience the loss of light, the failure of meanings, but later discovers, as he continues to respond to the beauty of nature, the return of vision and the kind of mutuality glimpsed on Snowdon:

> He feels that, be his mind however great
> In aspiration, the universe in which
> He lives is equal to his mind, that each
> Is worthy of the other; if the one
> Be insatiate, the other is inexhaustible.
> Whatever dignity there be [   ]
> Within himself, from which he gathers hope,
> There doth he feel its counterpart the same
> In kind before him outwardly express'd,
> With difference that makes the likeness clear,
> Sublimities, grave beauty, excellence,
> Not taken upon trust, but self-display'd
> Before his proper senses; 'tis not here
> Record of what hath been, is now no more,
> Nor secondary work of mimic skill,
> Transcripts that do but mock their archetypes;
> But primary and independent life,
> No glimmering residue of splendour past,
> Things in decline or faded. [   ]
> What hidden greater far than what is seen
> No false subordination, fickleness,
> Or thwarted virtue, but inveterate power
> Directed to best ends, and all things good
> Pure and consistent.

(1850 *Prel,* 576; 171–94)

The first twelve lines recapitulate almost to the letter the central idea of the Snowdon meditation. In the following lines, however, Wordsworth enters directly the ambience of the "Immortality" Ode, repeating its language but repudiating its central claims: " 'tis not here / Record of what hath been, is now no more . . . / No glimmering residue of splendour past." But the most important link in this passage is epistemological, the notion of imitative representation that Wordsworth anxiously tries to counter. He is at pains to establish that nature's workings show a "primary and independent life," that we are not looking at a "Record," "Transcripts," something "mimic." In another draft of these lines Wordsworth writes: "transcripts /And *imitations* are not here that mock / Their archetypes" (emphasis added).[4] His obsessive compunction to define precisely what he denies so emphatically evidently indicates that the concepts of resemblance, analogy and type, which, though problematic, worked to particular heuristic effect in March, are now perhaps proving to be exactly the question that cannot be ignored.

The issues Wordsworth explores in books 7 and 8 are continuous, in fact, with those of the spring, although he transposes them into a somewhat different form as he follows their implications. Having worked out the relation between mind and nature, especially in the Snowdon meditation, Wordsworth now proceeds to establish the relation between nature and human nature—an abstract question that he hopes to settle in the abstract in order to cope (with a mind made up, as Coleridge expected of the *Recluse* poet) with real-life particulars: other people in the landscape, in rural and urban environments. If Wordsworth thus moves toward the social criticism that was to be a major part of *The Recluse* (by the autumn of 1804 he had already begun treating history and politics in discussing revolutionary France in drafts of books 9 and 10, composed earlier in the summer), he nevertheless approaches the topic of other people epistemologically. Habitually, Wordsworth has come to understand nature by examining the self's response to natural objects in a natural landscape, during particular moments of perception. He now fathoms human nature in precisely the same way: by focusing on the self's response to human objects first in the natural landscape in book 8, and then in the human landscape in book 7. As a result, the epistemological passage becomes a bit more devious than the title of book 8 suggests. Love of nature leads to love of human nature which then supposedly leads to love of mankind. Moreover, because outward objects, both human and natural, are the focus of his attention, Wordsworth must establish ways for distinguishing between the human and the natural even as he strives to coordinate their meanings and effects. As the excerpt from MS. Y indicates, he consequently affirms various forms of presence—such as nature's "primary and independent life," the purity of origins, or autonomous inward meanings—in contrast to the threatening "mimic" show of "imitations" that a city like London presents. But insofar as Wordsworth seems half-intent on deducing the human from the natural in book 7, and then coordinating them in such a way that, as on Snowdon, each ends up resembling the other in essence, he unavoidably reopens the whole problem of imitative representation. In fact, the disruptive possibilities only intimated in the Snowdon and Alpine sequences are fully realized in books 7 and 8, and to devastating effect. As he sets out to extend a transcendental system to these new domains, the epistemology that is supposed to elaborate it completely subverts it.

We can best track these developments and see the relation of these books to the work of the spring if we take the books in compositional sequence. For evidently Wordsworth felt that he had too easily dispatched the disturbing reality of London in book 8 and that he needed to elaborate the problem to which he had found the answer (much as he had decided to expand *The Prelude* because he needed to show how imagination was impaired before showing how it was restored). By reading book 8 before book 7, we can see how the confident, abstract conclusions of book 8 get subverted by the particular, irrefragable examples of book 7. This way too, we will see how a confident transcendentalism comes under its strongest attack yet from an empiricist epistemology.

Wordsworth's argument in book 8 is inescapably circular. His intention is to explicate if not prove what he already feels is a *fait accompli*—the interfusion of the natural and the human—but the examples he cites, from which he tries inductively to argue his case, invariably beg the question epistemologically or rhetorically. Because he approaches the problem as a relation among external objects that he simply observes, casting himself in the privileged role of disinterested *spectator ab extra,* he must turn "inward meaning" (to use the apt term from *The Pedlar* and book 3 of *The Prelude*) into an unproblematic visible shape. Essentially, he makes his case by putting intrinsically different "beings" (mind and nature, subject and object, human nature and nature) on the same plane, converting one into the same kind of thing as the other in order to show that they are resolvable, identifiable, and in the end deeply interfused.

Wordsworth's opening sequence in book 8 serves as a telling illustration of these various ploys. He begins by describing how Helvellyn Fair looks to Mt. Helvellyn itself, putting himself on the very edge of the frame as he looks down from the summit on the panorama below:

> WHAT sounds are those, Helvellyn, which are heard
> Up to thy summit? Through the depth of air
> Ascending, as if distance had the power
> To make the sounds more audible: what Crowd
> Is yon, assembled in the gay green Field?
> Crowd seems it, solitary Hill! to thee,
> Though but a little Family of Men.

(8. 1–7)

Wordsworth first describes the "little Family of Men" as objects from the outside and at a distance: "How little They." But when looking at them as objects framed by the context that contains them, the ratios switch, and they suddenly radiate with meaning endued to them by their context. The "silent Rocks" and the "reposing Clouds," and "Old Helvellyn, conscious of the stir," look down in love upon the family of men, who then seem "great" (8. 50–61). As he makes the "circumambient World" embrace these people as if they were "tender Infants," and makes "all things serve them" and love them (8. 47–55), Wordsworth obviously personifies nature; but he also does the reverse: he naturalizes the human by figuring people in the landscape as quasinatural objects in harmony with their environment and reflecting its character and moods. Referring later in book 8 to his childhood when shepherds especially seemed like natural objects, Wordsworth remarks:

> Even then the common haunts of the green earth,
> With the ordinary human interests
> Which they embosom, all without regard
> As both may seem, are fastening on the heart
> Insensibly, each with the other's help,
> So that we love, not knowing that we love,
> And feel, not knowing whence our feeling comes.
>
> (8. 166–72)

The rhetorical sleight of hand also becomes epistemological. Personifying nature and naturalizing persons, Wordsworth finds that the natural and the human are inseparably given together; he cannot distinguish them here. But the point of discovery for Wordsworth is that, as they compose the one external phenomenon, he does not arbitrarily apply a subjective meaning to them but finds in them an "inward meaning" that they communicate to him. Meaning is already present in outside objects (the same meaning he might wish to see) and simply awaits his act of perception.

As he personifies nature and thereby enhances its own intrinsic presence and meaning (these are never questioned but taken as givens in book 8), Wordsworth casts the human figure in the landscape as a supplementary presence whose role is to express nature's inner spirit and articulate its meanings. The shepherds living in harmony with nature, fitting their lives to the rhythms of the seasons, clearly act out this principle, with the result that Wordsworth comes to value the human because it is the sign and measure of the natural. At a certain point in his development, Wordsworth says, he came to see "Man" as

> first
> In capability of feeling what
> Was to be felt; in being rapt away

> By the divine effect of power and love,
> As, more than anything we know instinct
> With Godhead, and by reason and by will
> Acknowledging dependency sublime.
>
> (8. 634–40)

Yet as an "index," the "first / In capability of feeling what / Was to be felt," "Man" signifies nature by doubling it, by imitating it. In the "pastoral Tract" (8. 325) near Goslar, for example, his "daily walk" (8. 350) when living in Germany, Wordsworth says that "there as for herself had Nature fram'd / A Pleasure-ground" (8. 328–29), "where at large / The Shepherd strays . . . telling there 'his hours' / In unlaborious pleasure" (8. 336–43). Pleasure reflects pleasure. There is nothing else for man to do in a self-complete nature but imitate it.

The circularity here may consist primarily in the both/and of a humanized nature and a naturalized humanity, but the chiasmus, as in this latter example, creates some interesting complications. The human imitates the natural, and by doubling it in this way confirms the autonomy and authenticity of the natural; but the identity of the natural is already human, either in part or whole, so that the natural humanizes the human in imparting its content to it. Love of nature leads to love of man because man, superadded to nature, is a redundant repetition of it—while, conversely, nature is constituted as human before man is made fully human too.

Moreover, by epistemologizing the both/and as predominantly an influx from nature to persons, and thereby positing the autonomy and authenticity of "inward meanings" in nature, Wordsworth can turn to the other side of the equation and make human objects work in the same way as natural ones. Wordsworth redeems London by putting this entirely human creation on a par with nature—not simply as an external object, but as an external object that also expresses autonomous inward meanings just like nature's:

> Never shall I forget the hour
> The moment rather say when having thridded
> The labyrinth of suburban Villages,
> At length I did unto myself first seem
> To enter the great City. On the Roof
> Of an itinerant Vehicle I sate
> With vulgar men about me, vulgar forms
> Of houses, pavement, streets, of men and things,
> Mean shapes on every side: but, at the time,
> When to myself it fairly might be said,
> The very moment that I seem'd to know
> The threshold now is overpass'd, Great God!
> That aught *external* to the living mind
> Should have such mighty sway! yet so it was
> A weight of Ages did at once descend

Upon my heart; no thought embodied, no
Distinct remembrances; but weight and power
Power growing with the weight: alas! I feel
That I am trifling: 'twas a moment's pause.
All that took place within me, came and went
As in a moment, and I only now
Remember that it was a thing divine.

(8. 689–710)

Despite Wordsworth's commitment to a transcendental belief in the sovereignty of mind, a mind that is lord and master of the senses, the success of his transcendental insights in the Alps and on Snowdon and here in book 8 has always depended on something external to the living mind having such sway. The remarkable thing here is that the visiting of awful promise comes from the absolute opposite of nature: the city, an absolutely human object. In fact, Wordsworth moves on to celebrate London as object, as "place" (8. 753): it is "That great Emporium, Chronicle at once / and Burial-place of passions and their home / Imperial, and chief living residence" (8. 749–51); and what Wordsworth found there is "power . . . / In all things; nothing had a circumscribed / And narrow influence; but all objects, being / Themselves capacious, also found in me / Capaciousness and amplitude of mind" (8. 755–59). Compact with inward meanings, London articulates "Human nature" itself, which Wordsworth then regards as identical in essence and attributes with nature itself:

The Human nature unto which I felt
That I belong'd, and which I lov'd and reverenced,
Was not a punctual Presence, but a Spirit
Living in time and space, and far diffus'd.

(8. 761–66)

[A] sense
Of what had been here done, and suffer'd here
Through ages, and was doing, suffering, still
Weigh'd with me, could support the test of thought,
Was like the enduring majesty and power
Of independent nature; and not seldom
Even individual remembrances,
By working on the Shapes before my eyes,
Became like vital functions of the soul;
And out of what had been, what was, the place
Was throng'd with impregnations, like those wilds
In which my early feelings had been nurs'd,
And naked valleys, full of caverns, rocks,
And audible seclusions, dashing lakes,
Echoes and Waterfalls, and pointed crags
That into music touch the passing wind.

(8. 781–96)

Human nature becomes a "Presence" and a "Spirit"—terms Wordsworth applies to nature at many points throughout *The Prelude;* and finally in the second passage he makes human nature, in the way it is enshrined in London, expressly equivalent to nature.

The success of this circularity, but also its problem—as Wordsworth encounters in book 7—consists in the apparent discovery not only that meaning can autonomously reside in objects but that the same meaning can fully inform both an object and a subject that are unrelated and at a remove from each other. Wordsworth presents this both/and serially, in the manner of an either/or, in the cavern simile, thereby exposing the problem as well as illustrating the success. After the ferment of shapes and forms subsides to leave the cavern roof exposed and lifeless as a written book, Wordsworth adds:

> But let him pause awhile, and look again
> And a new quickening shall succeed, at first
> Beginning timidly, then creeping fast
> Through all which he beholds; the senseless mass,
> In its projections, wrinkles, cavities,
> Through all its surface, with all colours streaming,
> Like a magician's airy pageant, parts
> Unites, embodying everywhere some pressure
> Or image, recognis'd or new, some type
> Or picture of the world; forests and lakes,
> Ships, rivers, towers, the Warrior clad in Mail,
> The prancing Steed, the Pilgrim with his Staff,
> The mitred Bishop and the throned King,
> A spectacle to which there is no end.
>
> (8. 728–41)

The object, autonomously, of its own accord, starts presenting human (and natural) shapes and forms that the observer can simply read off. His own imagination becomes nature's, but influx obscures the mind's own flux. As the cavern roof surges from full to empty and back to full again, we can see that meaning is a variable ratio that reveals no intrinsic coordination with the object. This observer sees what he wants to see, and sees as much as he wants to see. And the inward meanings he sees are in essence imitations. Wordsworth may hold firm to transcendental notions of nature and human nature in book 8 and dramatize his belief in their deep interfusion, but the epistemology he deploys to make his case, because of its circularity, unavoidably submits "presence" to the play of "imitations." In fact, it models one on the other, to the detriment of the entire argument. The same happens even more powerfully in book 7, where the endless "mimic" show of "imitations," "resemblances," "Transcripts" and "types" subverts "presence" altogether.

Feeling that he has not given sufficient treatment to London itself, Wordsworth therefore proceeds in book 7 with the task of describing the city's sights and sounds, the entertainments he enjoyed, and other encounters he had that he found important for one reason or another. But feeling that he has already resolved the question of London's meaning, he confidently opens himself to the city's relentless assault on his senses and sensibility. He opens himself to complete confusion and disorientation—not only because he knows already he has his bearings but more because he feels confident he can organize confusion into order and show how he reached the meanings he has already expounded. Given his overt claims in book 8 and his management of objects and meanings, this may seem like a calculated epistemological risk to take. It may begin that way, but the dangers eventually ensnare Wordsworth in the contradictions of his own procedures. Boldly letting epistemology take over—as completely as in the fragment "To Gaze" in the Alfoxden Notebook—Wordsworth in the end is overtaken by epistemology. He puts an end to his predicament—or rather closes the book —by wilfully reaffirming the conclusions of book 8 despite the glaring inconsistency of fact and theory. In short, Wordsworth stages confusion, disorientation and disruption, and safely assumes the stance of *spectator ab extra* only to find that the spectacle engulfs the spectator.

As a sequence in an epic progress, Wordsworth's sojourn in London corresponds to the classic descent into hell. Wandering through the phantasmagoria surrounding him, Wordsworth is, as Geoffrey Hartman points out, like Aeneas among the shades.[5] One may be surprised that London rather than Paris of the Reign of Terror should be presented as hell, but the substitution throws light on Wordsworth's philosophical predicament. On the surface, the substitution succeeds as a defensive response, a repetition in a finer tone, as it were, allowing Wordsworth to mediate at a safe distance what he cannot face directly.[6] The unspeakable acts of the Reign of Terror are replaced by noisy "mimic" shows on the streets of London; the public arena of political events and the guillotine on its platform by Bartholomew Fair and the "Showman's platform" elevated "Above the press and danger of the Crowd" (8. 658–59). In London, Wordsworth can confront what is threatening in Paris by transposing it into theatrical spectacle, into representation. That is, as we have seen in other instances, he reduces the psychological to the epistemological, making inward meaning entirely a matter of outward objects and their behavior, a spectacle of interactions that he can safely watch. But because Paris is half implicit in London, the spectacle becomes horrifying, the representation dangerous, the confusion overwhelming. As several commentators have pointed out, book 7 changes from a record of genuine delights to a stern satire on the corruption and degradation of urban civilization.[7] Here, the medium of hell's articulation becomes epistemology itself, for London comes close to reducing Wordsworth to epistemological incoherence.

Wordsworth opens his narrative by announcing his move to London as a new beginning:

> Return'd from that excursion, soon I bade
> Farewell for ever to the private Bowers
> Of gowned Students, quitted these, no more
> To enter them, and pitch'd my vagrant tent,
> A casual dweller and at large, among
> The unfenced regions of society.
>
> Yet undetermined to what plan of life
> I should adhere, and seeming thence to have
> A little space of intermediate time
> Loose and at full command, to London first
> I turn'd, if not in calmness, nevertheless
> In no disturbance of excessive hope,
> At ease from all ambition personal,
> Frugal as there was need, and though self-will'd,
> Yet temperate and reserv'd, and wholly free
> From dangerous passions. 'Twas at least two years
> Before this season when I first beheld
> That mighty place, a transient visitant:
> And now it pleas'd me my abode to fix
> Single in the wide waste, to have a house
> It was enough (what matter for a home?)
> That own'd me; living chearfully abroad,
> With fancy on the stir from day to day,
> And all my young affections out of doors.

(7. 57–80)

"[A]t large, among / The unfenced regions of society," and "living chearfully abroad, / With fancy on the stir from day to day," Wordsworth is as open to opportunity, as free of responsibility, as any picaresque hero of an eighteenth-century novel. Epistemologically this means that his mind is a perfect tabula rasa ready for any inscription. As he begins describing his experience in London, he shows how that tabula rasa was actually inscribed. That is, he unfolds a classic Lockean epistemology of primary and secondary qualities, sensations, impressions and ideas—all as a way to describe the object, London itself, an object so vast and unmanageable that it continuously suggests an ever-shifting array of meanings that can never be consolidated into one comprehensive idea.

In contrast to the simpler, even singular, objects composing the natural landscape, London appears to Wordsworth to be an object that is multifaceted and complex, incapable of being apprehended either as a whole or at once. As a phenomenon imprinting itself on the senses, it fulfills Locke's notion of a complex idea.[8] It is, however, as an "idea" in the popular sense of the word that Wordsworth first gains acquaintance with London. To the imagination of this northern school boy the distant southern capital ranks with the famed cities of history and the magical cities of fairy tales:

> There was a time when whatsoe'er is feign'd
> Of airy Palaces, and Gardens built
> By Genii of Romance, or hath in grave
> Authentic History been set forth of Rome,
> Alcairo, Babylon, or Persepolis,
> Or given upon report by Pilgrim-Friars
> Of golden Cities ten months' journey deep
> Among Tartarean Wilds, fell short, far short,
> Of that which I in simpleness believed
> And thought of London; held me by a chain
> Less strong of wonder, and obscure delight.
>
> (7. 81–91)

"Marvellous things," Wordsworth says, "My fancy had shap'd forth, of sights and shows, / Processions, Equipages, Lords and Dukes, / The King, and the King's Palace, and not last / Or least, heaven bless him! the renown'd Lord Mayor" (7. 108–12). Yet a fellow-schoolboy, "a Cripple from his birth" (95), returning unchanged from this magical city causes Wordsworth to face the discrepancy between fantasy and actuality when the report he gives of the city falls on Wordsworth's ears "flatter than a caged Parrot's note, / That answers unexpectedly awry, / And mocks the Prompter's listening" (7. 106–8). This childhood disappointment anticipates the ensuing dislocations that the "real scene" (7. 139) of London forces on the beholder—dislocations of a deeper order between external appearance and "inward meaning."

The imagined fantasies of childhood yield to the reality which the adult encounters:

> These fond imaginations of themselves
> Had long before given way in season due,
> Leaving a throng of others in their stead;
> And now I look'd upon the real scene,
> Familiarly perused it day by day
> With keen and lively pleasure even there
> Where disappointment was the strongest, pleased
> Through courteous self-submission, as a tax
> Paid to the object by prescriptive right,
> A thing that ought to be.
>
> (7. 136–45)

With London as with no other phenomenon anywhere else in *The Prelude*, not even Mont Blanc, Wordsworth confronts an overwhelming, intractable objectivity: as he says in book 8, "Great God! / That aught *external* to the living mind /

Should have such sway!" (8. 700–702; Wordsworth's emphasis). The sheer
vastness and profusion of the city elicit an ever-shifting complexity of responses. If by the end of book 7 he dismisses London as a "monstrous ant-hill
on the plain / Of a too busy world" (1850 *Prel,* 7. 149–50), at the beginning
he proclaims it to be "A vivid pleasure of my youth, and now . . . / A frequent
day-dream for my riper mind" (7. 151–53). His response, in fact, runs the gamut
from delight and astonishment to bewilderment, confusion, and finally disgust
and despondency. His wavering emotions are perhaps more important as an
index of the deeper epistemological difficulty of merely identifying and describing the object. The enormity of the task initially stops Wordsworth short at doing
nothing more than merely enumerating the wealth of sights and sounds assault-
ing his senses. He begins by attempting to describe "some portion of that motley
imagery" (7. 150):

> —And first the look and aspect of the place
> The broad high-way appearance, as it strikes
> On Strangers of all ages, the quick dance
> Of colours, lights and forms, the Babel din
> The endless stream of men, and moving things.

> (7. 154–58)

He is surrounded by a continuous array of scenes; he is engulfed by "the roar"
(7. 184), swept along in "the throng" (7. 205) or in a "thickening hubbub"
(7. 227), while "Here there and everywhere a weary throng / The Comers and
the Goers face to face, / Face after face" (7. 171–73) pass all around him.

The sights particularly engaging Wordsworth's attention are shows, exhibitions, or spectacles of some kind. In one street which he enters to escape "the
roar," he stumbles upon a "raree-show . . . / With Children gather'd round"
(7. 191–92); while another street

> Presents a company of dancing Dogs,
> Or Dromedary, with an antic pair
> Of Monkies on his back, a minstrel Band
> Of Savoyards, or, single and alone,
> An English Ballad-singer.

> (7. 191–96)

But besides semitheatrical entertainments of this kind, Wordsworth perceives
many other sights that are like spectacles or exhibitions in effect: sights that
intentionally aim to catch the attention of passersby and tell them something,
to make them stop and attend. For one, Wordsworth notices shop signs. "Shop
after shop" displays

> Symbols, blazon'd Names,
> And all the Tradesman's honours overhead;
> Here, fronts of houses, like a title-page
> With letters huge inscribed from top to toe;
> Station'd above the door, like guardian Saints,
> There, allegoric shapes, female or male;
> Or physiognomies of real men,
> Land-Warriors, Kings, or Admirals of the Sea,
> Boyle, Shakspear, Newton, or the attractive head
> Of some Scotch doctor, famous in his day.
>
> (7. 174–84)

Yet increasingly, as this passage suggests, Wordsworth notices signs that are written: the "files of ballads" dangling "from dead walls," where

> Advertisements of giant-size, from high
> Press forward in all colours on the sight;
> These, bold in conscious merit; lower down
> That, fronted with a most imposing word,
> Is, peradventure, one in masquerade,
>
> (7. 209–14)

and also some "written characters, with chalk inscrib'd / Upon the smooth flat stones" (7. 222–23) beside which a sailor lies. Wordsworth's tendency to be attracted by written signs finds its apotheosis later in the book in the figure of the blind beggar "Wearing a written paper" upon his chest "to explain the story of the Man, and who he was" (7. 614–15); while it also figures in the account of Bartholomew Fair where "staring pictures, and huge scrolls, / Dumb proclamations of the prodigies" throng "the midway region" above the heads of the crowd (7. 665–67).

All these signs call out for notice; generally they intend not only to convey information but to goad the passerby to some specific response. But even where "sights and sounds" (7. 189) are not so pointedly designed to provoke responsive action, they at least convey a considerable amount of information that Wordsworth automatically perceives as signifying something. In fact, even those sights and sounds that are not calling out for attention at all Wordsworth regards as signs, as significant in some way, or as emblematic or symbolic:

> Now homeward through the thickening hubbub, where
> See, among less distinguishable shapes,
> The Italian, with his Frame of Images
> Upon his head; with Basket at his waist
> The Jew; the stately and slow-moving Turk
> With freight of slippers piled beneath his arm.
> Briefly, we find, if tired of random sights

And haply to that search our thoughts should turn,
Among the crowd, conspicuous less or more,
As we proceed, all specimens of man
Through all the colours which the sun bestows,
And every character of form and face,
The Swede, the Russian; from the genial South,
The Frenchman and the Spaniard; from remote
America, the Hunter-Indian; Moors,
Malays, Lascars, The Tartar and Chinese,
And Negro Ladies in white muslin gowns.

(7. 227–43)

The individuals Wordsworth singles out from among "less distinguishable shapes" seem hardly more than animated versions of the "allegoric shapes, female or male" standing as signs or "symbols" over the tradesmen's shops. Wordsworth originally notices the Italian, Turk and Jew because their paraphernalia and the postures they assume to carry them make them appear "distinguishable" from the flux of "random sights." Yet Wordsworth's focus immediately shifts from the particular to the universal as he perceives these "random" individuals (and the others following them in the passage) not only as representative of their respective nationality or race but as indicative of the entire human species. In London can be seen "all specimens of man / Through all the colours which the sun bestows, / And every character of form and face." The intrinsic characteristics of the particular and the "random," "distinguishable" for accidental, arbitrary reasons from all other "random sights" that London offers, yield in importance to the general—the *universal*—which Wordsworth takes them collectively to represent and symbolize.

This passage suggests that visual properties alone make a shape "conspicuous less or more." And interpreting "distinguishable shapes" as in effect *"allegoric* shapes" (emphasis added)—that is, reading "random sights" as signs of the universal—relies on comparing the visual properties of one shape with those of another. This mode of looking, however, has a curious effect on the question of meaning. If it allows Wordsworth to proceed to general, overall meanings, it correspondingly requires him to disregard individual particular meanings. Wordsworth is less interested in the single item than in the whole series to which it belongs. In part, of course, the "sights" of London flow by faster than he is able to attend to them individually. But the sheer quantity of sights becomes an occasion for actively suppressing meaning. The shop signs, for example, appeal to Wordsworth not because of the commercial messages they convey but because of their visual variety. Even where he is looking at *words,* he is interested not in their meanings but in the style of the inscription: the size of the letters, for example. Individual items gain meaning, then, only by being put in context with others in their class. Whatever a "freight of slippers" and a "stately and slow-moving" gait might suggest about this particular Turk—or the Turkish character in general—is ignored in favor of the simpler idea of a representative ethnic type in characteristic posture, whose full significance consists in reminding Wordsworth of other representative ethnic types, and then indeed of the entire class of representative types.

This suppression effectively separates "sight" from meaning. If "shapes" are "distinguishable" on the basis of visual characteristics alone or in context with others in their class, then there obtains an epistemological detachment of "shapes" from any "inward meaning" that might be adduced as an intrinsic or local reason for finding them "distinguishable." Two other "random sights" exemplify this detachment quite sharply:

> As on the broadening Causeway we advance,
> Behold a Face turn'd up toward us, strong
> In lineaments, and red with over-toil;
> 'Tis one perhaps, already met elsewhere,
> A travelling Cripple, by the trunk cut short,
> And stumping with his arms.

(7. 215–20)

The "Face turn'd up toward us" on the causeway presents the same look as "one perhaps, already met elsewhere," a "travelling Cripple." Wordsworth allows that the two people may be one and the same, but he is not absolutely sure. He notices only the "shapes" themselves: the "Face turn'd up . . . , strong / In lineaments, and red with over-toil," and the cripple "by the trunk cut short, / And stumping with his arms."[9] Wordsworth's inability to connect precisely the specificity of one "shape" with that of the other argues an epistemological detachment or dislocation. If he can so vividly perceive the face "turn'd up" on the causeway, can he not also perceive whether the body it is attached to is that of the cripple "already met elsewhere"? If Wordsworth first finds the face "distinguishable" because of an "inward meaning"—the look of "over-toil" (which no doubt reminds him of the cripple who must also evince "over-toil" because he is reduced to "stumping with his arms")—the more important activity in this instance consists not in focusing on the idea of "over-toil" as suggested by the visual properties of one particular "shape" but only in connecting the two shapes separated in time and space. Wordsworth is less interested in the "sight" of "over-toil" than in relating a present sight to a remembered sight. In fact, "over-toil" as a common "inward meaning" is altogether separable from this primary activity of connecting two "distinguishable shapes." Such detachment figures quite explicitly on this occasion. The "turn'd up" face seems unattached to a body, while the cripple is quite literally truncated: "by the trunk cut short, / And stumping with his arms."

In London, Wordsworth finds the relation of visual shapes amongst themselves to be more important than their relation with any intrinsic "inward meaning." Dazzled by the press of "random sights," he has, to be sure, little opportunity to do more than distinguish features and shapes among the "motley imagery" flowing by. If the meaning of what he sees is an issue at all, then it is mediated entirely by this lateral movement as he determines one shape by juxtaposing it to another shape. Indeed, meaning for Wordsworth consists in recognizing that one shape in effect *represents* another shape, a shape adjacent to it, existing on the same plane with it. Face and cripple have meaning for Wordsworth only when juxtaposed; similarly, Italian, Turk and Jew become representative only when put in adjacency to each other and other ethnic types.

As Wordsworth continues his description of London, he gives us a literal illustration of the lateral movement of signification implicit in these examples:

> At leisure let us view, from day to day,
> As they present themselves, the Spectacles
> Within doors, troops of wild Beasts, birds and beasts
> Of every nature, from all climes convened;
> And, next to these, those mimic sights that ape
> The absolute presence of reality,
> Expressing as in mirror, sea and land,
> And what earth is, and what she has to shew;
> I do not here allude to subtlest craft,
> By means refin'd attaining purest ends,
> But imitations fondly made in plain
> Confession of man's weakness, and his loves,
> Whether the Painter fashioning a work
> To Nature's circumambient scenery,
> And with his greedy pencil taking in
> A whole horizon on all sides, with power,
> Like that of Angels or commission'd Spirits,
> Plant us upon some lofty Pinnacle,
> Or in a Ship on Waters, with a world
> Of life, and life-like mockery, to East,
> To West, beneath, behind us, and before:
> Or more mechanic Artist represent
> By scale exact, in Model, wood or clay,
> From shading colours also borrowing help,
> Some miniature of famous spots and things
> Domestic, or the boast of foreign Realms;
> The Firth of Forth, and Edinburgh throned
> On crags, fit empress of that mountain Land;
> St. Peter's Church; or, more aspiring aim,
> In microscopic vision, Rome itself;
> Or, else perhaps, some rural haunt, the Falls
> Of Tivoli,
> And high upon the steep, that mouldering Fane
> The Temple of the Sibyl, every tree

> Through all the landscape, tuft, stone, scratch minute,
> And every Cottage, lurking in the rocks,
> All that the Traveller sees when he is there.
>
> (7. 244–80)

The "troops of wild Beasts, birds and beasts / Of every nature, from all climes convened" further the concept of totality intimated by "all specimens of man" immediately preceding this passage. Wordsworth evidently views London as a microcosm of the whole world, for it contains not only representatives of every nationality and race but specimens of all animal and bird species too—and even representative depictions of earth's landscapes and famous features.[10] It is the latter class of "imitations," the panoramas and "miniature[s]," that particularly preoccupy Wordsworth in this passage. He praises them for their verisimilitude: they are faithful copies of complex intricate originals—"mimic sights that ape /The absolute presence of reality." Yet what is signified in these instances is itself an object, existing on the same plane together with the "miniature." Copy and original are both alike "sight" and "sight," posited in relation to each other. The one "sight" does no more than signify the other "sight"—while neither sight is posited in relation to any "inward meaning" or to anything other than "shapes" already featured in either the original or the copy.

But as Wordsworth turns to another class of "Spectacles / Within doors"—the theater—and explores the attraction it held for him during his stay in London, he begins to develop this epistemology in such a way as to incorporate the relation of meaning to sights. The theater quite obviously constitutes an example of "imitation." In staging "dramas of living Men, /And recent things, yet warm with life" (7. 313–14), it too presents "mimic sights that ape / The absolute presence of reality," exemplifying the same lateral movement of signification. Yet whether presenting a copy of real life or something patently fanciful, the theater inspires Wordsworth to ponder important epistemological questions: he wonders about the audience's willing suspension of disbelief, how self-evident artifice can work its magic and command belief in "The absolute presence" of a "reality" that is purely imaginary. Incipient surmise of this kind inevitably enters the realm of meanings: for Wordsworth finds himself asking what idea does this play of shapes signify and how:

> Nor was it mean delight
> To watch crude nature work in untaught minds,
> To note the laws and progress of belief;
> Though obstinate on this way, yet on that
> How willingly we travel, and how far!
> To have, for instance, brought upon the scene
> The Champion Jack the Giant-killer, Lo!

He dons his Coat of Darkness; on the Stage
Walks, and atchieves his wonders from the eye
Of living mortal safe as is the moon
'Hid in her vacant interlunar cave.'
Delusion bold! and faith must needs be coy;
How is it wrought? His garb is black, the word
INVISIBLE flames forth upon his chest.

(7. 297–310)

Adjacency and juxtaposition play their part here, as in previous instances. But the juxtaposition is clearly incongruous and offsets not so much a "distinguishable shape" as a "distinguishable" word—a word which, unlike the shop signs before, is now read for its meaning. The word "INVISIBLE" flames forth against the black costume Jack the Giant-killer wears, allowing him to achieve his "Delusion bold" of invisibility. This simple theatrical device is, however, an effective "Delusion bold" in context of the epistemology Wordsworth is developing. As a sign, a "distinguishable shape," the word conveys an idea— that is, a meaning which cannot, of course, be seen yet which profoundly affects what can be seen. As a "sight" labeling another "sight," the word tells the audience that the Jack whom they see is really invisible. A "sight" (i.e., a word, a label, affixed to another sight) functions, therefore, as a sign for invisibility. Meaning is thus contrary to "sight." Indeed, if we take this instance as "allegoric" of the whole question of meaning in London, we see that Wordsworth opposes meaning to "sight," making the word "INVISIBLE" be "allegoric" of the nature of meaning as such.[11]

Yet irony issues into paradox as Wordsworth compounds the "Delusion bold" by revealing the contrary way in which reference completes meaning. If meaning is in essence invisible, it is nonetheless a palpable presence—just as the invisible Jack is a palpable presence on stage. But inasmuch as Jack is of course clearly visible, then Wordsworth implies that meaning too is something which might be seen after all—a "sight," finally, even if of an order of "inward" visibility. The idea conveyed by the word "invisible" applies, refers, to Jack— so that, in this instance, reference works to equate meaning with sight. The meaning of the word "INVISIBLE," when fully understood and referred to its object, would translate into a sight.

This example may seem unimportant but it encapsulates the relation of meaning to sights and the epistemological maneuvers Wordsworth performs to construct meaning. Essentially, we have two opposite and contrary strategies: first, meaning in many of the examples Wordsworth gives is a double of the object, an imitative representation; but second, meaning can be the opposite of a sight, here something that is intrinsically invisible. The switch this example introduces is developed at length in the discussion that follows on the London theater. Wordsworth refers first to the play "Edward and Susan; or, The Beauty of Buttermere," produced at Sadler's Wells in 1803, a play he did not see (although he heard about it from the Lambs).[12] Having once met the subject of the play, Mary Robinson, the "Maid of Buttermere" herself, and speculating that her story would have been "doubtless treated with irreverence" (7. 319), Wordsworth moves into a protracted meditation on nature and the purity of origins versus the city and its corruptions.[13] The thought of the wronged innocent Mary and her dead infant reminds him by contrast of another woman he saw at the theater, whose cheeks were "A painted bloom" (7. 374), but who had a beautiful young boy who was "The pride and pleasure of all lookers-on" (7. 376):

> Upon a Board
> Whence an attendant of the Theatre
> Serv'd out refreshments, had this Child been placed,
> And there he sate, environ'd with a Ring
> Of chance Spectators, chiefly dissolute men
> And shameless women; treated and caress'd,
> Ate, drank, and with the fruit and glasses play'd,
> While oaths, indecent speech, and ribaldry
> Were rife about him as are songs of birds
> In spring-time after showers.
>
> (7. 383–92)

These theatrical examples suggest that diametric opposition and incongruous or contrary juxtaposition govern the epistemological procedures whereby Wordsworth responds to, and makes sense of, London. What he values about, or reads into, the sights he beholds is something which is either in reality not there and in essence diametrically opposed to what is there, or is only minimally present and under threat of imminent extinction from the antagonistic environment in which it finds itself. For example, Wordsworth envisions the innocent babe as dying at an early age in order to become

> no partner in the years
> That bear us forward to distress and guilt,
> Pain and abasement, beauty in such excess
> Adorn'd him in that miserable place.
>
> (7. 404–7)

Yet Wordsworth complicates these principles of opposition by making inward meanings take the form of sights—sights which, in the case of Mary of Buttermere, proceed laterally and in imitation of outward sights. As epistemological response takes the form of an interplay between, and juxtaposition of, two different orders of sights, Wordsworth finds that meaning becomes once again, as in book 8, a matter of ratios: the insignificant, the accidental or the random will suddenly open up a "world of thought" (7. 495)—whereas "More lofty Themes,/ Such as, at least, do wear a prouder face" cause "the imaginative Power [to] / Languish within [him]" (7. 496–500). When summing up his response to productions of Shakespeare he saw in London, Wordsworth acknowledges the disproportion between sight and meaning but still tries to retain the even balance of epistemological connection:

> If aught there were of real grandeur here
> 'Twas only then when gross realities,
> The incarnation of the Spirits that mov'd
> Amid the Poet's beauteous world, call'd forth,
> With that distinctness *which a contrast gives*
> *Or opposition,* made me recognize
> As by a glimpse, the things which I had shaped
> And yet not shaped, had seen, and scarcely seen,
> Had felt, and thought of in my solitude.
>
> (7. 508–16; emphasis added)

This passage aptly intimates the philosophical tensions at play in Wordsworth's treatment of London, for we can detect here the contradiction that has become increasingly evident in the course of book 7 between an inherently Lockean epistemology and a transcendental metaphysics of meaning that Wordsworth insists on superimposing on it. Engulfed in a world of imitations in which meanings end up being imitative representations of those imitations, Wordsworth struggles to affirm the categorical difference of his own "world of thought" from that world outside. If Wordsworth claims here a transcendental reliance on external objects for the mind to construct meanings it creatively half "shapes," he more than half fears absolute severance from external objects altogether. If he has "shaped" the meaning, if random insignificant things have opened up a "world of thought," then meaning not only is disproportionate to the object but potentially bears no relation to it at all. Conversely, if the meaning comes to him ready-shaped, then he is trapped in the circuit of passively imitating imitations. Wordsworth straddles the rift between these extremes—but does not close it—by claiming the both/neither of "shaped / And yet not shaped, had seen, and scarcely seen."

Moreover, it is all to the point that these tensions should be articulated in the theater, where representations on stage prompt Wordsworth to entertain different representations in the theater of his mind. For the theater is a classic metaphor for the mind in Hume: "The mind is a kind of theatre, where several perceptions successively make their appearance; pass, re-pass, glide away, and mingle in an infinite variety of postures and situations."[14] Hume's words accurately summarize Wordsworth's experience in London. But Hume's image essentially develops one of Locke's metaphors for the mind: a *"dark Room"* or "Closet wholly shut from light, with only some little openings left, to let in external visible Resemblances, or *Ideas* of things without" (Locke's emphases).[15] Curiously enough, Wordsworth echoes Locke's image when reminiscing about the pleasure he felt in his youth "When, at a Country-playhouse, [he] caught, / In summer, through the fractured wall, a glimpse / Of daylight" (7. 482–84). No doubt the echo is fortuitous, but the long run of the same epistemological drama is not. Wordsworth can easily find a transcendental exit when safely seated as a spectator on the other side of the footlights. But once outside the theater, he finds the theatricality of representation all the more oppressive and inescapable and transcendental passageways harder to find. We have already seen this earlier in book 7, but the most dramatic instance of all is Wordsworth's encounter with the blind beggar. On this occasion the spectator is engulfed by the spectacle, as he is plunged into utter confusion by the outward scene.

> O Friend! one feeling was there which belong'd
> To this great City, by exclusive right;
> How often in the overflowing Streets,
> Have I gone forward with the Crowd, and said
> Unto myself, the face of everyone
> That passes by me is a mystery.
> Thus have I look'd, nor ceas'd to look, oppress'd
> By thoughts of what, and whither, when and how,
> Until the shapes before my eyes became
> A second-sight procession, such as glides
> Over still mountains, or appears in dreams;
> And all the ballast of familiar life,
> The present, and the past; hope, fear; all stays,
> All laws of acting, thinking, speaking man
> Went from me, neither knowing me, nor known.

(7. 593–607)

All Wordsworth's epistemological efforts fail to organize the "overflowing" sight in any way. The faces passing by seem even more detached than the face upturned in the causeway—and far more inscrutable. "[O]ppress'd / By thoughts of what, and whither, when and how," as he "look'd, nor ceas'd to look," Wordsworth discovers that he cannot penetrate the "mystery" these faces present. All insight and explanation fail. In fact, the entire realm of inward meanings, including the knowledge of origins and originals, is utterly erased by the overwhelming sight:

> And all the ballast of familiar life,
> The present, and the past; hope, fear; all stays,

> All laws of acting, thinking, speaking man
> Went from me, neither knowing me, nor known.

The faculties of the mind—understanding, reason, memory—are immobilized; the only exception is the faculty of perception. Wordsworth is powerless to do anything but simply see, as he goes "forward with the Crowd."

The "shapes before [his] eyes," though removed from the theatrical context, show the essential characteristics of theatrical spectacle: they are a "procession," a "moving pageant" (7. 610), that turns Wordsworth from spectator to participant—to an actor whose role is dictated by the play.

It is in this state that he suddenly encounters a blind beggar. The experience powerfully dramatizes all the epistemological issues at play in book 7, for Wordsworth regards the beggar as an "emblem" (7. 619) of the whole problem of sight and meaning:

> And once, far-travell'd in such mood, beyond
> The reach of common indications, lost
> Amid the moving pageant, 'twas my chance
> Abruptly to be smitten with the view
> Of a blind Beggar, who, with upright face,
> Stood propp'd against a Wall, upon his Chest
> Wearing a written paper, to explain
> The story of the Man, and who he was.
> My mind did at this spectacle turn round
> As with the might of waters, and it seemed
> To me that in this Label was a type,
> Or emblem, of the utmost that we know,
> Both of ourselves and of the universe;
> And, on the shape of the unmoving man,
> His fixed face and sightless eyes, I look'd
> As if admonish'd from another world.

> (7. 608–23)

Contrary juxtaposition characterizes the experience at every point. Moving "forward with the Crowd" in the "overflowing Streets," Wordsworth suddenly encounters a fixed and stationary sight. This beggar, unlike the traveling cripple who moves from place to place, "Stood propp'd against a Wall"—but his face, like the one upturned toward us on the causeway, is "upright." The juxtapositions of motion and fixity, crowd and single individual, conduct to the more important kinds of "contrast or opposition" shaping the ratios of sight and meaning. Wordsworth states first of all that he was "Abruptly . . . smitten with the view / Of a blind Beggar," as if it were the beggar's sight of him as much as his sight of the beggar which surprises him.[16] But the beggar's sight is immediately unmasked, of course, to be its opposite: blindness. This blinding of sight, moreover, works by the same principle of "contrast or opposition" as

Jack the Giant-killer's "Delusion bold" of invisibility. With Jack, the visible signified a different order of invisibility in which the spectator might find the criterion for interpreting the visible. With the blind beggar, Wordsworth makes the same switch to an invisible inward realm by suggesting that blindness signifies *spiritual* insight.[17] As Wordsworth plainly emphasizes, he responds to the "fixed face and sightless eyes" of the beggar "As if admonish'd from another world." The implication is that the beggar sees "another world" but is blind to this world in which Wordsworth and all other sights reside. Correlatively, ordinary human vision is therefore a form of (spiritual) blindness because it cannot see into this other world.

But this conjunction of sight and blindness constitutes a more radical case of contrary juxtaposition than does Jack's. Whereas with Jack (and in "The Maid of Buttermere" sequence too) the visible and the invisible overlap or are contiguous, with the blind beggar they seem completely severed. In fact, the spectacle of the blind beggar would give no indication whether there even *is* a relation between the visible and the invisible were it not for the "written paper" which he wears on his chest and which, in explaining "The story of the Man, and who he was," explains his blindness and beggared state.[18] If in the beggar's "sightless eyes" Wordsworth sees evidence of "another world," on the "written paper" he reads the connection of that world to this one.

At first, then, there may appear to be no relation between the invisible and the visible, but the blind beggar and the label together show how the former has affected the latter. The invisible is implemented in the visible—and at the expense of the visible—resulting, in effect, in its negation: the drama of a living man warm with life ends in a "fixed and propp'd" spectacle that others might see. Moreover, reference completes meaning in this instance in the same way as in Jack's "Delusion bold." The "Label" is a sight affixed to another sight, instructing the spectator how to read the spectacle, but now the writing the beggar wears on his chest indicates that the invisible has been made visible. For Wordsworth takes the label to be "a type, / Or emblem, of the utmost that we know, / Both of ourselves and of the universe": all that can be known (especially about "another world") is summarized right here on the "written paper" the beggar wears. If the visible is "blinded" in the course of elaborating the invisible, then the invisible also undergoes a comparable fate as it is made visible by being put down in writing. The "utmost that we know" reduces to a few sentences, to next to nothing at all. "[A]nother world" suddenly seems thereby voided inasmuch as the invisible realm of inward meanings has been condensed into a simple sight, a "written paper."

The spectacle of the blind beggar dramatizes a crucial epistemological paradox: the invisible is of as wide a compass as the universe itself and yet is capable of being contracted within as little space as that of a mere label. All possible "inward meaning" ("the utmost that we know") is finally given as a sight. But this paradox unfolds a further "contrast or opposition." The label, as a record of the "utmost," fuses infinite possibility with severe limitation. The result, as it might be in a Kantian triad, is negation:[19] "the utmost that we know" proves to be almost nothing at all, something negligible—something which, like the sight itself that the label explains, has been reduced to near uselessness. But at precisely this point the paradox reverses its emphasis. If the "utmost" inward meaning is "blinded" in being made visible in the form of a label, just as the sight itself is also "blinded" in fulfilling it, then "inward meaning," "another world," "ourselves and the universe," having been reduced to virtually nothing, are freed to become as inscrutable, as extensive, and as full of possibility as before. Paradoxically, the spectacle undoes what it does; and fullness, reduced to emptiness, reverts to fullness once more.

The spectacle and all its imposing contrasts cause Wordsworth's mind to "turn round / As with the might of waters." But the "might" he faces is really that of his own mind, as he realizes that he himself has filled emptiness by construing the spectacle as an "allegoric" "type, / Or emblem." Aware that he has universalized from one example (as he did with Italian, Turk, and Jew before) and taken the spectacle to be "allegoric" of sight and meaning as such ("the utmost that we know"), Wordsworth now recognizes more clearly the things which he had shaped:

> Though rear'd upon the base of outward things,
> These, chiefly, are such structures as the mind
> Builds for itself. Scenes different there are,
> Full-form'd, which take, with small internal help,
> Possession of the faculties.

(7. 624–28)

This encounter is epistemologically crucial, then, because it shows Wordsworth wresting transcendental meaning from the dramatically antithetical ratios of contrast and opposition. Or rather he discovers meaning, is usurped by it, as the spectacle, "external to [his] living mind," suddenly exerts its sway. The distinction of this moment is that whereas inward meaning on previous occasions often seemed severed from outward sights, here meaning and sight are (inversely) commensurable and connected. Yet despite Wordsworth's confident transcendental theory about structures that the mind builds for itself on the base of outward things, the spectacle still stands on a base of imitative representations. As the label names the sight and represents the story that the beggar also represents, Wordsworth's antithetical ratios of "utmost" and next-to-nothing-at-all alternate in unending differential play because presence can never be anything other than a representation. Here, as the label and beggar mean him to do—and as he did in the "Maid of Buttermere" sequence—Wordsworth posits an antecedent presence to anchor and guide perception in the present: the label and its text, the beggar and his blindness, the spectacle as a whole point to some presupposed, antecedent "what, and whither, when and how." But this presence is only known insofar as it is represented—and that by representations that compound the case by representing each other.

Despite, then, his insistence in MS. Y on a world of "primary and independent life," Wordsworth finds himself immersed in London in a world of spectacle, "imitation" and "mimic" show—a world that in fact lives out its own independent, albeit secondary, life of representation. With presence an effect (sometimes a counter-effect) of representation, Wordsworth finds himself trapped in an either/or that unravels his whole system. Structures the mind builds for itself can often bear no relation to outward things, for the same object can be meaningful or meaningless for no intrinsic reasons; but conversely "Scenes" that are "Full-form'd," whose meanings "take, with small internal help, / Possession of the faculties," reduce the self to a passive imitative representation. The object, when full of meaning, can mean nothing to the perceiver. Under threat of absolute disconnection Wordsworth sides with "inward" transcendentalism and rejects the outside world of endless "types." As he says of Bartholomew Fair ("a type not false / Of what the mighty City is itself" [7. 696–97]), this world of endless types stages "the same perpetual flow / Of trivial objects, melted and reduced / To one identity, by differences / That have no law, no meaning, and no end" (7. 702–5). His response, as he increasingly reasserts that transcendentalism in the closing passages of book 7, is to claim, rather disingenuously and contrary to the evidence he has presented, that

> The Spirit of Nature was upon me here;
> The Soul of Beauty and enduring life
> Was present as a habit, and diffused,
> Through meagre lines and colours, and the press
> Of self-destroying, transitory things
> Composure and ennobling harmony.

(7. 736–41)

He claims the abiding continuity of presence and origins. But given the way his closing statement thoroughly presupposes the antecedent argument of book 8, we can see that nature will not solve but exacerbate the problem. For nature, an object like London (ultimately equal to it as "Spirit" and "Presence" in book 8), is as much subject to the swings of meaningfulness and meaninglessness as is this urban world of types and imitations, and as much determined one way or the other by the person observing it. There is no real reason, then, why any object—London or the natural landscape—should be meaningful or meaningless. Object, nature, self, meaning, and system are now farther apart than ever.

Confidently starting out with the intention of extending transcendentalism to new domains, Wordsworth articulates it on an inherently empiricist epistemology that only unravels the system. With this the philosophical outcome in November 1804, he obviously must emphasize next not only the sovereignty of mind but, more importantly, its energetic reciprocity with an external nature that is itself an autonomous mindlike presence. Clearly the "mighty Mind" passage of the Snowdon meditation, written within a month or two after book 7, is a move in this direction, as are other passages written about this time for later *Prelude* books. But the problems presented in books 7 and 8 and the strategies for resolving them extend beyond *The Prelude* to become the concern of later philosophical poems. In "Home at Grasmere," for example, a sustained paean to nature and its power, subtlety and variety, Wordsworth restores the object to full presence by dramatizing it as an animate, sentient being, with a voice and spirit of its own. But this solution comes too close to pantheistic fictionalizing in the style of the poetry of 1798. *The Excursion,* the majority of which was written between 1809 and 1814, offers Wordsworth's most balanced answer and his most sustained meditation on the range of issues emerging in *The Prelude* and the earlier poetry. In this poem, to which we turn next, Wordsworth thinks through the problem of representation in the larger theological context of emblem and symbol, a rubric under which he rethinks the role and functioning of nature. As this task draws him closer once again to his theories in the climactic *Prelude* passages, it satisfactorily allows him to formulate a comprehensive transcendental system. But although he adroitly circumvents epistemology for the most part, his new thinking on nature, emblem and symbol raises more urgently the problem of being. In *The Excursion* ontology proves the more disruptive empiricist force.

6

Transcendental Argument and Empirical Evidence in *The Excursion*

The Excursion, published in July 1814, comes closest to fulfilling the plans for *The Recluse* as formulated with Coleridge sixteen years earlier. If *The Prelude* and the other poems we have examined so far show Wordsworth treating man as man, a subject of eye, ear, touch and taste, in contact with external nature, and from such interaction attempting to work out a system of philosophy, *The Excursion* marks the culmination of those efforts in successfully establishing Wordsworth as "a man in mental repose, one whose principles [are] made up, and so prepared to deliver upon authority [that] system of philosophy."[1] Although Wordsworth concedes in his preface to *The Excursion* that it is not his "intention formally to announce a system," the reader does indeed "have no difficulty in extracting the system for himself" from the "clear thoughts, lively images, and strong feelings" Wordsworth engages to convey his settled principles (*PW,* 5: 2). That system is a Christian philosophy of "Man, Nature, and Society" (*PW,* 5: 2).

Surveying in the first four books (as in the previous poetry) man's response to nature, Wordsworth establishes feeling and imagination as principles of natural religion and then as supports of Christian faith in God and immortality; in the remaining books he turns to the practical implementation of that faith in the form of a moral "strength of mind" enabling people to cope with the difficulties of life.[2] This individualistic ethic, connected to "Nature" and metaphysical issues on the one hand, connects with "Society" and social theory on the other. The Pastor's graveyard narratives of various individuals' lives conducts to a trenchant critique of contemporary society, both pastoral and urban. As Wordsworth writes in his preface, *The Excursion* "was designed to refer . . . to passing events, and to an existing state of things" (*PW,* 5: 1). Although Wordsworth does not explicitly show "a redemptive process in operation," as Coleridge hoped he would, he at least holds out the hope that the right strength of mind, the right imaginative faith, can lead to "future glory and restoration," to the renovation of society as well as of individual lives.[3]

The first difference we notice between *The Excursion* and *The Prelude*—apart from that of form, which I discuss below—is the pronounced religious feeling that pervades the poem and the self-confidence and authority of those speakers who articulate it: the Wanderer, the Pastor and, to a lesser extent, the Poet, all of whom see it as their task to redeem the Solitary from his misanthropic melancholy by demonstrating the realities and benefits of the Christian faith. Whereas in *The Prelude* and earlier poetry Wordsworth talked of a pantheistic One Life, Being, one mind, or a mighty Mind, now he talks only of God, the Christian God, maker of heaven and earth, origin and end of all being. Clearly Wordsworth's earlier metaphysical formulations have enabled him to reach the present new position—and we can see how he relies on and consolidates his earlier philosophical investigations in the way he repeatedly puts to use the "Immortality" Ode and the Snowdon vision in particular. But the new certainty of belief in *The Excursion* generates problems of its own, problems stemming from that very certainty. Whereas *The Prelude* is a poem of exploration and discovery, presenting the processes themselves of induction and deduction and offering philosophical formulations that are as often tentative and provisional as authoritative and final, *The Excursion* insistently offers only the settled doctrines of a worldview that has an answer for everything. While Wordsworth painstakingly derives theory from experience in *The Prelude,* he reverses the ratios in *The Excursion:* he cites experience only to corroborate theories whose truths are already established and never called into question in the present. A poem of product and not process, *The Excursion* does not obviate or transcend philosophical problems, however, but exacerbate them, for the relation of theory to experience—or, more broadly and accurately, of argument to evidence—*becomes* problematic in this poem precisely because the poem proceeds as if there were no problem.

Although inherently philosophical, the problem is also literary, a function in some measure of the poem's form. Whereas "the first and third parts of The Recluse," Wordsworth writes in the preface to *The Excursion,* were to "consist chiefly of meditations in the Author's own person," in the present poem "the intervention of characters speaking is employed, and something of a dramatic form adopted" (*PW,* 5: 2). The dramatic form adopted is the philosophical dialogue, a form first developed by Plato and used to particular literary effect by Enlightenment philosophers, Berkeley and Hume most importantly. Perhaps Berkeley's *Alciphron* served Wordsworth as model for *The Excursion:* both texts have a similar setting, cast of characters, and argumentative movement from discussion of natural religion to "An Apology for the Christian Religion."[4] As already mentioned, Wordsworth owned a copy of *Alciphron,* the only work of Berkeley's on his shelves, as well as copies of Plato's Dialogues (although he owned none of Hume's philosophical works, only his *History of England*). But regardless of which work or works may stand behind *The Excursion,*

Wordsworth seems to be working both within and against the form of the philosophical dialogue. Inevitably he takes on its implicit problem of how to make interesting dramatic action out of abstract argument, where someone who is in the right all along is proved right while someone else, who is in the wrong, is proved wrong. Most importantly, he must try to make the triumph of true logic over false both dramatic and genuine and not simply a rhetorical victory exacting mere verbal assent from the loser. Furthermore, he must decide whether the loser's recognition of his error should amount to no more than a change of mind or be something deeper—a change of heart, or perhaps an inner conversion. Admittedly, the topic of debate will determine the dramatic propriety. In Berkeley's *Three Dialogues between Hylas and Philonous,* where belief in corporeal substance is the topic and the thing that Hylas must give up, no spiritual conversion follows from the admission of his error, only gratitude and pleasure at being made to see the light. But in *The Excursion,* as in *Alciphron,* where belief in God, his wisdom, and the glory and beneficence of his creation are all at issue, assent to persuasive reasoning should carry important consequences. The Solitary is sufficiently persuaded by the Wanderer's arguments to have his "Despondency Corrected," as the title of book 4 claims; but Wordsworth leaves the Solitary's final conversion to the Wanderer's and Pastor's religious perception a matter of doubt at the end of *The Excursion.* (Similarly, Alciphron concedes the argument to Euphranor by the end of *Alciphron* but remains a curmudgeonly "Minute Philosopher.") Despite the different ways the plot can turn out, the strategy that is fundamental to the philosophical dialogue, for Wordsworth as for Berkeley, is the humanization of abstract argument, the characterization of theory: theory is given to a character (and a character to a theory), and different theories given to distinctly different characters. On the literary, dramatic level this humanizing strategy pays philosophical dividends by showing the practical implementation of abstract argument, the human consequences of ideas and beliefs. But the literary dramatization also runs philosophical risks—and it is to the extent that *The Excursion* is more obviously literary and dramatic than Berkeley's dialogues that Wordsworth not only works against the form (as he follows through on its premises) but undermines its philosophical authority. For Wordsworth takes the next logical dramatic step by entirely commuting questions of theory to questions of character: the theories and ideas his characters espouse are not the fanciful promptings of the moment, associations or hypotheses to which they have no more than an intellectual commitment, but the deeply considered and deeply felt products of their lifelong experiences. The man and his life are summed up in the theory, just as the theory is demonstrated by the man in his life. For this reason Wordsworth gives us at length the Wanderer's and Solitary's biographies (the Pastor, as the voice of religious authority, needs no biography). Yet Wordsworth thereby turns what is still in the philosophical dialogue proper a contest of good and bad theories, true and false logic, into a contest of characters, their lives and experiences (insofar as experience, that is, has already yielded proven theories). Logical argument is thus transformed into argument by example; objective proof becomes subjective because the final proof is the man. How he lives, feels and sees in the present moment articulates his understanding. In essence, the evidence therefore becomes unassailable because we are left with the relativity of people's perceptions and the incomparability of their lives. On what basis, then, can the Wanderer justifiably prove that he is right and the Solitary wrong?

If the methods of philosophical argument are blurred by so closely identifying theoretical positions with characters, then the ostensible topic of philosophical debate becomes equally blurred. Is the focus of the plot the therapeutic task of cheering up the Solitary and bringing him back within the human fold, or that of persuading him of the truth of transcendental arguments about God, Man, Nature and Society? To be sure, the two tasks go hand in hand, but they further the philosophical diffusion. Given the Solitary's reticence from book 6 on, and behind that his lingering skepticism, it is unclear how far he endorses the transcendentalism of the Wanderer and the Pastor. Is that transcendentalism the final, official statement of *The Excursion,* or is it put into question by the Solitary's hesitation?[5]

The topic of debate, the methods of arguing it, the nature and presentation of the evidence are all so various and diffuse, and often in conflict with one another, as to compromise the system Wordsworth seeks to deliver. From one point of view one could say that a system as strong and comprehensive as Christianity can tolerate disruption and even incoherence. From another point of view, however, the very excursiveness to which systematic comprehensiveness commits Wordsworth proves uncontrollable. Exactly as in books 7 and 8 of *The Prelude,* the attempt to apply and extend system—here to a field as all-inclusive as Man, Nature and Society, "passing events, and . . . an existing state of things"—runs aground on the materials that are supposed to support it.

The *philosophical* problems of *The Excursion,* then, deriving from Wordsworth's development of the philosophical dialogue form, are all to do with the topic, argumentative method and the evidence. These are my main concern here. And the general principle apparent throughout *The Excursion* is, to put it in its strongest terms, subversive deflection. We may see what looks like simply a turn, a development, or a progression, as the move from argument to example or objective proof to subjective may suggest, but these moves invariably involve a detour that disrupts philosophical intentions. The argumentative line often gets deflected as Wordsworth transposes it into new forms, introduces new topics, or seeks further proof. There are two large areas where this process is most in evidence. First, Wordsworth turns to psychology to prove

Christian transcendental arguments; he appeals to the feelings and sensory perception as evidence. Second, he turns to the object of those feelings and perceptions: nature. More than man or society, nature is offered as the realization and proof of the Wanderer's and Pastor's arguments, the direct evidence from which much can be inferred. Neither psychology nor nature, however, provides the conclusive demonstration Wordsworth desires—either because their evidence is ambiguous or because it is so overdetermined, so *certain,* as to be suspicious (one senses the force of what has to be excluded to yield such untroubled interpretations). The philosophical result is that Wordsworth's attempts to ground transcendentalism in human psychology and external nature, to give it a tangible foundation and show the realization of Christian system, only evoke a new empiricism.

Indeed, Wordsworth's movement beyond transcendentalism to a new kind of empiricism is in part a function of historical circumstance—both his own and philosophy's. Writing books 2 through 9 of *The Excursion* between 1809 and 1814 during a time when the Allies' eventual victory over Napoleon became ever more certain and his own politics steadily more conservative, Wordsworth expresses his ideological bias in a celebration of all things English and traditional: the village, its church, the countryside, traditional occupations and institutions—indeed, a whole way of life. Pro-English feeling precipitates recurrent anti-French sentiment in *The Excursion,* in particular a denunciation of the French philosopher Voltaire. If correlatively Wordsworth also denounces the positivistic scientism of his time (the school of Locke and Hartley and the "Mechanic Dogmatists," as Coleridge calls them), he nevertheless praises philosophy itself as equal to poetry as a way towards the truth. Wordsworth leaves unclear who these right-thinking philosophers might be. But since there is nothing in the poem to suggest that they might be German, then it can only be inferred that the philosophy he values is also English: quite probably the writings of seventeenth- and eighteenth-century divines (and behind them the Platonic tradition in general), many of which he had in his library, but perhaps as well, ironically enough, the writings of the empiricists themselves, whose Christian spirit (in the case of Berkeley, Locke and Hartley) could be distinguished from the letter of their particular theories.[6] A native, Christian philosophical tradition should obviously be the beneficiary of the poem's celebration of all things English. But there is also reason to suspect that, despite his overt transcendentalism in the poem, Wordsworth might be decidedly turning away from German philosophy as well as French—because of Coleridge. Coleridge was back in the Lake District at Keswick between September 1808 and October 1810. While working on *The Friend,* he would doubtless have encouraged Wordsworth to resume work on *The Recluse,* as Kenneth Johnston points out.[7] Coleridge's own Christianized transcendentalism may well have influenced Wordsworth's, but Wordsworth may have conceived at this time his later vaunted antipathy to German metaphysics because of the example of Coleridge. Becoming increasingly addicted to opium and increasingly addicted to German metaphysics—Fichte and Schelling are his major interests during these years—Coleridge may well have served Wordsworth not only as model for the touchy withdrawn Solitary (as Kenneth Johnston astutely observes)[8] but as a poor advertisement for the life of philosophy in general and German metaphysics in particular. Wordsworth could see firsthand the deleterious effects of metaphysics on one of its most devoted practitioners.

If the political and personal circumstances of Wordsworth's life at the time of writing *The Excursion* may have turned him away from most things continental, his own philosophical development up to this point may have only furthered the trend. *The Prelude* proceeds towards moments of breakthrough into transcendentalism and traces the dialectical unfolding of the self's dynamic activity as Wordsworth realizes its infinitude and limitation—a journey that Mark Kipperman has characterized as a "quest romance."[9] But the quest comes to an end; self-realization is achieved (as far as it can be); limitations, boundaries and infinity are confronted and negotiated. The result is system—and next, a return to the everyday world in order to implement the vision, consolidate the gains. Having secured transcendentalism, Wordsworth now seeks to set down the transcendentalism of everyday life. But, as we will see, the very process of materializing system in the human, natural and social realms results in transcendentalism Englished according to empiricist principles. Even more than in the *Prelude* texts we examined, transcendentalism ends up as empiricism. But before seeing how psychology and nature in particular introduce empiricism as the consequences of a completed transcendental quest, we should first look at how extensive the transcendentalism of *The Excursion* is, for nearly all the arguments the Wanderer and Pastor offer elaborate a transcendental idealism.

A good place to start is in medias res with the Pastor. As a man of the church he expounds, as we would expect, the basic doctrines of the Christianized transcendentalism central to the poem: belief in God, the soul, immortality and a transcendent realm. If this transcendentalism—identical with orthodox Christianity—comes so far as no surprise, the nearly orthodox Kantianism permeating his opening speech in book 5, in which he begins elaborating this Christian system, does indeed come as a surprise. Asked to "Accord . . . the light / Of [his] experience to dispel [the] gloom" (5. 481–82) of the "cogitations" (5. 480) the Wanderer, Poet and Solitary have been engaging in—cogitations on such questions as "Are we a creature in whom good / Preponderates, or evil? Doth the will / Acknowledge reason's law?" (5. 469–71), is life meaningless and miserable, ending in decay and nothingness?—the Pastor begins by asserting the sound Kantian principle that, as a thing in itself, life, human nature, cannot be known:

> "Our nature," said the Priest, in mild reply,
> "Angels may weigh and fathom: they perceive,
> With undistempered and unclouded spirit,
> The object as it is; but, for ourselves,
> That speculative height *we* may not reach.
> The good and evil are our own; and we
> Are that which we would contemplate from far."

(5. 485–91)

Soon turning to the question of the will's acknowledgment of reason's law, the Pastor invokes something like an intellectual intuition of noumenal reality (something strictly impossible in Kant) in order to realize the categorical imperative of conscience:

> Yet for the general purposes of faith
> In Providence, for solace and support,
> We may not doubt that who can best subject
> The will to reason's law, can strictliest live
> And act in that obedience, he shall gain
> The clearest apprehension of those truths,
> Which unassisted reason's utmost power
> Is too infirm to reach.

(5. 515–22)

The Wanderer elaborates the same ideas even more eloquently at the beginning of book 4. Telling the Solitary, who has just finished the "mournful narrative" of his life (4. 2), that faith in God and his benevolence provides the "One adequate support / For the calamities of mortal life" (4. 10–11), the Wanderer then expatiates on the glory of God and the splendor of his law—laws of the intellect, that is, which delimit and realize his infinity:

> Duty exists;—immutably survive,
> For our support, the measures and the forms,
> Which an abstract intelligence supplies;
> Whose kingdom is, where time and space are not.
> ....
>   —Thou, dread source,
> Prime, self-existing cause and end of all
> That in the scale of being fill their place;
> Above our human region, or below,
> Set and sustained. . . .
> ....
>   . . . —thou, thou alone
> Art everlasting, and the blessed Spirits,
> Which thou includest, as the sea her waves:
> For adoration thou endur'st; endure
> For consciousness the motions of thy will;

> For apprehension those transcendent truths
> Of the pure intellect, that stand as laws
> (Submission constituting strength and power)
> Even to thy Being's infinite majesty!

(4. 73–99)

Forasmuch as both Pastor and Wanderer discourse on transcendent knowledge, they more often center their arguments on the human mind and its power to shape its world. Faith, love, hope, feeling, an imaginative responsiveness to nature (the basis of mythology and natural religion, as the latter half of book 4 explains), fleeting intellectual intuitions and "shock[s] of awful consciousness" (4. 1157) all express the outward-directed activity of mind, its dynamic *"excursive* power" (4. 1263; Wordsworth's emphasis) to transform the world, give it shape, or transcend the limiting conditions of mortal existence. Illustrated and analyzed at length throughout *The Excursion,* these transcendental faculties (if they may be called that) articulate the essential Wordsworthian transcendentalism: a priori capacities, powers, tendencies or structures given in the mind or soul that define the human and determine how the world is known.

In the letter Coleridge wrote Wordsworth (at Wordsworth's request) giving his critique of *The Excursion* and explaining his disappointment, he describes what he felt should have been the poem's philosophical intentions in such a way as to suggest how transcendental system may result in spite of itself in empiricism:

> I supposed you first to have meditated the faculties of Man in the abstract, in their correspondence with his Sphere of action, and first, in the Feeling, Touch, and Taste, then in the Eye, & last in the Ear, to have laid a solid and immoveable foundation for the Edifice by removing the sandy Sophisms of Locke, and the Mechanic Dogmatists, and demonstrating that the Senses were living growths and developements [sic] of the Mind & Spirit in a much juster as well as higher sense, than the mind can be said to be formed by the Senses—. . . . and to conclude by a grand didactic swell on the necessary identity of a true Philosophy with true Religion, agreeing in the results and differing only as the analytic and synthetic process, as the discursive from intuitive, the former chiefly useful as perfecting the latter—in short, the necessity of a general revolution in the modes of developing and disciplining the human mind by the substitution of Life, and Intelligence . . . for the philosophy of mechanism which in everything that is most worthy of the human Intellect strikes *Death,* and cheats itself by mistaking clear Images for distinct conceptions, and which idly demands Conceptions where Intuitions alone are possible or adequate to the majesty of the Truth.—In short, Facts elevated into Theory—Theory into Laws—& Laws into living & intelligent Powers—true Idealism necessarily perfecting itself in Realism, & Realism refining itself into Idealism.[10]

Of course, as Kenneth Johnston points out, "this tall order" expresses Coleridge's own ideal plans and ones that his later prose works realize in only piecemeal, partial ways.[11] Wordsworth, on the other hand, to give him his due, does fulfill more of Coleridge's demands than Coleridge gives him credit for, even if he proceeds in a discursive rather than orderly, systematic way in *The Excursion*. There is much discussion (although not meditation "in the abstract") of "Feeling," the "Eye" and "Ear" and of the relation of the senses to "Mind & Spirit." One could say that Wordsworth's central theme is indeed "the necessary identity of a true Philosophy with true Religion," that "clear Images," "distinct conceptions" and "Intuitions" play decisive roles in the argument, and that he sets up a Jacob's Ladder of "Facts," "Theory," "Laws," "living & intelligent Powers" perhaps even more effectively than Coleridge does in his prose works because Wordsworth emphasizes the descent of immanence as well as the ascent of transcendence. Yet Coleridge's dichotomizing procedure in his letter (you should distinguish *x* from *y*) precisely traces the fissure that runs through *The Excursion*. In his stress on eye and ear, Wordsworth tends towards forming a mind from the senses, thereby helplessly slipping into the "sandy Sophisms of Locke"; and in calling on "analytic" and "discursive" processes to "perfect" the "synthetic" and "intuitive," Wordsworth finds that the former undermine rather than substantiate the latter, causing powers, theories and laws to defecate into "Facts" and a unifying transcendental system of "Life, and Intelligence" to revert to a "philosophy of mechanism," or something like it.

We can see this slippage even in ostensibly transcendental passages of *The Excursion*. When the Pastor turns to the Wanderer's question about whether life is meaningful or meaningless, he gives an answer that predicates the identity of the object on the relativity of perception:

> [H]uman life
> Is either fair and tempting, a soft scene
> Grateful to sight, refreshing to the soul,
> Or a forbidding tract of cheerless view;
> Even as the same is looked at or approached.

(5. 526–30)

The answer is so far Kantian in that the world conforms to the categories the mind imposes on it. Summing up the Pastor's point, the Wanderer replies, "We seen, then, as we feel" (5. 558)—a broad comment that not only reemphasizes the relativity of perception featuring so frequently in *The Excursion,* or implicitly thereby categorizes the Solitary's gloomy worldview as willful perversity, but also empiricizes knowledge by radically sensationalizing it. We have seen how in *The Pedlar* seeing, believing and feeling, at their most intense, are all equivalent, differing less importantly in kind than in degree. If a roughly Lockean notion of the straightforward passage from sensation to reflection underlies the Wanderer's statement, the result, if anything, is a Berkeleyan theory of vision itself. Here, to feel is to see because the object of vision is known by and as the sensations it occasions in the perceiver. The object exists according as it is perceived and changes according as it is "looked at" from a distance or "approached," almost as if approaching the object allows "ideas of touch" to supplement those of sight to give a different sense of the object.[12] We see, then, as we feel or touch. But what begins as a point of transcendental epistemology has now evolved, in the course of being illustrated by an example taken from nature, into an instance of empiricist "mechanic" dogma.

This example illustrates a typical philosophical maneuver in *The Excursion* and one that is generally the reverse of what obtains in *The Prelude*. In *The Prelude,* Wordsworth proceeds from epistemology to metaphysics, from a self-conscious analytical use of method to the development of system by means of that method. In *The Excursion,* with system already in place and its demonstration and elaboration the issue at hand, Wordsworth proceeds from metaphysics to epistemology. But, significantly, epistemology itself never becomes the issue in this poem. In an environment where everyone is so busily and efficiently reading all the signs, no question is ever raised about the problems of reading itself. The characters contest each other's readings, but disagreement is always over either the signs they are reading or the meanings they derive from them— never over the activity of reading. Epistemological issues, then, are transposed into semiotic or psychological issues: nature as object and sign occupies one large part of the argument, while the affective coordinates of epistemology (the senses, the responsive passions) occupy another. Because perception is treated as unproblematic, Wordsworth moves directly from metaphysics via this transposed or suppressed epistemology to ontology. With metaphysical system already in place, his concern is with the reality of what things are, both natural things and human things.

The effects of this maneuver are evident in the way Wordsworth draws ontological conclusions from his psychological argument. To be sure, Wordsworth makes his argument psychological in order to show the human consequences of system and theory, how they are lived. The Wanderer fulfills this intention, for example, in the first half of *The Excursion* in trying to get the Solitary to see how strong feelings, in harmony with and responsive to the glories of nature, prove the truths of religion (a psychological case, that is, about the uniformity and universality of the feelings). But by admitting the relativity of perception and its linkage to psychological disposition, his conclusion "We see, then, as we feel" only becomes all the more ontologically unsettling. Nothing can be resolved if we all see and feel differently. Yet instead of exchanging a psychological argument for a straightforward epistemological one that would apply uniformly in all cases, Wordsworth follows his inherently Berkeleyan tendency to its conclusion: after establishing in books 2 through 4 the universality of the feelings involved in the case of natural religion and response to nature, he progressively organizes his characters' feelings into a consensus, thereby ontologically securing sign and meaning. If all are feeling the same way, then they must all be seeing the same thing, agreeing further on what it is they are seeing and what it means. The sunset that closes book 9 finally delivers this consensus. Having shared the pleasures of a picnic, the Pastor, his wife, his son and his son's friend, the Wanderer, the Solitary and the Poet, all feeling "the repose / Of the still evening" (9. 359–60), climb a hill to look at the valley and the landscape. All are rapt in

> admiring quietly
> The general aspect of the scene; but each
> Not seldom over anxious to make known
> His own discoveries; or to favourite points
> Directing notice, merely from a wish
> To impart a joy, imperfect while unshared.

(9. 582–87)

But the Poet immediately adds, "That rapturous moment never shall I forget / When these particular interests were effaced / From every mind!" (9. 588–90). The sudden transfiguring effect of the sunset on the clouds and their reflection in the lake, providing an effect of "unity sublime" (9. 608), transfixes all the onlookers: "We gazed, in silence hushed, with eyes intent / On the refulgent spectacle, diffused / Through earth, sky, water, and all visible space" (9. 610–12). Speaking for all of them and naming what they feel and see, the Pastor addresses a prayer to God, designating the sunset scene "this effluence of thyself" (9. 617), "this local transitory type / Of thy paternal splendours" (9. 619–20), "The faint reflections only of thy face" (9. 626). The Pastor offers, that is, a confident reading of the scene, based on seeing and feeling but closed to any epistemological questioning. Furthermore, he boldly ontologizes the objects of vision as he openly treats them as signs.

If Wordsworth's attempt to ground transcendentalism in psychological theories of the senses and feelings disposes his argument towards empiricism, his use of nature as evidence does so even more. Nature is repeatedly cited as the realization of the transcendental arguments the Wanderer and Pastor put forth, but as empirical proof, as physical embodiment of those arguments, it pushes those arguments towards an unavoidable materialism. Wordsworth may try to rescue his case from this tendency by asserting a Christian semiotics of emblem and symbol, as the sunset from book 9 can show. Yet even these counterattempts are unavailing. As we shall see, despite the Christianity, which we might too easily presume to be inseparable from transcendentalism, nature, as signs to be read and as an object ontologically defined by those signs, works according to empiricist principles.

Nature plays several roles and fulfills several different functions in *The Excursion*—more, really, than in *The Prelude* or "Home at Grasmere." It is proof, evidence, example, source and goal, comforter and healer, emblem and allegory yet at other times symbol of God's love and presence; it is everything that Wordsworth predicates of it in "Tintern Abbey" (nurse, guide, guardian, heart, soul of one's moral being). It is also personified, at times speaks a language or is a writing to be read, sometimes seems to sympathize with or even respond to the humans in its midst, and is invariably more feelingful, subtle and elusive than those humans. As richly figurative as all these uses and representations become, nature is also quite simply the literal scene, the setting in which the action takes place (and therefore a necessary topic of description) and, more broadly, the environment in which people live. To mention these ordinary functions of nature as landscape may be to state the obvious, but it is from these that Wordsworth's more problematic, inherently empiricist presentations of nature develop. As physical space, extension, site, or material object, nature becomes increasingly subversive of transcendental intentions.

Curiously enough, nature turns out to be so diverse in role and function because the primary roles evident in *The Prelude* are largely repressed. Geoffrey Hartman remarks that "After the first book . . . the visual and visionary divide, the first being curiously neglected, and the second being rendered by an oblique and self-conscious voice. The Wanderer only occasionally makes us feel the earth he stands on or the heaven he stands under, and for whose sake he sermonizes." While ordinary scene-setting mostly appropriates the visual, the visionary reduces to emblematic moments that come as no surprise. "Sometimes, in fact," Hartman continues, "Nature ironically punctuates the Wanderer's speech with its truly visionary sounds," but more often its usurpations of the speaker's consciousness are few and far between.[13] The one notable exception is the Solitary's vision of a heavenly city in book 2. Otherwise, such shocks of awful consciousness or mild surprise as nature delivers in this poem are no sooner registered than authoritatively interpreted as emblems of divine presence or purpose. Nature's spontaneity and autonomy thereby become thoroughly subordinated to the spectator's transcendental intent. The raven cawing at dusk unseen in the distance at the end of book 4, the snow-white ram reflected in the still pool of water in book 9, and even the sunset in book 9 with its unfolding gradations of radiance all function as exempla, as ostensible proof, the given evidence for ready answers instead of the surprises that should prompt questioning.[14]

Geoffrey Hartman, like Kenneth Johnston and Frances Ferguson after him, links Wordsworth's abrogation of the visionary to a determined renunciation of the apocalyptic imagination. Vision of this order has happened to the characters, but Wordsworth shows us its "effects . . . and rarely the substance." His desire is to "speak of nothing more than what we are" (Prospectus, *PW* 5, 59), to treat not the exceptional sublime moments but the ordinary and everyday, and thereby coordinate imaginative vision with common experience.[15] As we have seen in *The Prelude,* the apocalyptic imagination and the visionary sublime closely correlate with transcendentalism, so that their abrogation could already be construed as implying Wordsworth's withdrawal from the transcendental highpoint of the Snowdon climb or Crossing the Alps. If Wordsworth's intent here is, as in the case of the feelings, to show us transcendentalism embodied, to give us the ordinary empirical evidence of the visual instead of the extreme, unique case of the visionary, the attempt runs the same risk of empiricizing imagination into mere matter. The visual, then—that is, nature as landscape, setting or environment—is made to bear the burden of the argument, domesticating and democratizing the visionary whose effects are still detectible in the mild surprises or slight shifts in mood the landscape evokes in the characters.

These effects are most pronounced in books 2 through 4, where nature plays a fairly prominent role, closest to that in *The Prelude*. Every commentator has mentioned the sudden ironic reversals that pervade book 2, often involving a chiastic switching or doubling between characters and situations.[16] But these switches and reversals also extend to the landscape as well—and continue through books 3 and 4. The house the Solitary lives in, in the "Urn-like" valley, (2. 333) looks to the Poet and the Wanderer from the height of the mountain ridge like a perfect picture of order, harmony and tranquility (2. 330–69); but inside—in the Solitary's room, at least—there is mess and muddle (2. 660–70). Furthermore, the Solitary's account of the circumstances leading to the Pensioner's death intimates a certain moral carelessness in the house: the landlady, her husband and the Solitary himself are all culpable to different degrees. It would seem, then, that the difference between appearance and reality depends on distance or proximity. A scene can be "Grateful to sight" or "a forbidding tract of cheerless view" depending on whether "the same is looked at, or approached." Such criteria apply most importantly to the urnlike valley itself. When the Poet sees it, he rapturously exclaims (echoing almost verbatim the language used at the beginning of book 8 of *The Prelude*):

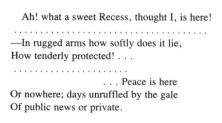

> Ah! what a sweet Recess, thought I, is here!
> . . . .
> —In rugged arms how softly does it lie,
> How tenderly protected! . . .
> . . . .
> . . . Peace is here
> Or nowhere; days unruffled by the gale
> Of public news or private.

(2. 349–66)

The Poet repeats the same sentiment when leaving the valley at the beginning of book 5: the "spot seemed / Like the fixed centre of a troubled world" (5. 15–16). But the Solitary is at pains to counter such impressions. He denies that the valley is a reclusive haven from the troubles of the world:

> Dissevered from mankind,
> As to your eyes and thoughts we must have seemed
> When ye looked down upon us from the crag,
> Islanders mid a stormy mountain sea,
> We are not so;—perpetually we touch
> Upon the vulgar ordinances of the world.
>
> (2. 732–37)

Later too, the mountain's "rugged arms" by which the valley is "How tenderly protected" become (perhaps less than half-jokingly) a means of restraint, according to the Solitary: "Ye have left my cell,—but see / How Nature hems you in with friendly arms! / And by her help ye are my prisoners still" (3. 13–15).

Wordsworth is quick to ascribe such different perceptions to different feelings. We see, then, as we feel. But the incipient Berkeleyanism here affects the identity and status of the object as well. For the matter is not simply one of feeling and response. Book 3 sharply delineates this ontologizing tendency, as we are given particular description of the landscape-setting and a contest of readings in which the Poet joins the Wanderer and Solitary too. Deciding to "trace [a] streamlet to its source" in a spring (so they imagine) "haply crowned with flowerets and green herbs" (3. 30, 33), the three find instead that

> —A quick turn
> Through a strait passage of encumbered ground,
> Proved that such hope was vain:—for now we stood
> Shut out from prospect of the open vale,
> And saw the water, that composed this rill,
> Descending, disembodied, and diffused
> O'er the smooth surface of an ample crag,
> Lofty, and steep, and naked as a tower.
>
> (3. 35–42)

The landscape changes, then, according as it is "looked at" from below "or approached." The "semi-cirque of turf-clad ground" (3. 50) in which they find themselves, however, contains some singularly shaped stones, some like pillars, and three forming a natural "altar" on which a holly tree is growing, having "found / A hospitable chink" (3. 77, 62–63). To the Poet, the holly looks as if it has been "inserted by some human hand / In mockery, to wither in the sun, / Or lay its beauty flat before a breeze, / The first that entered" (3. 64–67). But where the Poet sees only cause for pessimism, the Wanderer sees cause for optimism: "Boldest of plants that ever faced the wind, / How gracefully that slender shrub looks forth / From its fantastic birthplace!" (3. 85–87). Presumably the Wanderer is right, since the holly has so far thrived (even the Poet describes it as "tall and shiny" [3. 62]). But as slight as this instance is, it anticipates the larger contest of readings between the Wanderer and Solitary.

Looking around at the place, the Wanderer exclaims, "Behold a cabinet for sages built, / Which kings might envy!" (3. 74–75), and then elaborates:

> Among these rocks and stones, methinks, I see
> More than the heedless impress that belongs
> To lonely nature's casual work: they bear
> A semblance strange of power intelligent,
> And of design not wholly worn away.
> . . . .
> . . . And I own,
> Some shadowy intimations haunt me here,
> That in these shows a chronicle survives
> Of purposes akin to those of Man,
> But wrought with mightier arm than now prevails.

$$(3.\ 80\text{--}91)$$

The Solitary, however, flatly retorts that "The shapes before our eyes / And their arrangement, doubtless must be deemed / The sport of Nature, aided by blind Chance / Rudely to mock the works of toiling Man" (3. 124–27). Explaining how he has named one rock "My Theban obelisk" and the altarlike grouping "A Druid cromlech" (3. 132–33), he subsequently relents in part by making concessions to the Wanderer's feelings—but not to his ontological judgment:

> —Forgive me, if I say
> That an appearance which hath raised your minds
> To an exalted pitch (the self-same cause
> Different effect producing) is for me
> Fraught rather with depression than delight,
> Though shame it were, could I not look around,
> By the reflection of your pleasure, pleased.

$$(3.\ 152\text{--}58)$$

The parenthesis is all-important. If the "self-same cause" can produce radically different effects, is it really the self-same cause? The two men can resolve their difference of feeling but not their different determinations of the object. Their different readings, in fact, leave the object undetermined, for the issue is never settled. The Wanderer offers a transcendental explanation: design in nature as a kind of Kantian purposiveness without purpose;[17] but the Solitary counters that with what sounds like the voice of matter-of-fact scientific skepticism, only really to provide his own sense of purposes: Nature, in its "sport," "aided by blind Chance," has arranged these shapes in order "to mock the works of toiling Man." Such design as there is in the place is no design and is intended to oppose the idea of design, which is inherently human. Both the Solitary and the Wanderer, then, each in his own way, technically anthropomorphize the scene. But their antithetical answers do not generate a synthetic solution. Instead, they philosophically deconstruct the object, leaving it ontologically undetermined. The Solitary's further references to the "wandering Herbalist" (3. 161) and the geologist and the different kinds of pleasure they would take in the place only entrench the tendency; and the Poet joins in the process too by mentioning the "cottage-boy" (3. 197) and the "delight" (3. 206) he would find there. To be sure, each extracts pleasure from different phenomena, looking at or approaching the object to different degrees and in different ways. But the result is that the object itself is different for each. Different effects have *not* been produced by the self-same cause, because no single cause is identifiable.

If this debate between the Wanderer, Solitary and Poet emphasizes the relativity of perception in a Berkeleyan kind of way, it more radically implies that under the pressure of close scrutiny the object itself changes, fractures into different objects, or even slips from sight altogether. It becomes unknowable in any straightforward way. This slippage suggests Wordsworth's uncertainty about what nature really might be. As nature's many changing roles may indicate, Wordsworth seems to be trying out different theories and concepts, developing few of them very far because they mostly fail to fit. Despite the characters' many confident readings, nature remains indifferent, even recalcitrant. The attempt to localize meaning, to locate the active principle in an object, results in a delocalization of meaning, its dispersal from thing to thing, from place to place. These effects are traceable in the latter half of *The Excursion*. While Wordsworth insists all the more pointedly on nature as phenomenal object, even as material substance, he simultaneously develops from this an increasingly generalized sense of nature as surface, space, extension, as landscape and geography in the ordinary, everyday understanding of those words. Both senses of nature, like both the localizing and delocalizing tendencies, end up establishing an empiricist deconstruction of transcendental notions of nature and meaning.

Taking the delocalizing tendency first, we notice that the Pastor, when telling the series of epitaphic biographies in the churchyard in books 5 through 7, occasionally directs his listeners' attention to particular graves or to houses or points in the landscape visible from where they are standing. Besides referring ostensively to the landscape in this way, the Pastor also refers discursively to other places and environments to explain various events in his narratives. What emerges from this visual and mental "excursiveness" is a vigorous environmental determinism, a strong sense of how nature in a particular place determines the conditions of people's lives by bringing them poverty or bounty, adversity to be overcome or opportunities to be seized. Behind this, moreover, stands an implicit belief in an ideal correspondence between nature and human nature: an austere moral integrity, for example (known by its failures as well as successes in the Pastor's epitaphs), mirrors the austerity of the landscape, a correspondence further enhanced, of course, by the Pastor's frequent personifications of nature and naturalization of persons (his metaphors and similes make people into animals, birds, plants, rocks, etc.). While the latter strategies ramify meaning *through* phenomena, the former track it *across* surfaces. This delocalization and dispersion are significant because the books of epitaphs lead in to almost two books of social criticism of "passing events, and . . . an existing state of things" obtaining outside the immediate domain of the Lake District but profoundly affecting life within its borders. We have seen how the Solitary's urnlike valley prompts reflection on whether or not it can or should be a reclusive refuge from the troubles of the world. In the social criticism of books 8 and 9 we are made to see how the outside impinges on the inside, and that the sharper the contrast between the two the less secure is the division. The Napoleonic Wars on the continent, for example, have already claimed the life of one young man who joined the army. Industrialization is drastically transforming the landscape and the lives of families and towns in areas close to the Lake District, its effects being seen and felt in the secluded valleys of the Lake District itself. And urban behavior, institutions, and civilization in general, although repeatedly contrasted with those of the Lake District, exert an influence even there, suggesting a closer continuity than the characters wish to recognize.[18]

A minor but telling example of the latter is the way praise of the country churchyard leads to a self-cancelling comparison with urban churchyards. Commenting on how

> Green is the Churchyard, beautiful and green,
> Ridge rising gently by the side of ridge,
> A heaving surface, almost wholly free
> From interruption of sepulchral stones,
> And mantled o'er with aboriginal turf
> And everlasting flowers

> (6. 605–10)

the Poet contrasts the situation with that

> in less simple districts, where we see
> Stone lift its forehead emulous of stone
> In courting notice; and the ground all paved
> With commendations of departed worth;
> Reading, where'er we turn, of innocent lives,
> Of each domestic charity fulfilled,
> And sufferings meekly borne—I, for my part,
> Though with the silence pleased that here prevails,
> Among those fair recitals also range,
> Soothed by the natural spirit which they breathe.
> And, in the centre of a world whose soil
> Is rank with all unkindness, compassed round
> With such memorials, I have sometimes felt,
> It was no momentary happiness

To have *one* Enclosure where the voice that speaks
In envy or detraction is not heard;
Which malice may not enter; where the traces
Of evil inclinations are unknown;
Where love and pity tenderly unite
With resignation; and no jarring tone
Intrudes, the peaceful concert to disturb
Of amity and gratitude.

(6. 624–45)

Their self-conscious showiness apart, urban churchyards fulfill the same function as rural ones by providing *"one* Enclosure where the voice that speaks / In envy or detraction is not heard"—an enclosure "in the centre of a world whose soil / Is rank with all unkindness." The logic of the comparison demands that this rank soil begins the other side of the fence in the present churchyard as well as in those in less simple districts.[19]

Such comparisons establish continuities and connections rather than the uniqueness and significance of the local. It is for this reason, in the last two books, that Wordsworth angrily acknowledges the likely death of a traditional way of life. Asking where are now "The old domestic morals of the land, / Her simple manners, and the stable worth / That dignified and cheered a low estate?" (8. 236–38), the Wanderer replies, "Fled! . . . Fled utterly! or only to be traced / In a few fortunate retreats like this" (8. 252–54). Under threat of erosion from the outside, this fortunate retreat can maintain only a precarious hold on the special, the meaningful, the unique.

This literally extensive strategy of delocalization carries the argument far away from any concept of nature as usurping transcendental presence (*Nature* with a capital *N*) towards a more matter-of-fact sense of nature as environment affecting the course of human affairs. Such a normalization of nature certainly implies a turn away from transcendentalism—not an active, conscious turn so much as a shift of focus towards phenomena that do not immediately come within its parameters. Yet the move brings Wordsworth closer to empiricism by according the object rather than the subject the greater power, the larger determining role. Even if the active principle in things cannot be precisely located, Wordsworth still privileges nature as source, as cause. This tendency fosters, of course, the counterstrategy of localization. In his linear pursuit of meaning, Wordsworth will stop and assert its presence at a particular spot. Embodiment, incarnation and materialization thus become important topoi in the poem. If they show Wordsworth renegotiating transcendental notions of presence, they nevertheless affirm empiricism by his sheer insistence on the materiality of the object. As a result, Wordsworth gives us several highly charged moments in the poem where nature communicates powerful meanings that are usually subject to disabling slippage even as they are localized in particular phenomena. Despite the transcendental intent, the ontology and semiotics become inherently empiricist. Four instances from the poem can show us the precise pattern: the concern with death, epitaphs and funerary monuments in book 5; the copy of *Candide* in the children's playhouse in book 2; and the two complementary sunset visions, both modeled on the Snowdon sequence in *The Prelude:* the Solitary's vision in book 2 and the closing sunset in book 9.

After the Wanderer's "eloquent harangue" (4. 1276) on nature, mythology and natural religion, on love of nature leading to love of life and love of man, the group moves to the village church and its churchyard to find a different kind of empirical evidence. After the Pastor appears on the scene and after their initial discussion with him about "Our nature" (5. 485), the Wanderer asks him:

> The mine of real life
> Dig for us; and present us, in the shape
> Of virgin ore, that gold which we, by pains
> Fruitless as those of aery alchemists,
> Seek from the torturing crucible. There lies
> Around us a domain where you have long
> Watched both the outward course and inner heart:
> Give us, for our abstractions, solid facts;
> For our disputes, plain pictures.
> . . . .
> Or rather, as we stand on holy earth,
> And have the dead around us, take from them
> Your instances . . .
> . . . .
> Epitomise the life; pronounce, you can,
> Authentic epitaphs on some of these
> Who, from their lowly mansions hither brought,
> Beneath this turf lie mouldering at our feet.
>
> (5. 630–53)

They are to learn, then, what death can tell them about life; the Pastor agrees to their request, saying,

> True indeed it is
> That they whom death has hidden from our sight
> Are worthiest of the mind's regard; with these
> The future cannot contradict the past:
> Mortality's last exercise and proof
> Is undergone; the transit made that shows
> The very Soul, revealed as she departs.
>
> (5. 661–67)

The epitaphs will be "Authentic" because meaning is completed, closed, thoroughly knowable and therefore true. With the transcendental signified so unproblematically in evidence, attention focuses on the signifier: the body, the grave, the spot, the churchyard. In "A village church-yard, lying as it does in the lap of nature,"

> The sensations of pious cheerfulness, which attend the celebration of the sabbath-day in rural places, are profitably chastised by the sight of the graves of kindred and friends, gathered together in that general home towards which the thoughtful yet happy spectators themselves are journeying. Hence a parish-church, in the stillness of the country, is a visible centre of a community of the living and the dead; a point to which are habitually referred the nearest concerns of both. (*PrW*, 2: 55–56; "Essays upon Epitaphs," 1)

This broad concentering emphasis on the churchyard in these books and the preoccupation with death, not just as the closure of life but as a state of being that is integrally linked to a set of physical phenomena, show that the localizing tendency manifests itself here as a fascination with forms of material reduction. Material substance, in the Lockean sense, is the terminus to which the tendency leads. But although specifiable—Hamletlike, one could hold a Yorick's skull in one's hand and discourse on essence—the material substance eludes cognitive capture that would yield understanding of the continuity between the physical and the metaphysical. It is for this reason that Wordsworth's insistent attention to matter is written across with conflicting figures. The Wanderer, for instance, upon first entering the churchyard, nicely expresses the ironic juxtaposition of metaphysical and physical, transcendent and immanent. He remarks on

> the unvoyageable sky
> In faint reflection of infinitude
> Stretched overhead, and at my pensive feet
> A subterraneous magazine of bones,
> In whose dark vaults my own shall soon be laid.
>
> (5. 342–46)

His awareness of the "subterraneous magazine of bones" becomes more pronounced in his speech to the Pastor requesting him to "pronounce . . . Authentic epitaphs." He mentions how they "stand on holy earth, / And have the dead around us," how the dead "Beneath this turf lie mouldering at our feet." But he begins his speech with a metaphor that radically conflicts with these ideas: "The mine of real life / Dig for us; and present us, in the shape / Of virgin ore, that gold which we . . . Fruitless . . . Seek." Admittedly, the Wanderer's reference is at first general; it is the substance of "real life" he is after. But since his ostensive references are then immediately to the churchyard and "mouldering" bodies under the turf, the "mine" becomes the subterraneous magazine of bones and the virgin ore that is to render up its gold the corpse in whom "The very

Soul [was] revealed as she depart[ed]." The location of substance, then, has already been delocalized by the figures that would name its meaning.

We have here an essentially Lockean concept of substance. The physical object is known to be the locus of some forms of power and presence; it can be pointed to, seen and felt, just as the power and presence it exerts can be sensed. But neither the Wanderer nor the Pastor can specify exactly in what the power and presence consist or name them with anything other than metaphors—and metaphors that slip, clash and delocalize. Material substance remains unknown, although it is known to be the support of primary and secondary qualities that they can indeed specify and name in considerable detail: the various sensory surfaces and appearances of the object that make it add up to an intricate, composite sign. The Wanderer and Pastor describe, often quite analytically, the particular graves, the churchyard and its amenities, its relationship to its environment, and so on. As the Wanderer says, "There lies / Around us a domain where you [the Pastor] have long / Watched both the outward course and inner heart." The domain, the churchyard, the grave all contribute as signs to the meaning of life, the full signified the Pastor authoritatively pronounces. They distribute the meaning around and on a particular site, ramifying it in the form of secondary qualities that the Wanderer and Pastor read. Wordsworth expatiates on the way the concentric qualities of place and landscape contribute to the overall effect and distribute the meaning in the first "Essay upon Epitaphs." Talking about the ideal rural setting of funerary monuments, he says:

> We might ruminate upon the beauty which the monuments, thus placed, must have borrowed from the surrounding images of nature—from the trees, the wild flowers, from a stream running perhaps within sight or hearing, from the beaten road stretching its weary length hard by. Many tender similitudes must these objects have presented to the mind of the traveller leaning upon one of these tombs. . . . And to its epitaph also must have been supplied strong appeals to visible appearances or immediate impressions, lively and affecting analogies of life as a journey—death as a sleep overcoming a tired wayfarer. . . . These, and similar suggestions, must have given, formerly, to the language of the senseless stone a voice enforced and endeared by the benignity of that nature with which it was in unison. (*PrW,* 2: 53–54)

Moreover, the epitaph writer often employs the "tender fiction" of having the epitaph "personate the deceased, and represent him as speaking from his own tomb-stone" (*PrW,* 2: 60). Such factors all go to make the monument, connected to, speaking for, and representing a person who is now continuous with the rocks and stones and trees with which the monument is also continuous, into a classic, archetypal Wordsworthian sign—but one in which the presumed continuities of substance are figured by juxtapositions, annexations and associations that cannot counteract the dispersal of meaning even as they concenter it in, on and around one location.[20]

The case of the copy of *Candide* in the "penthouse" (2. 417) that children have built for their play, which the Poet discovers as he and the Wanderer descend into the urnlike valley, elaborates the same idea but introduces new elements that further empiricize the configuration. The Poet relates how he found

> a cool recess,
> And fanciful! For where a rock and wall
> Met in an angle, hung a penthouse, framed
> By thrusting two rude staves into the wall
> And overlaying them with mountain sods;
> To weather-fend a little turf-built seat
> Whereon a full-grown man might rest, nor dread
> The burning sunshine, or a transient shower;
> But the whole plainly wrought by children's hands!
> Whose skill had thronged the floor with a proud show
> Of baby-houses, curiously arranged;
> Nor wanting ornament of walks between,
> With mimic trees inserted in the turf,
> And gardens interposed.
>
> (2. 415–28)

While showing this find to the Wanderer, "Who, entering, round him threw a careless glance / Impatient to pass on" (2. 430–31), the Poet notices "A book, that, in the midst of stones and moss / And wreck of party-coloured earthen-ware, / Aptly disposed, had lent its help to raise / One of those petty structures" (2. 433–36). The book turns out to be Voltaire's *Candide,* prompting a tirade from the Wanderer who, as Frances Ferguson points out, "see[s] *Candide* as yet another symptom of the Solitary's misery."[21] The scene suggests that the book has been "put . . . in its place":

> The book . . . in my hand
> Had opened of itself (for it was swoln
> With searching damp, and seemingly had lain
> To the injurious elements exposed
> From week to week,). . . .
>
> (2. 438–42)

But, if anything, the book, as Ferguson explains, ironically reads its own situation. Its mouldering state suggests "a novel interpretation for the famous final line of the book. 'Il faut cultiver notre jardin' becomes 'it [the book] must cultivate our garden.'"[22] The garden here is the miniature garden with its houses that the children have created under the penthouse, a garden that duplicates the real-life house and garden in the "sweet Recess" below. This episode is fraught with "misplaced meaning," according to Ferguson,[23] for whereas a book has been literally misplaced it finds itself in a setting which, by contributing to it its own new meaning, it helps to make more paradisiacal than the original of which the setting is a copy (the house and garden in the recess below look more austere and cheerless when approached). The misplacement amounts to the delocalization we have been considering—here, more properly, a relocalization and one that results again in concentric juxtapositions (the various objects assembled under one roof and adding up to a curiously powerful image). Yet the book's primary value now is as a material object. To the extent that the "injurious elements" have caused it to decay, it is like a body "mouldering" underground in the churchyard, its substantial continuity with its physical environment also evident in the way it is a crucial part of the children's miniature landscape. This material reduction characterizes the miniature landscape with its houses and gardens, too. Although presenting a series of representations (much like the panoramas Wordsworth viewed in London in book 7 of *The Prelude*), a series of objects recognized as "mimic" by the relation and proportions of their primary qualities (extension, shape, bulk), perception shifts away from resemblances to the material substances from which they are composed: "stones and moss / And wreck of party-coloured earthenware" and book. Various disparate objects compose, then, an elaborate concentration of signs in which the construction of coherent meaning (possibly a single unifying meaning) cannot but give way to its own deconstruction into its constituent material parts. Meaning cedes to matter.

The ironic misplacement of *Candide,* the mimic landscape, the penthouse built by children for their play yet large enough to hold "a full-grown man" who could rest on its "turf-built seat" and be shielded from "burning sunshine, or a transient shower," all strongly suggest that the moment, the place, can be read as an allegory. The Wanderer, of course, acts on such suggestions in his diatribe against the novel, and nature too lends its support by ironically withholding in this instance any suggestion of its own status as book. Moreover, the similarity that Ferguson points out between this playful penthouse-refuge and the refuge the Pensioner builds over himself with "tufts / Of heath-plant . . . / To baffle . . . the watery storm" (2. 818–20)—and where the search party find him "Snug as a child that hides itself in sport" (2. 822)—only extends the allegorical intimations. But although we can pursue the associations and resemblances and note, as Ferguson does, the rapid alternation between play and earnest (throughout book 2 as well as in these two instances),[24] an adequate allegorical interpretation is difficult to construct from the various materials. Play and earnest, to which should be added the sense of danger, would seem to reflect the changing character of nature itself, duplicated by being materialized in human form in much the same way as the children's "mimic" landscape realizes the essentially paradisiacal quality of the actual landscape better than the latter. A reductive relocalization would thus appear to achieve a more concentrated substantialization of meaning. But any meanings (allegorical or otherwise) one can construct from such moments never quite free themselves from their objects, which insistently ask to be considered only as objects. Something similar happens in the case of the sunset vision given to the Solitary immediately after helping the Pensioner from his refuge. Here the allegorical intent is more obvious.

Lagging behind the group taking the Pensioner back to the house, the Solitary steps out of the enshrouding "blind vapour" (2. 831) and suddenly sees "opened to [his] view / Glory beyond all glory ever seen / By waking sense or by the dreaming soul!" (2. 831–33). He sees a "mighty city" (2. 835) with domes, spires, terraces, pavilions, avenues and battlements:

> By earthly nature had the effect been wrought
> Upon the dark materials of the storm
> Now pacified; on them, and on the coves
> And mountain-steeps and summits, whereunto
> The vapours had receded, taking there
> Their station under a cerulean sky.
> Oh, 'twas an unimaginable sight!
> Clouds, mists, streams, watery rocks and emerald turf,
> Clouds of all tincture, rocks and sapphire sky,
> Confused, commingled, mutually inflamed,
> Molten together, and composing thus,
> Each lost in each, that marvellous array
> Of temple, palace, citadel, and huge
> Fantastic pomp of structure without name,
> In fleecy folds voluminous, enwrapped.
> Right in the midst, where interspace appeared
> Of open court, an object like a throne
> Under a shining canopy of state
> Stood fixed; and fixed resemblances were seen
> To implements of ordinary use,
> But vast in size, in substance glorified;
> Such as by Hebrew Prophets were beheld
> In vision—forms uncouth of mightiest power
> For admiration and mysterious awe.
> This little Vale, a dwelling-place of Man,
> Lay low beneath my feet; 'twas visible—
> I saw not, but I felt that it was there.
> That which I *saw* was the revealed abode
> Of Spirits in beatitude: my heart
> Swelled in my breast.—"I have been dead," I cried,
> "And now I live! Oh! wherefore *do* I live?"
> And with that pang I prayed to be no more!—

(2. 846–77)

This apocalyptic, transcendental vision almost forces its allegorical meaning on the Solitary and the reader. As Geoffrey Hartman remarks, "He seems to see the glory-seat of God. Its footstool is the little valley in which he dwells."[25] More precisely one might say he sees the City of God as well as his court and glory-seat, or, as the Solitary himself emphatically claims, "That which I *saw* was the revealed abode / Of Spirits in beatitude." The vision, prompting the Solitary's reassessment of his life, seems to hold out illustrative proof of salvation, the promise of personal "future glory and restoration" (in Coleridge's phrase). The pictorial detail of the vision, moreover, only enhances the allegory, making it a true "picture-language" (as Coleridge calls allegory)[26] for transcendental desires. Yet there is much in the experience that baffles allegorical intent. Well aware of the vision's import for himself, though seeming to flee this demonstration of the apocalyptic force of his own imagination,[27] the Solitary nonetheless recounts the vision in such a way as to successively qualify it before resoundingly reaffirming its transcendental theme at the close. In ways that resemble those of the Snowdon climb, the Solitary tells us that "by earthly nature had the effect [the vision of the heavenly city] been wrought." Having described the intricately figured architectural vision, he describes it a second time, but now literally in terms of its material constituents: "Clouds, mists, streams, watery rocks and emerald turf, / Clouds of all tincture, rocks and sapphire sky." This material reduction of the vision does not as yet undermine its visionary pretension because we can easily infer the power of the Solitary's imagination in his perceiving the scene in so figurative a way. But when he resumes his figurative description (like the man looking again at the cavern's roof in the epic simile in book 8 of *The Prelude*), then the reduction resumes, causing the vision to disperse into objects. It is one thing to see the throne of God (suitably vacant at this particular moment), but quite another to see near it "resemblances . . . / To implements of ordinary use, / But vast in size." The apotheosis of household implements notwithstanding, the juxtaposition is incongruous and in every way collapses into bathos. In fact, the vision begins to resemble the jumbled look of the Solitary's own room:

> What a wreck
> Had we about us! scattered was the floor,
> And, in like sort, chair, window-seat, and shelf,
> With books, maps, fossils, withered plants and flowers,
> And tufts of mountain moss. Mechanic tools
> Lay intermixed with scraps of paper, some
> Scribbled with verse: a broken angling-rod
> And shattered telescope, together linked
> By cobwebs, stood within a dusky nook;
> And instruments of music, some half-made,
> Some in disgrace, hung dangling from the walls.
>
> (2. 660–70)

The throne of God becomes just another intricate resemblance in a series of resemblances in the clouds. Imagination dissipates into mere fancy, and the vision into different material objects on which the Solitary must work to impose meaning by comparing their shape, extension, bulk and color (their primary and secondary qualities) to those of random objects already known from everyday life. While the tendency to locate a transcendental reality at the center is figured here by the throne that "Stood fixed," the Solitary says, in an "open court" "Right in the midst," this figuration itself sets going an almost uncontrollable dispersive play of figuration, causing the transcendental idea to disintegrate into an associative stream of empiricist representations. These material ends of transcendental figuration can only check the allegory, fixing it as mere picture-language and no more—in fact as a picture-language that does not spell out anything but its own pictures.

It would seem, then, that the Solitary's impulse towards naturalistic honesty qualifies his visionary pretension (despite his closing emphasis that what he saw was the revealed abode of spirits in beatitude). But philosophically these opposing tendencies result in a deconstruction of transcendentalism. The Solitary leaves his vision as simply figure; and he makes no claims for its ontological reality apart from what passionate affirmation can do. The case is entirely different with the visionary sunset that is the climax of *The Excursion.* In this case figuration is as intricate and rich as it is in book 2, but the difference is that the Pastor fully supplies to signs the ontological dimension missing before.

The sunset scene in book 9 closely resembles the Snowdon scene in book 13 of *The Prelude,* and it plays an identical role as both definitive proof and authoritative summary statement of the poem's philosophical program. Again, Wordsworth describes a climb to a commanding eminence from which a vision unfolds, surprising and transporting the spectators. The vision, which is all-pervasive, is entirely "wrought by nature," being described in naturalistic terms before being interpreted emblematically (the reverse sequence, then, of the Solitary's vision in book 2). Wordsworth takes interpretation further here, however, than on Snowdon by directly discussing God's agency, which he sees at work in a particular metaphysical movement that is the real signature of the Snowdon scene: the emergence from an abyss, or from below the other side of some boundary, of a power (usually sounds, but here it is light) which the spectators, on their eminence, catch suddenly. This upward movement is complemented by a downward one: on Snowdon the moon looks down in solitary splendor high in the heavens, while here the setting sun irradiates the clouds that are then reflected in the lake below. The point and effect of this movement become clear in Wordsworth's use of it in other places in *The Excursion.*

At the end of book 4 the Wanderer mentions how at dusk one might hear the cry of "the solitary raven, flying / Athwart the concave of the dark blue dome, / Unseen, perchance above all power of sight" (4. 1178–80), until its plaintive anthem fades as it flies away, off into the distance. But just as its "iron knell" (4. 1181) "seemed / To expire . . . yet from the abyss [it] is caught again, / And yet again recovered!" (4. 1185–87). The Wanderer immediately classifies the experience as belonging to the category of "imaginative heights, that yield / Far-stretching views into eternity" (4. 1188–89). His categorization explicitly shows how the movement transcendentalizes as it connects origin and tendency: in this experience, the perceiver's senses all tend towards the transcendental point that is at once origin and goal, a point that is located in the "abyss" of heaven, the other side of the perceived horizon, from which a form of power emerges to pervade, transfigure, if not transcendentalize, the entire space (now with the assistance of the downward movement). The Wanderer delineates this configuration and its transcendentalizing effect at length in an extended simile at the beginning of book 9, a simile that repeats the details of the Snowdon scene almost to the letter. Calling old age "a final EMINENCE" (9. 51), the Wanderer recuperates it as an imaginative height yielding far-stretching views into eternity. He compares it to reaching the top of a peak commanding far-stretching views of the landscape. Thanks to distance and elevation, "the gross and visible frame of things / Relinquishes its hold upon the sense, / Yea almost on the Mind herself, and seems / All unsubstantialized" (9. 63–66). Yet then to the climber there suddenly comes "how loud the voice / Of waters, with invigorated peal / From the full river in the vale below, / Ascending" (9. 66–69). Having elaborated his simile's vehicle, the Wanderer unsubstantializes it further in next supplying its transcendental tenor: from this height, in old age, we have

> Fresh power to commune with the invisible world,
> And hear the mighty stream of tendency
> Uttering, for elevation of our thought,
> A clear sonorous voice, inaudible
> To the vast multitude.

(9. 86–90)

In the climactic sunset scene at the end of book 9, the Wanderer, the Solitary, the Poet, the Pastor, his wife and the children have also climbed an imaginative height, "a green hill's side" (9. 570) above the lake, from which, as the sun sets, they gain a far-stretching view into eternity. Here is the Poet's description of the vision and the first part of the prayer the Pastor utters in interpretation of it:

> —Already had the sun,
> Sinking with less than ordinary state,
> Attained his western bound; but rays of light—
> Now suddenly diverging from the orb
> Retired behind the mountain-tops or veiled
> By the dense air—shot upwards to the crown
> Of the blue firmament—aloft, and wide;
> And multitudes of little floating clouds,
> Through their etherial texture pierced—ere we,
> Who saw, of change were conscious—had become
> Vivid as fire; clouds separately poised,—

Innumerable multitude of forms
Scattered through half the circle of the sky;
And giving back, and shedding each on each,
With prodigal communion, the bright hues
Which from the unapparent fount of glory
They had imbibed, and ceased not to receive.
That which the heavens displayed, the liquid deep
Repeated; but with unity sublime!

    While from the grassy mountain's open side
We gazed, in silence hushed, with eyes intent
On the refulgent spectacle, diffused
Through earth, sky, water, and all visible space,
The Priest in holy transport thus exclaimed:

    "Eternal Spirit! universal God!
Power inaccessible to human thought,
Save by degrees and steps which thou hast deigned
To furnish; for this effluence of thyself,
To the infirmity of mortal sense
Vouchsafed; this local transitory type
Of thy paternal splendours, and the pomp
Of those who fill thy courts in highest heaven,
The radiant Cherubim;—accept the thanks
Which we, thy humble Creatures, here convened,
Presume to offer; we, who—from the breast
Of the frail earth, permitted to behold
The faint reflections only of thy face—
Are yet exalted, and in soul adore!
Such as they who are in thy presence stand
Unsullied, incorruptible, and drink
Imperishable majesty streamed forth
From thy empyreal throne, the elect of earth
Shall be—divested at the appointed hour
Of all dishonour, cleansed from mortal stain."

                                                    (9. 590–633)

The Pastor explicitly allegorizes the scene as a figure of God's glory. But more than that, as John Hodgson has carefully elaborated, he turns nature as emblem into a synecdochal symbol. The principle of analogy that rules the Snowdon scene is replaced here by claims of identity: not only is nature an emblem of God's presence; it is also continuous with it as his actual "effluence." As John Hodgson points out, "what the universe expresses is mysterious union, synecdochal identification, with its creator"—a belief the Wanderer expresses repeatedly, as when, for example, he calls the universe a monitor shell to "the ear of Faith" (4. 1142) or cites the far-stretching views into eternity that the raven and other natural shocks of consciousness afford.[28]

Nature's identification with God, declared triumphantly here in the poem's peroration, would thus seem to be Wordsworth's most important point in *The*

Excursion, a claim at once religious and philosophical. Certainly it serves as comprehensive ground for all aspects of the transcendentalism Wordsworth wishes to put across. But once again, here at the poem's climax, the natural objects and, more importantly, the figures the Pastor uses to describe them ground the transcendentalism in an empiricist ontology and semiotics.

A hint of this is apparent in the partly Neoplatonic, partly Berkeleyan way in which the Pastor opens his prayer. The "degrees and steps" whereby "human thought" can ascend to knowledge of Godhead recalls the Neoplatonic notion of the steady derivation of the many from the One, an idea Berkeley deploys in *Siris,* where God's "effluence," a "celestial fire," irradiates and permeates nature and is the source of life itself.[29] The suggestion of Berkeleyanism may prepare us for empiricism, but the empiricism comes into view as the bedrock ontology when we tread the "degrees and steps" of the figuration.

If a characteristic tropology can be assigned to a particular philosophical system or tendency, then it should seem that the symbol, so privileged and praised in the Romantic era, should accord with transcendentalism, while allegory, repeatedly denigrated and repudiated, should accord with empiricism. The reverse is really the case. With its insistence on limits and the a priori, transcendentalism establishes precisely the same kind of absolute division that is constitutive of allegory, which relies on a categorical separation between the picture-language vehicle and its abstract tenor. We have seen, when examining "Tintern Abbey," how metonymy and metalepsis emerge as the figures connecting phenomena and noumena in a relation that cannot be known for certain or specified as causal. Synecdoche may ground metonymy if there is a vital link between appearance and reality; but strictly speaking the relation cannot be known. By observing various divisions, then, transcendental tropology is thoroughly compatible with orthodox Christianity, which insists on a "chasm," as Coleridge calls it, between God and his creation, between "I AM" and "it is."[30]

Clearly, though, in his would-be transcendental prayer the Pastor closes the chasm and runs down the "degrees and steps" to "it is." In essence, he has acted out Coleridge's wish in his letter that *The Excursion* show "true Idealism necessarily perfecting itself in Realism, & Realism refining itself into Idealism" as he argues for the immanence of "living & intelligent Powers" in the "Laws," "Theory," and "Facts" of the sunset scene. Yet the emphasis in the scene falls unmistakably on immanence rather than transcendence—on symbol and synecdoche and therefore on empiricism.

The Berkeleyan theory of vision Wordsworth intermittently features in *The Excursion* coordinates, as we have noticed (and despite the flagrant contradiction from the Berkeleyan point of view), with a distinctly Lockean theory of substance. Appearances, however shifting when looked at or approached, inhere in a material substance always regarded as the terminus of any philosophical excursion. While the substance itself is an unknowable "support" of appearances, it gives off powers that determine those appearances and then reach the perceiver, partly determining in him or her the variable subjective component of the secondary qualities. This ontology inscribes, therefore, a continuous tropic movement from object to subject, from substance to powers to qualities to sensations to ideas in the mind (to complex ideas, judgments, and so on). The appearance of the object is a part of a whole, integrally connected to it and realizing it as far as possible (to the extent that an unknowable substance can be made known). Certainly the distance between an idea in the mind and the unknowable substance is great enough to strain the linkage to breaking point, but the synecdochal symbol, Lockean empiricism's operative trope, easily negotiates any ontological gap by making each phase of the transaction into a simple subset of itself: the idea, sensation, or quality is each part of a whole that extends backwards from this location. If technically, at the very least, a metaphor, it takes its station as a symbol in an extensive synecdochal continuum.

Precisely this empiricist semiotic defines the Pastor's emblematic interpretation of the sunset scene. Transfigured by the setting sun, nature as God's "effluence" articulates the synecdochal continuum from substance to powers to appearances to powerful effects on the perceivers. For already "exalted" by the vision, they will be numbered among "the elect of the earth" (so the Pastor implies), who, like those already standing purified in God's presence, will *"drink /* Imperishable majesty *streamed forth /* From thy empyreal throne" (emphasis added). The following figures the Pastor offers may seem to qualify the boldness of the first claim about God's "effluence," but while reinstalling gaps they do not revert to transcendentalism, however Christian the claims. Thanking God for "this local transitory type / Of thy paternal splendours, and the pomp / Of those who fill thy courts in highest heaven, / The radiant Cherubim," the Pastor designates the phenomena resemblances, much in the same way as the Solitary does in his sky-scape vision in book 2; and his inclusion of the Cherubim as filling God's courts and radiating a "pomp" all their own ramifies resemblances by referring to the "Innumerable multitude" of clouds in the scene, all "Vivid as fire" and mutually irradiating one another. More complicated, however, is the final figure. Gazing at the vision, the Pastor says, is equivalent to "behold[ing] / The faint reflections only of thy face." If "reflections" might seem to unsubstantialize "effluence" by making God as distantly connected to nature as is an object to its image in a mirror, it really perfects the continuity by troping resemblance as identity. Effluence, then, consists not only in a substance's radiation of its powers but in a successfully communicated representation of itself. It is not only the light shining from God's face that they see, but his face itself, caught, albeit faintly, in the mirror of nature. That the scene itself actually contains a mirror and reflections only adds to the "perfection," to use Coleridge's term. The clouds and their radiance are in "the liquid deep / Repeated; but with unity sublime," creating a "refulgent spectacle, diffused / Through earth, sky, water, and all visible space." It is through resemblances, appearances, visible qualities, caused by the effluence of his divine substance, that God is "known" here. Effluence, type and reflection thus correspond to different phases in the synecdochal continuum, to different tropes that all insistently refer to their origin in divine substance.

The same dispersal of presence, moreover, is evident here in the Pastor's prayer as before, and if it directs attention all the more to the physical environment it unerringly becomes once again a delocalizing tendency that empiricizes still further. After delivering his prayer the Pastor conjures up the vision of Druid worship and human sacrifice that once took place on the shores of this very lake. Now only "A few rude monuments of mountain-stone / Survive" (9. 710–11), but then

> the loudest voice
> Of the swoln cataracts (which now are heard
> Soft murmuring) was too weak to overcome,
> Though aided by wild winds, the groans and shrieks
> Of human victims, offered to appease
> Or to propitiate. And, if living eyes
> Had visionary faculties to see
> The thing that hath been as the thing that is,
> Aghast we might behold this crystal Mere
> Bedimmed with smoke, in wreaths voluminous,
> Flung from the body of devouring fires.
>
> (9. 693–703)

The Pastor means the comparison to point up the difference between then and now, affirm human progress and suggest that in this present time and place "paradise" has been "here restored" (9. 717–19). But given the long persuasive excursus on superstition, mythology and natural religion in book 4, the comparison becomes more subversive than the Pastor would intend. And indeed, as an imaginative vision it is hardly less impressive than the naturalistic one the sunset has just staged. Given, then, that it too is prompted by the eye's excursion across the scene—now from ridge to lake to shore—it ironically counters the sunset vision by uncovering yet another skeleton mouldering under the turf in a section of ground not too distant from where they are standing. God's effluence may diffuse through all *visible* space, but physical space contains matter that antedates his reign in England. The empiricism into which Wordsworth's transcendentalism unavoidably condenses in *The Excursion* in turn solidifies into almost outright materialism.

Although Wordsworth emphasizes throughout *The Excursion,* and makes his cardinal point, the power of the human self to feel, imagine, love, hope and believe, this emphasis does not carry through his implicit philosophical intentions. Wordsworth's celebration of these human powers and strengths leads one to expect restatement of the kind of triumphant claim that closes *The Prelude,* that "the mind of man becomes / A thousand times more beautiful than the earth / On which he dwells" because it is "In beauty exalted, as it is itself / Of substance and of fabric more divine" (*Prel*, 13. 439–45). But with his mind made up about such steady transcendental principles, Wordsworth ends up jeopardizing the system as he extends and applies it. Merely by consistently turning to nature as evidence and proof, and by illustrating its numerous roles and functions, he starts establishing instead that nature is more beautiful than the human mind because it is "Of substance and of fabric more divine."

Wordsworth's turn to nature takes him back to empiricism because his emphasis on phenomena and their particularity privileges the object over the subject, matter over mind. Although it is obviously an oversimplification to align nature with one philosophy and mind with another, this is nevertheless the outcome of Wordsworth's philosophical tendencies. Throughout his career the physical reality of the object-world has always acted as antidote to more extreme forms of idealism. Clutching a gate or tree would bring him back from "the abyss of idealism," he tells us in the Isabella Fenwick note to the "Immortality" Ode. Any consideration of the things that simply exist and the power of their mere being encourages, in Wordsworth's case, the distinctly empiricist responses we have been tracing here. Ontology, semiotics and psychology thus deliver a nature instinct with inherent powers to which the human self is once again secondary and supplementary.

Indeed, one can say that Wordsworth never really relinquishes empiricism, perhaps most of all because of its simplicity, its semiscientific appeal to common sense (however problematic that common sense). Talking of common things and of nothing more than what we are invariably gets Wordsworth thinking along Lockean-Hartleyan lines about associations, responsive feelings and the qualities and substances of the external world. When he makes the transition to transcendentalism and fully explores the power of mind to shape its world, he falls, if anything, into a binaristic trap in which his frequent praise of the mind alternates with somewhat guilty, compensatory gestures towards nature. In this later stage of his career, praise of nature can proceed unchecked because Christianity takes over the functions of transcendentalism. Tensions, inconsistencies, tendencies and persuasions persist, but given the centrality of Christianity as a comprehensive, authoritative system from this point on in Wordsworth's life and writings (however we judge the authenticity of his "faith"), then the philosophical issues we have followed here, issues in which Wordsworth has been openly interested from 1798 to 1814, cease to be of importance after *The Excursion*. If we believe that the vitality of Wordsworth's poetry during this sixteen-year period owes much to his engagement with philosophy, then we can correlate his putative "decline" after 1814 with the absence of philosophical engagement and the acceptance of orthodox Christianity. But however we construe the achievement of his later years, it is not the kind of philosophical poetry that inspired his best writing and thinking during his youth and maturity.

Notes

Introduction

1. See *The Anxiety of Influence: A Theory of Poetry* (New York: Oxford University Press, 1973); *A Map of Misreading* (New York: Oxford University Press, 1975); and *Poetry and Repression* (New Haven: Yale University Press, 1976).

2. While all of Derrida's writings can be said to be about the relation between philosophy and literature, the books that treat the topic most explicitly are *Margins of Philosophy* (1972), trans. Alan Bass (Chicago: University of Chicago Press, 1982); *Dissemination* (1972), trans. Barbara Johnson (Chicago: University of Chicago Press, 1981); and *Glas* (1974), trans. John P. Leavey and Richard Rand (Lincoln: University of Nebraska Press, 1987). The extent to which "philosophy as literature/literature as philosophy" has become a major area of critical investigation can be gauged by the existence of such institutions as the International Association for Philosophy and Literature, which has held annual conferences since 1975, the journal *Philosophy and Literature,* inaugurated in 1976 and, in recent years, the publication of several important volumes of essays: for example, A. Phillips Griffiths, ed., *Philosophy and Literature* (Cambridge: Cambridge University Press, 1984); Donald G. Marshall, ed., *Literature as Philosophy/ Philosophy as Literature* (Iowa City: University of Iowa Press, 1987); and Anthony J. Cascardi, ed., *Literature and the Question of Philosophy* (Baltimore: Johns Hopkins University Press, 1987). With Derrida at the origin of much of this critical debate, interest in Derrida himself as a philosopher and "historian" of philosophy has accordingly been growing, even while deconstruction as a method of literary criticism has declined in popularity. See, for example, Geoffrey H. Hartman, *Saving the Text: Literature, Derrida, Philosophy* (Baltimore: Johns Hopkins University Press, 1981); Sarah Kofman, *Lectures de Derrida* (Paris: Galilée, 1984); John Llewelyn, *Derrida on the Threshold of Sense* (London: Macmillan, 1986); Rodolphe Gasché, *The Tain of the Mirror: Derrida and the Philosophy of Reflection* (Cambridge: Harvard University Press, 1986); and Christopher Norris, *Derrida* (Cambridge: Harvard University Press, 1987).

3. The New Historicism, frequently taking its cue from the theories of Foucault and its point of departure from predominantly deconstructive readings of literary texts, should be differentiated from the new Marxist historicism and materialism, which, following Marxist theory closely, *ground* discourse in socio-politico-economic conditions. For a useful discussion of the differences see Marjorie Levinson, *Wordsworth's Great Period Poems: Four Essays* (Cambridge: Cambridge University Press, 1986), 1–13 and especially 135–36.

4. See Arthur Beatty, *William Wordsworth: His Doctrine and Art in Their Historical Relations* (Madison: University of Wisconsin Press, 1922); Melvin Rader, *Wordsworth: A Philosophical Approach* (Oxford: Clarendon Press, 1967): M. H. Abrams, *The Mirror and the Lamp: Romantic Theory and the Critical Tradition* (1953; rpt. New York: W. W. Norton, 1958) and *Natural Supernaturalism: Tradition and Revolution in Romantic Literature* (New York: W. W. Norton, 1973); Earl R. Wasserman, "The English Romantics: The Grounds of Knowledge," *Studies in Romanticism* 4 (1964): 17–34; H. W. Piper, *The Active Universe: Pantheism and the Concept of Imagination in the English Romantic Poets* (London: Athlone Press, 1962); Jonathan Wordsworth, *The Music of Humanity: A Critical Study of Wordsworth's "Ruined Cottage"* (London: Nelson, 1969); and Alan Grob, *The Philosophic Mind: A Study of Wordsworth's Poetry and Thought, 1797–1805* (Columbus: Ohio State University Press, 1973).

5. Melvin Rader stresses Wordsworth's affinity with Kantian epistemology and metaphysics (66–71, 145–47). Studies of the sublime, moreover, have invariably coordinated Wordsworth's theory and practice of the sublime with Kant's theory in the *Critique of Judgment:* see Thomas Weiskel, *The Romantic Sublime: Studies in the Structure and Psychology of Transcendence* (Baltimore: Johns Hopkins University Press, 1976), 1–62 and 167–204. Theresa M. Kelley points out the precise parallel between Kantian theory, especially in *Of the Beautiful and Sublime,* and Wordsworth's theory in his fragmentary essay "On the Sublime" (a theory more precisely Kantian, as Kelley shows, than is Coleridge's): see "Wordsworth, Kant, and the Romantic Sublime" *Philological Quarterly* 63 (1984): 130–40. On Wordsworth's affinity with Fichte's theories, see Daniel Stempel, "Revelation on Mount Snowdon: Wordsworth, Coleridge, and the Fichtean Imagination," *Journal of Aesthetics and Art Criticism* 29 (1971): 371–84. On Wordsworth's affinities with Schelling's theories, see E. D. Hirsch, Jr., *Wordsworth and Schelling: A Typological Study in Romanticism* (New Haven: Yale University Press, 1960). René Wellek discusses the "mathematical" problems of source and influence study (in the case of Coleridge) in Frank Jordan, Jr., ed., *The English Romantic Poets: A Review of Research and Criticism,* 3rd ed. (New York: Modern Language Association of America, 1972), 238–39.

6. *Correspondence of Crabb Robinson with the Wordsworth Circle,* ed. Edith Morley, 2 vols. (Oxford: Clarendon Press, 1927), 1: 401.

7. Hirsch, 8–9 (his more frequent term is "typification"); Abrams, *Natural Supernaturalism,* 11–12.

8. *Anxiety of Influence,* 29–45.

9. Derrida discusses the distinction between the literal and the figurative in "White Mythology: Metaphor in the Text of Philosophy" in *Margins of Philosophy,* 207–71. See also his sequel to this essay, in which he discusses metaphysics as originally a trope: "The Retreat of Metaphor," *enclitic* 2 (1978): 5–34.

10. For a useful discussion of intertextuality see Jonathan Culler, *The Pursuit of Signs: Semiotics, Literature, Deconstruction* (Ithaca: Cornell University Press, 1981), 100–118. It is worthwhile repeating what Christopher Norris points out: "intertextuality [is] *not* the kind of open-ended textual 'freeplay'—the farewell to rigorous protocols of reading—that literary critics often make of it" (*Derrida,* 43).

11. Besides Weiskel and Kelley (see note 5), see also Raimonda Modiano, *Coleridge and the Concept of Nature* (Tallahassee: Florida State University Press, 1985), 101–37; Steven Knapp, *Personification and the Sublime: Milton to Coleridge* (Cambridge: Harvard University Press, 1985); and Frances Ferguson, "The Sublime of Edmund Burke, or the Bathos of Experience,"

Glyph 8 (1981): 62–78, and "Legislating the Sublime" in Ralph Cohen, ed., *Studies in Eighteenth-Century British Art and Aesthetics* (Berkeley: University of California Press, 1985), 128–47. See also the recent issue of *Studies in Romanticism* devoted to the sublime (Vol. 26, No. 2, Summer 1987).

12. See Mark Kipperman, *Beyond Enchantment: German Idealism and English Romantic Poetry* (Philadelphia: University of Pennsylvania Press, 1986), 119–41. Kipperman does raise the question of "historical antecedents" to Romanticism in his first chapter (6) but not in any great detail. The second book is Andrew M. Cooper, *Doubt and Identity in Romantic Poetry* (New Haven: Yale University Press, 1988).

13. See Jerome J. McGann, *The Romantic Ideology: A Critical Investigation* (Chicago: University of Chicago Press, 1983).

14. Feeling compelled to justify his discussion of "Alice Fell," "Beggars," and especially "Gipsies," David Simpson remarks that it is not his "ambition to set the canon on its head" (*Wordsworth's Historical Imagination: The Poetry of Displacement* [New York and London: Methuen, 1987], 8). Even so, a shift in interests and paradigms inevitably entails a shift in one's sense of the canon. Although recent historicist criticism makes no claims for the special literary merits of the poems it focuses on, it is nonetheless making "minor" poems more important by showing how they embody in a particularly telling way certain socio-historical tensions. A good example is the coincidental publication of two articles on "Poor Susan": see David Simpson, "What Bothered Charles Lamb about Poor Susan?" *SEL* 26 (1986): 589–612; and Peter J. Manning, "Placing Poor Susan: Wordsworth and the New Historicism," *Studies in Romanticism* 25 (1986): 351–69.

15. *Collected Letters of Samuel Taylor Coleridge,* ed. Earl Leslie Griggs, 6 vols. (Oxford: Clarendon Press, 1956–71), 4: 574. For an account of Wordsworth's and Coleridge's Somerset year together, see Coleridge's informative remarks in chapter 10 of *Biographia Literaria* (where he relates his own philosophical situation in 1797 as well as the amusing "Spy Nozy" story, that establishes he discussed Spinoza with Wordsworth) and chapter 14 (in which he gives the genesis of *Lyrical Ballads*). See Samuel Taylor Coleridge, *Biographia Literaria; Or Biographical Sketches of My Literary Life and Opinions,* ed. James Engell and W. Jackson Bate, *The Collected Works of Samuel Taylor Coleridge,* 7, 2 vols. (Princeton: Princeton University Press, 1983), 1: 168–222, and 2: 5–18. See also Mary Moorman, *William Wordsworth, A Biography: The Early Years: 1770–1803* (Oxford: Clarendon Press, 1957), 321–407.

16. *The Table Talk and Omniana of Samuel Taylor Coleridge,* H. N. Coleridge (London: Oxford University Press, 1917), 188.

17. For a complete discussion of *The Recluse* project see Kenneth R. Johnston, *Wordsworth and "The Recluse"* (New Haven: Yale University Press, 1984). See also Jonathan Wordsworth, *William Wordsworth: The Borders of Vision* (Oxford: Clarendon Press, 1982), 340–77.

18. Traditionally metaphysics is "first philosophy," but, as Anthony J. Cascardi writes (paraphrasing Heidegger), "in Descartes, philosophy was first brought to the insight that it must begin with reflection on the possibility of knowledge before it could proceed with any other matter" (*Literature and the Question of Philosophy,* 242). See René Descartes, *Meditations on First Philosophy* (1641) trans. Laurence J. Lafleur (1951; rpt. Indianapolis: Bobbs-Merrill, 1980), 17–33.

19. See, for example, Earl R. Wasserman, "Grounds of Knowledge"; and Geoffrey H. Hartman, *Wordsworth's Poetry: 1787–1814,* 6th ed. with essay "Retrospect 1971" (1964; rpt. New Haven: Yale University Press, 1977), 163–83.

20. Mary Jacobus, *Tradition and Experiment in Wordsworth's "Lyrical Ballads" (1798)* (Oxford: Clarendon Press, 1976), 121.

21. Jacobus, 68.

22. Paul Sheats, *The Making of Wordsworth's Poetry, 1785–98* (Cambridge: Harvard University Press, 1973), 163.

23. Jacobus, 59.

24. *Music of Humanity,* 194. Mary Jacobus fully discusses "Reflections on Having Left a Place of Retirement" and its role in Wordsworth's and Coleridge's dialogue (71–77).

25. Letter to J. H. Reynolds, 3 May 1818, in *Letters of John Keats,* ed. Robert Gittings (London: Oxford University Press, 1970), 93.

26. See *The Friend,* ed. Barbara E. Rooke, *The Collected Works of Samuel Taylor Coleridge,* 4, 2 vols. (Princeton: Princeton University Press, 1969), 1: 127, 148–49.

27. See, for example, Alan Grob, *Philosophic Mind* (see note 4).

28. See Chester L. Shaver and Alice C. Shaver, *Wordsworth's Library: A Catalogue* (New York: Garland, 1979). For a full coverage of the range of Wordsworth's reading see Joseph Warren Beach, *The Concept of Nature in Nineteenth-Century English Poetry* (New York: Macmillan, 1936), 569–77; and Melvin Rader, *Wordsworth: A Philosophical Approach,* 39–80. Besides the examples of philosophers I quote in the text, Wordsworth's library contained some other interesting selections: the only works of Hume's on his shelves were *The History of England* (1793–94) and *Political Discourses* (1752, 1782); the only work of Berkeley's he had was *Alciphron;* but in addition to Locke's *Essay* (1690 edition) and *Of the Conduct of the Understanding* (1706), both borrowed from Coleridge (see the following note), he owned Locke's *Letter to Edw. Stillingfleet, Bp. of Worcester* (1697) and *Mr. Locke's Reply* (to Stillingfleet's second letter; 1699). (One wonders whether the Locke-Stillingfleet correspondence on spiritual substance and the immortality of the soul had a bearing on the "Immortality" Ode.) Perhaps most interesting of all is that Wordsworth owned almost as many works of seventeenth- and eighteenth-century theology as of philosophy: Boehme, Burnet, Cudworth, etc.

29. Shaver and Shaver point out that the books belonging to Coleridge were lent to Wordsworth— or left with him—when Coleridge departed for Malta in early 1804. They were in Wordsworth's possession for about twenty years. On 17 September 1829, Coleridge drew up his will, and Wordsworth separated his books from his own in October 1829. See *Wordsworth's Library,* xxi. Significant philosophical works belonging to Coleridge include those by Proclus, Ficino, Gassendi, More, Malebranche, Newton, Leibniz, Hartley, Paley and Tucker.

30. Ben Ross Schneider, Jr., *Wordsworth's Cambridge Education* (Cambridge: Cambridge University Press, 1957), 105.

31. Schneider, 111.

32. Schneider, 230. Schneider points out that "Nearly all of the moral questions asked of degree-candidates on examination Wednesday [June 1789] dealt with subjects of [Locke's] *Essay*" (106). He also half implies that the Lockean-inspired and Cambridge-produced Hartley's *Observations on Man* and Paley's *Moral Philosophy* might have been on the Cambridge curriculum (106). Schneider furthermore quotes a letter from a student in 1791 who complains that one examination "Question (of all things in the world) is to defend Berkeley's immaterial system" (33).

33. Coleridge discusses his enthusiasm for Hartley and Spinoza in 1798 in his *Biographia Literaria*. His enthusiasm for Berkeley is evident in "Religious Musings" (1796), lines 395–401, "The Destiny of Nations" (1796), lines 13–26, and the Conversation Poems, particularly "This Lime-Tree Bower My Prison" (1797) and "Frost at Midnight" (1798), where he extensively draws on Berkeley's theory of nature as God's language (in a transcription of "This Lime-Tree Bower My Prison" in a letter to Southey, 17 July 1797, Coleridge adds the footnote "You remember, I am a *Berkleian*" [*Collected Letters,* 1: 335]). If Berkeleyanism was an integral part of the Conversation Poems, and the Conversation Poems an integral part of the dialogue between Coleridge and Wordsworth in 1797–98, then Berkeleyanism would surely have been a major topic of conversation between the two poets. On Coleridge's study of Kant and Fichte (he began seriously studying the two of them in February-March 1801), see G. N. G. Orsini, *Coleridge and German Idealism: A Study in the History of Philosophy with Unpublished Materials from Coleridge's Manuscripts* (Carbondale: Southern Illinois University Press, 1969), 47–48 and passim (Kant), and 179–83 (Fichte). See also, Thomas McFarland, *Coleridge and the Pantheist Tradition* (Oxford: Clarendon Press, 1969), 107–90, who establishes that Kant is a more lasting influence on Coleridge than Fichte (and traces Coleridge's lifelong ambivalent attitude towards Spinozism and the problem of pantheism). Interestingly, on 9 February 1801, Coleridge included in a letter to Dorothy Wordsworth he had translated from Fichte's *Wissenschaftslehre,* making light of it by commenting that "nothing in Touchstone ever equalled this" (*Collected Letters,* 2: 379). If he treated Dorothy to his knowledge of Fichte, there is all the more reason to assume that he shared a lot more of it with Wordsworth (the same goes for his knowledge of Kant).

34. See *The Letters of William and Dorothy Wordsworth; The Early Years; 1787–1805,* ed. Ernest de Selincourt, rev. Chester L. Shaver (Oxford: Clarendon Press, 1967), 452. See also Wordsworth's even more anxious request in a letter of 29 March 1804 (*Early Years,* 464). McFarland discusses these letters and their place in the *Recluse* project in *Romanticism and the Forms of Ruin: Wordsworth, Coleridge, and the Modalities of Fragmentation* (Princeton: Princeton University Press, 1981), 97–98.

35. See the series of letters he writes to Josiah Wedgwood in February 1801 (*Collected Letters,* 2: 677–703), in which he discusses Descartes as well as Locke and establishes Locke's reliance on Descartes. Griggs cites the conclusion of a commentator that Coleridge "gives evidence of having studied book 1 and the opening chapters of book 2 of the *Essay,* [but] he does not seem to have read the rest of the work with much care" (678).

36. For Locke's epistemology see book 2 of the *Essay.* Hartley's necessaritarian psychology is based in a mechanistic physiology of "vibrations." Although Wordsworth could have skipped Hartley's first two chapters elaborating his "Doctrine of Vibrations" in order to get to the psychology proper and the discussion of the "Moral Sense," he could not have avoided the physiology altogether. He makes some use of it in "Tintern Abbey" (see chapter 3, below) but his interest is always in the psychological and not the mechanical. See David Hartley, *Observations on Man, His Frame, His Duty, and His Expectations* (1749), introd. Theodore L. Huguelet (Gainesville: Scholars' Facsimiles and Reprints, 1966), ix-xi, 493–99. For a broad-ranging discussion of how books of philosophy were read and understood in the eighteenth century, how they were popularized and the expectations they encouraged in the reading public as to style and method, as well as their influence on various writers throughout the period, see John Valdimir Price, "The Reading of Philosophical Literature" in *Books and Their Readers in Eighteenth-Century England,* ed. Isabel Rivers (New York: St. Martin's Press, 1982), 165–96. Writing about Newtonian science books in the eighteenth century, G. S. Rousseau points out that "two types of Newtonian books need to be distinguished: the interpretations,

or reinterpretations, and the popularizations." "Far more influential were the outright popularizations" because they "were capable of effecting cultural secularization by reaching large
audiences." See G. S. Rousseau, "Science Books and Their Readers in the Eighteenth Century," in *Books and Their Readers,* 216. The same situation applies to philosophy. Given that
Lockean empiricism would have been popularized and secularized not only by philosophical
writers but by literary authors too, then Wordsworth would have received the broad, general
understanding of his century's philosophy that I am arguing for here.

37.   While the essence of empiricism is a method of inference from experience and experiment,
transcendentalism focuses, in Wendell Harris' words, on "a structure which is not only invisible
but which cannot be deduced from the phenomena of experience. To those who hold the
[transcendentalist] view, the world often seems more purposive, more mysteriously wonderful
than to the [empiricists] and is more likely to be seen as a structure of 'vital' or 'spiritual'
forces. . . ." See Wendell V. Harris, *The Omnipresent Debate: Empiricism and Transcendentalism in Nineteenth-Century English Prose* (DeKalb: Northern Illinois University Press,
1981), 7–8. Prompting Kant to effect his "Copernican Revolution" in philosophy is the extreme
skeptical, solipsistic impasse reached by Hume (and empiricism in general). If our only certain
knowledge is our sensations, then we have no way of knowing that objects really exist outside
us to cause those sensations, that our ideas represent and correspond to an objectively existing
external world. See *Immanuel Kant's Critique of Pure Reason,* trans. Norman Kemp Smith
(1929; rpt. London: Macmillan, 1964), 22–23. On the "veil of perception" that characterizes
empiricism, see Jonathan Bennet, *Locke, Berkeley, Hume: Central Themes* (Oxford: Clarendon
Press, 1971), 69; and Richard Rorty, *Philosophy and the Mirror of Nature* (Princeton: Princeton University Press, 1979), 45–69. John W. Yolton dissents from this monolithic view of
empiricist epistemology. See his *Perceptual Acquaintance from Descartes to Reid* (Minneapolis: University of Minnesota Press, 1984), 204–23 (especially 222–23). For a full discussion
of Kant's response to extreme empiricist skepticism and his deduction of both "transcendental
idealism" and "empirical realism" as the appropriate answer to empiricist idealism, see Barry
Stroud, *The Significance of Philosophical Scepticism* (Oxford: Clarendon Press, 1984), 128–
69.

38.   I am giving here a Fichtean account of self and nature and their interaction. For Fichte's
explanation of how the self posits itself absolutely (as infinite) and how in making itself
receptive to itself it thereby posits absolutely a not-self that is opposed to itself (and equally
infinite—a not-self that becomes nature), see *Fichte: Science of Knowledge (Wissenschaftslehre), with the First and Second Introductions,* ed. and trans. Peter Heath and John
Lachs (New York: Appleton-Century-Crofts, 1970), 93–119. See also Kipperman's clear exposition of Fichte's system in *Beyond Enchantment,* 61–81. Via Coleridge's mediation, the actual
philosophical sources for Wordsworth's transcendentalism up to and through *The Prelude* of
1805 would be Kant and Fichte. Even if Wordsworth displays a remarkable parallelism with
Schelling, the similarity more likely proceeds metaleptically: Schelling's philosophy resembles
Fichte's sufficiently closely such that Fichte would more likely be the true point of origin. It
is important to bear in mind too that Coleridge did not begin reading Schelling until some time
after he had left the Lake District and Wordsworth's company. His earliest reference to
Schelling is in January 1806. See *The Notebooks of Samuel Taylor Coleridge,* ed. Kathleen
Coburn, 3 vols. (Princeton: Princeton University Press, 1957–73), 2: 2784.

Chapter 1

1.　Coleridge, *Collected Letters,* 1: 209. Coleridge quotes lines 38–43 of the poem.

2.　Jonathan Wordsworth, *The Music of Humanity,* 198–99.

3.　Hartman, *Wordsworth's Poetry,* 163.

4.　Hartman, *Wordsworth's Poetry,* 166

5.　*The Prelude,* 3. 106.

6.　I use the term "errancy" rather than "error" here and throughout the book, because what I wish to point to is less categorical than outright error and closer to the condition of wandering that the Latin root specifies. An accurate synonym would be "dislocation," as some epistemological barrier separating subject from object (and usually involving it in uncertainty) is always implied.

7.　Hartman, *Wordsworth's Poetry,* 9.

8.　Hartman, *Wordsworth's Poetry,* 176.

9.　Sheats, 176. Sheats states that "A Night Piece" is "clearly and forcefully presentational. It seeks to reenact the presentation of phenomena to the mind in experience." I omit discussion of "A Night Piece" and "The Discharged Soldier" (also in the Notebook) largely because they have received extensive discussion already. Besides Sheats, see also Kenneth R. Johnston, "The Idiom of Vision," in *New Perspectives on Coleridge and Wordsworth: Selected Papers from the English Institute,* ed. Geoffrey H. Hartman (New York and London: Columbia Univ. Press, 1972), 1–39; and Michael C. Jaye, "William Wordsworth's Alfoxden Notebook: 1798," in *The Evidence of the Imagination: Studies of Interactions between Life and Art in English Romantic Literature,* ed. Donald H. Reiman, Michael C. Jaye, et al. (Gotham Library) (New York: New York University Press, 1978), 42–85.

10.　The text of the Alfoxden Notebook fragments I use is that given in William Wordsworth, *"The Ruined Cottage" and "The Pedlar,"* ed. James Butler, *The Cornell Wordsworth* (Ithaca: Cornell University Press, 1979), 112–25. The passage quoted is on 15ᵛ of the Notebook (112–13). Future references to the Notebook appear in the text, where I cite leaf numbers only. I reproduce the transcriptions of the Notebook passages only where Wordsworth's deletions and emendations are pertinent to my argument. Otherwise I follow the intended final version (as best as it can be established), which mostly coincides with de Selincourt's transcription in *PW,* 5: 340–42. Although, as Butler judiciously points out in his introduction, "Placement in the manuscript is not a good criterion for determining the order of entry in Wordsworth's notebooks" (7), I nevertheless discuss the fragments in the sequence in which they appear on the leaves.

11.　See Jaye (63), who also mentions this point.

12.　Sheats (165–66) discusses the fine balance between activity and passivity in this fragment. Hartman (*Wordsworth's Poetry,* 166) mentions how the verb *stand* "gains a new emphasis here as in other fragments." It should be noted too that Wordsworth's lines echo the movement of Coleridge's "This Lime-Tree Bower My Prison," where the interplay of activity and passivity in the act of "gazing" results (via the conjunction "till") in the landscape appearing "Less gross than bodily" (39–43).

13.　For Locke's account of influx see *An Essay Concerning Human Understanding,* book 2, chapters 1–10 in particular. The "secondary qualities" of sensible phenomena (color, sound, smell, temperature) derive from some "power" or "powers" in the phenomena, but their effect on different people can vary widely. Secondary qualities are therefore more subjective than objective; and insofar as some indeterminable power produces these variable effects, Locke argues that these qualities are incidental to our "idea" of the phenomena. Only "primary qualities" (extension, figure, solidity and mobility) give an "adequate idea," a true "resemblance" of the object. John Locke, *An Essay Concerning Human Understanding,* ed. Peter H. Nidditch (Oxford: Clarendon Press, 1975), book 2. 8. 134–43, and book 2, 31–32. 375–94. Inhibition and distortion are also attributable to other variables: the state of feeling, physical constitution, and so on.

14. *"Ruined Cottage" and "Pedlar,"* 371 (MS. D, 56ᵛ).

15. Jaye focuses on this aspect of the Notebook. He discusses it as "a document in itself," one that "preserves the traces of the creative imagination in first flow . . . hold[ing] both the struggling transcription of creative thought in the immediacy of conception and the poet's revisionary attempts to reshape his initial visionary utterance" (42, 43).

16. The final version of these lines is to be found in *PW,* 5: 342.

17. "What she felt" is, of course, the conscious thoughts present in the mind at the time. This content yields to a more generalized feeling which the self can remember later. The distinction between "what" and "how" is roughly that between thought and feeling, and, to an extent, content and form.

18. *PrW,* 1: 124.

19. I am adapting Derrida's concept of the "Supplement": "whether it adds or substitutes itself, the supplement is *exterior,* outside of the positivity to which it is super-added, alien to that which, in order to be replaced by it, must be other than it. Unlike the *complement,* dictionaries tell us, the supplement is an '*exterior* addition.' " Jacques Derrida, *Of Grammatology,* trans. Gayatri Chakravorty Spivak (Baltimore and London: Johns Hopkins University Press, 1977), 145. The term *supplement* is roughly interchangeable in meaning with *trace* and *différance.* A definition of *trace* which Derrida gives in the course of *Of Grammatology* helps to explain the concept and its functioning: the trace "is the opening of the first exteriority in general, the enigmatic relationship of the living to its other and of an inside to an outside: spacing. The outside, 'spatial' and 'objective' exteriority which we believe we know as the most familiar thing in the world, as familiarity itself, would not appear without the gramme, without differance as temporalization, without the nonpresence of the other inscribed within the sense of the present, without the relationship with death as the concrete structure of the living present" (70–71). Throughout Wordsworth's writings, self and nature alternately function as supplements of one another—to the confusion of the issue of priority. Frequently the self derives its content from nature (so that nature seems prior, and the self a supplement of it); but the situation can suddenly be reversed (and nature seem to be a supplement of the self and dependent on the self's commutations). The supplementarity between self and nature does not mean, however, that the two are interchangeable or equivalent—which is what Geoffrey Hartman has argued (Hartman, *Wordsworth's Poetry,* 174). For more on the Derridean concept of the supplement, see *Of Grammatology,* 141–64; and Jacques Derrida, *Speech and Phenomena,* trans. David B. Allison (Evanston: Northwestern University Press, 1973), 88–104.

20. See Derrida, *Speech and Phenomena,* 32–47, 70–87.

21. Derrida focuses his critique in *Of Grammatology* on the traditional metaphysical and linguistic theories of the differential relation between writing and speech, and he argues that writing is not a corrupting supplement of speech (as Western thought has generally conceived it to be)

but is in essence constitutive of it: language—whether writing or speech—relies on the expressive medium of an outside, whether visible mark or audible sound. Indeed, he argues that this outside, reducible to the trace, to differance, opens the possibility of meaning, of understanding and of experience in general. At the same time, however, he stresses that meaning or presence—in whatever form—is not to be had without the mediation of an outside. Derrida's terms are especially applicable to Wordsworth, for notions of writing and speech repeatedly structure the presentation of self and nature in his poetry, while the difference and interaction between self and nature are often modeled on the relation between inside and outside (a dichotomy which features prominently in empiricist epistemology in its concern with primary and secondary qualities, etc.). The self, as an inside in this Alfoxden fragment, comes to know itself by means of the outside. The outside ("The mountain's outline and its steady form") is also a bounding line. On this topic, see Jacques Derrida, " 'Ousia and Grammè': A Note to a Footnote in *Being and Time*," trans. Edward S. Casey, in *Phenomenology in Perspective*, ed. F. J. Smith (The Hague: Martinus Nijhoff, 1970), 54–93.

22. In later versions of this passage (i.e., the opening for the reconciling addendum in MS. B of *The Ruined Cottage* [46ʳ] and later as part of book 4 of *The Excursion* [1207–98]) Wordsworth changes the line to read "things that hold / An *inarticulate* language" (emphasis added).

23. *Modes, combination,* and *link* are readily identifiable as standard philosophical terms which Locke and the empiricists frequently deploy. Even if the term *soul* appears more rightfully to belong to theology, it nevertheless features in Locke's system. In book 2, chapter 1 of his *Essay*, Locke questions the relationship between consciousness, thinking and the soul. He argues that there is no thinking without being conscious of it and that thinking is not the soul's "Essence, but one of its Operations" (2. 1. 10, 108). In effect, Locke equates the soul with consciousness, the "I" which is self-aware—a proposition which Coleridge attacks at length in a letter to Josiah Wedgwood in February 1801 (*Collected Letters*, 2: 696). Wordsworth's use of the word *soul* in this passage then, does not indicate any breach with Locke. In fact, Wordsworth appears almost to be answering a question which Locke cannot resolve. Locke states, "But whether the Soul be supposed to exist antecedent to, or coeval with, or some time after the first Rudiments of Organization, or the beginnings of Life in the Body, I leave to be disputed by those who have better thought of the matter" (2. 1. 10, 108). Wordsworth's lines suggest that the soul is imbued "some time after the first rudiments of organization," after the "modes" have joined into "combinations"—a position differing from that espoused in *The Prelude* and the "Immortality" Ode.

24. See, for example, Alan Grob, who claims that "whatever Wordsworth learns of life on this occasion depends upon the 'pleasant consciousness' that accompanies his visual sensations, while introspection can yield no knowledge of life's character when it delves into pure mind, that is, a mind devoid of images" (*The Philosophic Mind*, 28). But, as I argue below, "a mind devoid of images" does "yield . . . knowledge of life's character" even if only in an indeterminate, hazy fashion. As Geoffrey Hartman argues, it is clear that in returning from "pure mind" to consciousness of the outside the self becomes aware of having undergone a change, of having undergone an experience it can barely articulate. The last four lines of the fragment do not constitute "a mere return to duality. If the données of ordinary perception are reconstituted, it is with the difference that 'the One Life, within us and abroad' is now directly sensed and even activated by changing polar distinctions" (Hartman, *Wordsworth's Poetry,* 178).

25. While Locke (and Grob) may entertain the idea of "pure mind, . . . a mind devoid of images," it is for them a blank which cannot be known or described. Although Kant would agree that pure mind cannot become an object of experience, he nevertheless is able to deduce its formal

structure, its a priori constitution (see, in particular, the "Transcendental Analytic" in *Critique of Pure Reason*).

26. I am borrowing from (and adapting) Kant's famous statement here: "Without sensibility no object would be given to us, without understanding no object would be thought. Thoughts without content are empty, intuitions without concepts are blind." (*Critique of Pure Reason*, 93.) Kant argues in the "Transcendental Analytic" that the categories of the understanding are empty unless sense experience fills them with content; correlatively, mere sense data are unintelligible unless mediated by the categories of the understanding. Kant's theory is applicable to this fragment, for Wordsworth quite clearly presents a separation of mind from sense experience, a notion whose theoretical feasibility Kant is concerned to discuss in this section of the *Critique*.

27. Locke's metaphors for the mind include not only the *tabula rasa* (on which characters are to be written) but also the wax tablet on which impressions are stamped (104), as well as the "empty Cabinet" (55) and the "dark Room" (162–63).

28. De Selincourt conjectures that the Christabel fragments are contemporary with the Alfoxden ones and date, therefore, from early 1798 (*PW*, 5. 369 and 480). Mark Reed, however, argues that they were written after 6 October 1798 (when Wordsworth arrived at Goslar in Germany) but before October 1800. See Mark L. Reed, *Wordsworth: The Chronology of the Early Years: 1770–1799* (Cambridge: Harvard University Press, 1967), 322–25.

29. Hartman, *Wordsworth's Poetry*, 180.

30. Timothy Bahti, "Figures of Interpretation, the Interpretation of Figures: A Reading of Wordsworth's 'Dream of the Arab,'" *Studies in Romanticism* 18 (1979): 606–7.

31. William Wordsworth, *The Prelude, 1798–1799*, ed. Stephen Parrish, *The Cornell Wordsworth* (Ithaca: Cornell University Press, 1977), 67.

32. It seems that the coincidence of inside and outside is understood as the two separate upon the reemergence of self-consciousness. To apply what Coleridge says of the identity of subject and object in *Biographia Literaria*, the self "must in some sense dissolve this identity, in order to be conscious of it" (*Biographia Literaria*, 279).

33. *Prelude, 1798–99*, 206–7.

Chapter 2

1. Charles Lamb, Letter to William Wordsworth, 9 August 1814, *The Letters of Charles and Mary Anne Lamb*, ed. Edwin W. Marrs, Jr. (Ithaca: Cornell University Press, 1978), 3. 95.

2. See *"The Ruined Cottage" and "The Pedlar,"* x–xii and 3–35, for detailed information about the MSS and order of composition. The text I follow is that of MS. D (338–68) as given by Jonathan Wordsworth in *The Borders of Vision*, 378–87. Line references appear in the text after quotations.

3. Geometry features in *The Pedlar* in lines 140–203. There has been some controversy about the precise meaning of the word *form* in Wordsworth's poetry. H. W. Piper, exploring the pantheist forerunners of Coleridge and Wordsworth in the eighteenth century, considers Wordsworth's use of the word to be in accord with that of the later *philosophes* (*The Active Universe*, 73). Piper concludes that *form* for Wordsworth "seems to mean any organized natural body, and the implication is that such bodies have life and sensibility" (74), although he also points out that in associationist philosophy *forms* meant "those shapes which were perceived as simple ideas,

and it might as well refer to a table as a tree" (74). Colin C. Clarke has argued that *forms*—like *shapes, images, sense* and *sensation*—takes on increasingly ambiguous connotations in Wordsworth's poetry, and "can be applied, interchangeably and accurately, to mind *and* nature." Colin C. Clarke, *Romantic Paradox: An Essay on the Poetry of Wordsworth* (New York: Barnes & Noble, 1963), 25. Clarke argues that Wordsworth's poetry exploits to the full the equivocal meaning of these words, but his stress on their perceptual denotation does not necessarily preclude the persistence of a precise technical meaning of the order that Piper is concerned to isolate. The major attraction of such words for Wordsworth, it seems to me, is that they are general and reductive: they classify phenomena according to their lower common denominator—which, in reality, is the criterion both Piper and Clarke are applying (Piper that of "life," and Clarke that of visibility). In the *Pedlar* passage under discussion, "shapes and forms" have an ideal (insofar as mental) meaning; yet the sense of the general, the schematic and even of the abstract, is important here too, and features more prominently in other passages in the poem (e.g., 92–114).

4. Geoffrey Hartman discusses "surmise" as a figure central to Wordsworth's poetry. It is a questioning attitude most often expressed in "'whether . . . or' formulations, alternatives rather than exclusions, echoing conjecture (Keats's 'Do I wake or sleep?') rather than blunt determinateness" (*Wordsworth's Poetry,* 8). As Hartman point out, surmise is originally a classical rhetorical figure: "Fallor, an . . . ?" ("Am I mistaken, or . . . ?"), which is precisely the form of the questions in *The Pedlar* (Hartman, *Wordsworth's Poetry,* 347, n. 17). Surmise functions throughout Wordsworth's poetry as a major method of philosophical insight and discovery.

5. Jonathan Wordsworth, *The Music of Humanity,* 212.

6. Jonathan Wordsworth claims the opposite. He follows the sentence quoted above by saying that "At this stage in his [Wordsworth's] thought only the One Life matters, and how it is perceived is relatively unimportant" (212).

7. Wordsworth himself gives authority for using the term "redundancy" in this epistemological way. In the "glad preamble" (*Prelude,* 7. 4) to the 1805 *Prelude* he mentions that "while the sweet breath of Heaven / Was blowing on [his] body, [he] felt within / A corresponding mild creative breeze" which became "a redundant energy / Vexing its own creation" (*Prel,* 1. 41–47). The root idea here is as much that of redounding, of a reflexive recoiling, as of superfluity. My epistemological interpretation of the term is supported by a fragment from MS. 18A entitled "Redundance":

> Not the more
> Failed I to lengthen out my watch. I stood
> Within the area of the frozen vale,
> Mine eye subdued and quiet as the ear
> Of one that listens, for even yet the scene,
> Its fluctuating hues and surfaces,
> And the decaying vestiges of forms,
> Did to the dispossessing power of night
> Impart a feeble visionary sense
> Of movement and creation doubly felt.

(*PW,* 5: 346)

I use the term "redundancy" here and in later chapters to mean a reflexive reiteration, which characterizes the self's response to nature during the trance.

8. Acts 17: 28.

9. See Peter F. McInerney, "Natural Wisdom in Wordsworth's *The Excursion,*" *The Wordsworth Circle* 9 (1978): 188–99, who discusses the section of *The Pedlar* in a way similar to my own. McInerney argues the relevance of this passage to *The Ruined Cottage* as a whole, however. See also Charles Sherry, *Wordsworth's Poetry of the Imagination* (Oxford: Clarendon Press, 1980), 47–50.

10. *The Excursion,* 1. 1617 (*PW,* 5: 8).

11. Wordsworth discusses his interest in geometry at length in book 6 of *The Prelude* (6. 135–87). In book 5, he explicitly figures the kind of epistemological dislocation that books cause in the way I have been discussing it here. Concentration on the page before his eyes shuts him off from the surrounding beauties of nature:

> Full often . . . I have lain
> Down by thy side, O Derwent! murmuring Stream,
> On the hot stones and in the glaring sun,
> And there have read, devouring as I read,
> Defrauding the day's glory, desperate!
> Till, with a sudden bound of smart reproach,
> Such as an Idler deals with in his shame,
> I to my sport betook myself again.
>
> (*Prel,* 5. 505–15)

12. Wordsworth's discussion of "books" in the middle section of *The Pedlar* anticipates his more amplified discussion of the same subject in book 5 of *The Prelude,* where again the relation of books and book-learning to nature and truth is conceived according to the metaphysics of immanence and transcendence and expressed in precisely the same language. Fearing the apocalyptic destruction of books and all their "adamantine holds of truth" (5. 38), Wordsworth exclaims:

> Oh! why hath not the mind
> Some element to stamp her image on
> In nature somewhat nearer to her own?
> Why, gifted with such powers to send abroad
> Her spirit, must it *lodge* in shrines so frail?
>
> (5. 44–48; emphasis added)

In book 5, however, he offers transcendence as the answer; he commits the phenomenal to the charge of the intelligible medium of language:

> Visionary power
> Attends upon the motions of the winds
> Embodied in the mystery of words.
> There darkness makes abode, and all the host
> Of shadowy things do work their changes there,
> As in a mansion like their proper home;
> Even forms and substances are circumfus'd
> By that transparent veil with light divine;
> And through the turnings intricate of Verse,
> Present themselves as objects recognis'd,
> In flashes, and with a glory scarce their own.
>
> (5. 619–29)

13. MS. RV, 10ᵛ (*Prelude, 1798–1799,* 206–7). In a variant of these lines in D.C. MS 33, Wordsworth says: "In which all beings live with god themselves / Are god existing in one mighty whole" (50ʳ; *Prelude, 1798–99,* 164–65).

14. Paul Sheats has discussed the "abyss of idealism" Wordsworth mentions in the Isabella Fenwick note to the "Immortality" Ode (*PW,* 4: 463), and has drawn attention to the Berkeleyan form of "subjective idealism" that gripped Wordsworth during his childhood (*Making of Wordsworth's Poetry,* 18). John Hodgson, however, makes a strong case for seeing this Berkeleyanism as an adult superinscription: "not once before 1804 does Wordsworth allude to such a remembrance [of the soul's immortality] or such a childhood experience [of grasping at a wall or tree to dispel the feeling of the immateriality of the external world]." (John A. Hodgson, *Wordsworth's Philosophical Poetry, 1797–1814* [Lincoln: University of Nebraska Press, 1980], 102).

Chapter 3

1. See McGann, 85–88; Levinson, 14–57; and Simpson, *Wordsworth's Historical Imagination,* 109–13.

2. Levinson, 40. Levinson goes on to say that " 'Tintern Abbey' invents and idealizes a procedure whereby the mind's extension (denotation, object representation, quantitative knowledge) is experienced as intension (connotation, valorization, qualitative knowledge)" (51). She also uses the term *empirical idealism* (42).

3. On the eighteenth-century interest in the picturesque and visiting England's beauty spots, see, among others, Charles Norton Coe, *Wordsworth and the Literature of Travel* (New York: Bookman Associates, 1953), 14, 101–2; and Donald Wesling, *Wordsworth and the Adequacy of Landscape* (London: Routledge & Kegan Paul, 1970).

4. Richard J. Onorato, *The Character of the Poet: Wordsworth in "The Prelude"* (Princeton: Princeton University Press, 1971), 46.

5. Mary Moorman, 402–3. Levinson discusses at length the industrialization of the Wye Valley, charcoal burning, the Tintern ironworks, the pollution of the river, poverty and vagrancy (29–37).

6. *King Lear,* 3. 4. 28–32. Geoffrey Hartman points out that the Hermit is a reflection of Wordsworth's own "buried (naturalized) self" (*Wordsworth's Poetry,* 175). Even if "Wordsworth's self-projection [is a] hollowed-out emblem of uncompromised consciousness" (Levinson, 41), the Hermit is still in part, I feel, a "picturesque prop" (Hartman, *Wordsworth's Poetry,* 384, n.39).

7. John Locke, *Essay concerning Human Understanding,* 151. In chapter 10, "Of Retention," Locke talks of "paint[ing]" (150) ideas and particularly colors in the memory. In an associated image that he uses more extensively, he says that if our ideas are not "sometimes renewed by the repeated Exercise of the Senses . . . the Print wears out, and at last there remains nothing to be seen" (151):

> *The Pictures drawn in our Minds, are laid in fading Colours;* and if not sometimes refreshed, vanish and disappear. How much the Constitution of our Bodies, and the make of our animal Spirits, are concerned in this; and whether the Temper of the Brain make this difference, that in some it retains the Characters drawn on it like Marble, and in others like Free-stone, and in others little better than Sand, I shall not enquire here, though it

> may seem probable, that the Constitution of the Body does sometimes influence the Memory. (152; Locke's italics)

8. On the significance of the title and the dates and anniversaries it records, see J. R. Watson, "A Note on the Date in the Title of 'Tintern Abbey,'" *The Wordsworth Circle* 10 (1979): 379–80. See also Levinson, 16–17 and 53–55. Levinson half suggests that Wordsworth can see the Abbey, but it should be stressed that it is invisible from his putative location. Even if Wordsworth were reclining on the cliff tops overlooking the scene (and there is little other than his view of the hedgerows and the "one green hue" to suggest that he might be; in fact his reference to the river's "soft inland murmur" and to standing on its "banks" [114] imply proximity to the water's edge), the steep, wooded, winding narrow valley would hide the building from view.

9. See Levinson, 29–32.

10. This movement is an example of "Hartley Transcendentalized by Coleridge" that de Selincourt mentions. See *1850 Prel*, lxix. See also Newton P. Stallknecht, *Strange Seas of Thought: Studies in William Wordsworth's Philosophy of Man and Nature* (Bloomington: Indiana University Press, 1958), 33–72. On Wordsworth's Hartleyanism in "Tintern Abbey," see Beatty, 106–9; Grob, 33–72; and Robert Brainard Pearsall, "Wordsworth Reworks His Hartley," *RMMLA Bulletin* (1970): 73–83.

11. For a discussion of Wordsworth's syntax and its problematic undertow in the poem, see, besides Onorato, Susan J. Wolfson, "The Speaker as Questioner in *Lyrical Ballads*," *Journal of English and Germanic Philology* 77 (1978): 546–68.

12. Kant discusses the understanding's architectonic structure and deduces its a priori categories and their applicability to phenomenal experience in the "Transcendental Analytic," the first part of the "Transcendental Logic." See *Critique of Pure Reason*, 92–175.

13. *Wordsworth's Poetry*, 27.

14. Levinson links this kind of language to Descartes and Wordsworth's "Cartesian epistemology" (48; see also 40–49), but it is also standard empiricist terminology. See John W. Yolton, *Thinking Matter: Materialism in Eighteenth-Century Britain* (Minneapolis: University of Minnesota Press, 1983), 14–28 and 90–106.

15. The poem parallels Psalm 23 at a few points. Actually quoting a line from the psalm—"For thou art with me" (114; Ps. 23: 4)—Wordsworth sees Dorothy as providing him with the same comfort and support that the Lord provides to the speaker of the psalm. Moreover, Wordsworth is lying down "in green pastures . . . beside the still waters" and believes that "Surely goodness and mercy shall follow [him] all the days of [his] life" because he "will dwell" not "in the house of the Lord for ever" but in the "house" of Dorothy's mind for ever (Ps. 23: 2, 6).

Chapter 4

1. For a full discussion of the chronology of *Prelude* composition during the spring of 1804, see Mark L. Reed, *Wordsworth: The Chronology of the Middle Years, 1800–1815* (Cambridge: Harvard University Press, 1975), 628–55. I follow here Jonathan Wordsworth's decisions about when particular passages were written. See his "The Five-Book *Prelude* of Early Spring 1804," *Journal of English and Germanic Philology* 76 (1977): 1–25, especially 15–25. See also William Wordsworth, *The Prelude: 1799, 1805, 1850*, ed. Jonathan Wordsworth, M. H. Abrams, and Stephen Gill (New York: W. W. Norton, 1979), 515–25.

2. Jonathan Wordsworth, "Five-Book *Prelude*," 18.

3. All the quotations in this paragraph are from Jonathan Wordsworth, "Five-Book *Prelude,* 24; except for the final one, which is from page 18.

4. Among the recent scholarly work on Wordsworth's engagement with politics and history, see in particular, James K. Chandler, *Wordsworth's Second Nature: A Study of the Poetry and Politics* (Chicago: University of Chicago Press, 1984); Alan Liu, "Wordsworth: The History in 'Imagination,'" *ELH* 51 (1984): 505–48; Kenneth Johnston, *Wordsworth and "The Recluse"*; and Simpson, *Wordsworth's Historical Imagination.*

5. Jonathan Wordsworth argues that the Snowdon sequence probably was not consolidated until late December 1804 or as late as February 1805. He also speculates that two missing notebooks from mid-1804 may have contained work on the Snowdon sequence. See "Five-Book *Prelude,*" 23; and Reed, *Middle Years,* 641–44.

6. *Biographia Literaria,* 1: 141–42.

7. Coleridge habitually uses the Berkeleyan term *outness,* meaning externality or the sense of objects existing outside us. For typical examples of his usage of the term, see *Notebooks,* 1: 1387, and 3: 3325. Wordsworth himself expressly calls attention to the problem of "outness" in his Isabella Fenwick Note to the Ode in 1842:

   > I was often unable to think of external things as having external existence, and I communed with all that I saw as something not apart from, but inherent in, my own immaterial nature. Many times, while going to school have I grasped at a wall or tree to recall myself from this abyss of idealism to the reality. At that time I was afraid of such processes. In later periods of life I have deplored, as we all have reason to do, a subjugation of an opposite character. (*PW,* 4: 463–64)

8. The celestial light has been variously interpreted as a metaphor for the imagination or poetic power—and the Ode itself as an "elegy" on "growing up." See, especially, Lionel Trilling, "The Immortality Ode," in *The Liberal Imagination* (1950; rpt. Garden City: Doubleday Anchor, n.d.), 135, and, in rebuttal, Helen Vendler, "Lionel Trilling and the Immortality Ode," *Salmagundi* 47 (1978): 66–86. For discussion of light and light imagery in the Ode, see Cleanth Brooks, "Wordsworth and the Paradox of the Imagination," in *The Well-Wrought Urn: Studies in the Structure of Poetry* (1947; rpt. London: Methuen, 1968), 101–23. Ferguson judiciously points out that celestial light "has all the elusiveness of a tenor without a vehicle" (*Wordsworth: Language as Counter-Spirit,* 104). In this section, I interpret celestial light not metaphorically but literally: I take it to mean simply "light." For an interesting aside on the issue—and on the implicitly metaphorical status of the "literal," such as I am claiming here— see Jacques Derrida, "Force and Signification," in *Writing and Difference,* trans. Alan Bass (Chicago: University of Chicago Press, 1978), 27, where he argues that the "metaphor of darkness and light (of self-revelation and self-concealment) . . . [is] the founding metaphor of Western philosophy as metaphysics. The founding metaphor not only because it is a photological one—and in this respect the entire history of our philosophy is a photology, the name given to a history of, or treatise on, light—but because it is a metaphor . . . the passage from one existent to another."

9. These lines, in their context, apply, of course, to the mortal youth who has already journeyed a considerable distance from the light. But they equally as accurately characterize the situation of the immortal child, as stanza 8 reveals.

10. My use of the term *semblance* and my discussion of stanza 8 owe much to Jerome Christensen's article, "'Thoughts That Do Often Lie Too Deep For Tears': Toward a Romantic Concept of Lyrical Drama," *The Wordsworth Circle* 12 (1981): 52–64.

11. *Formed* and *fixed* are terms Coleridge uses in a notebook entry when describing the difference between fluid, evolving form and static, realized form. See *Notebooks*, 2: 3159.

12. Wordsworth, MS. JJ, in *The Prelude, 1798–1799*, 124.

13. In a fine discussion of stanza 9 of the Ode, Kenneth R. Johnston argues that Wordsworth celebrates the memory of a memory, or remembering forgetting. See "Recollecting Forgetting: Forcing Paradox to the Limit in the 'Intimations Ode,'" *The Wordsworth Circle* 2 (1971): 59–64.

14. Wordsworth mentions in the Isabella Fenwick note to the Ode that he regards "that dream-like vividness and splendour which invest objects of sight in childhood" as "presumptive evidence of a prior state of existence" (*PW*, 4: 463–64). Wordsworth uses the term "index" when talking about man in book 8 of *The Prelude* (8: 415) and "utmost" when describing the blind beggar in book 7 (7: 619). I introduce these terms here in order to suggest the continuities, semiological and strategic, between the Ode and the transcendental poetry of 1804 and books 7 and 8. See the following chapter for further elaboration.

15. In an early MS. of the Ode, line 152 is followed by: "Throw off from us, or mitigate, the spell / Of that strong frame of sense in which we dwell" (*PW*, 4: 283, app. crit.).

16. Christensen mentions that this vision is an intimation of immortality ("Too Deep for Tears," 59).

17. See Wordsworth's letter of December 1814 to Catherine Clarkson in *The Letters of William and Dorothy Wordsworth: III, The Middle Years; Part II, 1812–1820*, 2nd ed., ed. Ernest de Selincourt, rev. Mary Moorman and Alan G. Hill (Oxford: Clarendon Press, 1970), 619.

18. Note to Isabella Fenwick, *PW*, 4: 463.

19. Presumably Wordsworth's line alludes to St. Paul, 1 Cor. 9:24–27, although another possible source is Eccl. 9:11–12.

20. See Christensen (52–55) for a discussion of Wordsworth's opinions on the appropriateness of tears as a response to tragedy. See also James H. Averill, *Wordsworth and the Poetry of Human Suffering* (Ithaca: Cornell University Press, 1980), 120–24, and John Beer, *Wordsworth and the Human Heart* (New York: Columbia University Press, 1978), 109–12.

21. Line 120 of stanza 8 was originally followed (1807–15) by the lines: "To whom the grave / Is but a lonely bed without the sense or sight / Of day or the warm light, / A place of thought where we in waiting lie" (*PW*, 4: 282, app. crit.). For a discussion of the connection of flower to thought, of the problem of connections in general in the Ode and especially that between metaphysics, memory and ontology, see Ferguson, *Language as Counter-Spirit*, 112–14 and 122–25. Moreover, Ferguson argues that the epitaph is central to Wordsworth's theory of language in general (155–72).

22. Johnston shrewdly points out "the great significance of the Ode is that it is one of the few Romantic poems to satisfactorily answer the essential Romantic question of what to do in the face of the cost, the transiency, of visionary experience." Wordsworth "can build firm consolations upon" his lost "visionary experience" because he knows that he did at one time *have* the experience, even if he "was in fact always in the process of forgetting it" ("Recollecting Forgetting," 63).

23. *PW*, 4: 464.

24. *Biographia Literaria*, 1: 285.

25. MS. W, 6–17. Jonathan Wordsworth reprints the MS. W text in *The Prelude: 1799, 1805, 1850*, 496–500. Quotations will be cited by line numbers in the text. See also 1850 *Prel, 482–86*, app. crit., and 620–29 for passages Jonathan Wordsworth does not reprint. Quotations from these passages will likewise be cited by line number in the text.

26. For a discussion of the analogies and why they break off, see Joseph F. Kishel, "The 'Analogy' Passage from Wordsworth's Five-Book *Prelude*," *Studies in Romanticism* 18 (1979): 271–85.

27. On the potential pantheism and related implications of the Snowdon scene, see Donald Gutierrez, *Subject-Object Relations in Wordsworth and Lawrence* (Ann Arbor: UMI Research Press, 1987), 45–54.

28. As W. J. B. Owen points out, "Most of the operations here attributed to Nature [i.e., moulding, enduing, combining, separating, etc.] have parallels in Wordsworth's standard discussion of the workings of the literary Imagination, the Preface to his *Poems* published in 1815." "The Perfect Image of a Mighty Mind," *The Wordsworth Circle* 10 (1979): 4. Coleridge defines imagination as the "shaping or modifying power" and fancy as the "aggregative or associative power" (*Biographia Literaria*, 1: 293). Coleridge takes Wordsworth to task for subsuming the fancy under the imagination (*Biographia*, 1: 294). For a far-reaching study of the problem of imagination and fancy, its philosophical background, and the debate between Coleridge and Wordsworth on the topic, see Thomas McFarland, *Originality and Imagination* (Baltimore: Johns Hopkins University Press, 1985).

29. See the series of passages reprinted in 1850 *Prel*, 620–23. Wordsworth is evidently working on defining the nature of the self observing the scene—ideas that go into the latter part of the meditation (roughly 13: 97–116).

30. See *Wordsworth's Poetry*, 39–69. Subsequent quotations from Hartman's interpretation will be cited by page number in the text. On Crossing the Alps as a consummate instance of the Wordsworthian sublime, see Weiskel, 195–204.

31. For a discussion of the geographical terrain and Wordsworth's representation of it, see Max Wildi, "Wordsworth and the Simplon Pass," *English Studies* 40 (1959): 224–32, and Wildi's further article, with the same title, in *English Studies* 43 (1962): 359–77. For a rejoinder to Wildi, see Ernest Bernhardt-Kabisch, "Wordsworth and the Simplon Pass Revisited," *The Wordsworth Circle* 10 (1979): 381–85. For a full account of Wordsworth's walking tour of France, Switzerland and Italy, see Donald E. Hayden, *Wordsworth's Walking Tour of 1790*, Monograph Series 19 (Tulsa: University of Tulsa, 1983).

32. Wordsworth had already written about the Alps in *Descriptive Sketches* (1791–93), actually describing Gondo Gorge in lines 263–80. If Wordsworth's 1799 date for the poem "The Simplon Pass" is reliable, then the Gondo Gorge passage in book 6 was already in existence *in toto* when Wordsworth began writing about the Alps in 1804. However, I follow Reed here, who believes that the 1799 date, added by Wordsworth to the poem in 1845, is suspect. He believes that the passage was composed in sequence with the rest of Crossing the Alps in book 6. See *Wordsworth: The Chronology of the Early Years, 1770–1799* (Cambridge: Harvard University Press, 1967), 31, 261. If he had not written the Gondo Gorge lines before Imagination's usurpation interrupted him, the gist of it must surely have been in Wordsworth's mind (as text as well as experience) if he had a sense of where "the eye and progress of [his] Song" (6: 526) were leading when he broke off to utter the apostrophe. In either a literal or also a

figurative sense, then, Wordsworth can be said to "reread" as he writes in March 1804. For convenience's sake, I refer to the entire passage (5: 525–48) as the "apostrophe," even though, technically, only the first 2½ lines constitute an apostrophe.

33. The draft in question is MS. WW. See Jonathan Wordsworth, *The Prelude: 1799, 1805, 1850,* 216 n.3, 508. See also Mark Reed, *Middle Years,* 641.

34. "The Speaker of *The Prelude,*" in *Bicentenary Wordsworth Studies in Memory of John Alban Finch,* ed. Jonathan Wordsworth (Ithaca: Cornell University Press, 1970), 283–89.

35. On the essentially Fichtean nature of the mighty Mind, see Daniel Stempel, "Revelation on Mount Snowdon: Wordsworth, Coleridge, and the Fichtean Imagination," *Journal of Aesthetics and Art Criticism* 29 (1971): 371–84.

36. Hartman points out that Wordsworth "does not project the image of an agent but at most the image of an action" (*Wordsworth's Poetry,* 65).

37. By locating imagination and soul in the Snowdon scene, describing one or two features of its face, exhaustively enumerating nature's imaginative workings, and then telling us the whole composes a *perfect* image of a mighty Mind, Wordsworth invites allegorical interpretation of the scene's "hieroglyphics," as Stempel has called them (372). But any consistent or thorough interpretation is impossible, precisely because any one analogy exerts only a partial sway. For example, Wordsworth writes:

> [A]bove all
> One function of such mind had Nature there
> Exhibited by putting forth, and that
> With circumstance most awful and sublime,
> That domination which she oftentimes
> Exerts upon the outward face of things.
>
> (13: 73–78)

Imagination is the tenor of this description, but what in nature is its vehicle? If we take "above all" literally, then clearly it is the moon; but since the sound of waters usurps the moon and is identified with imagination in the scene, then Wordsworth confounds a literalizing decoding of the scene. In the 1850 text he revises to accommodate both interpretations; he now mentions "mutual domination" and "interchangeable supremacy" (1850 *Prel,* 485; 14: 81, 84). Because any analogy exerts a limited sway, we are still encouraged to discover more analogies. Two general ones are inscribed in the scene and are of importance to the philosophical themes I am tracing in this study. Stempel glosses the ways in which the mighty Mind is the Fichtean Ego, but empiricist pictures of the mind are discernible in the scene. Standing inside the mighty Mind, Wordsworth is also standing inside what looks like a gigantic camera obscura, a standard image of the mind in Locke (*Essay,* 163). The fracture in the vapor is the lens letting in the image of the outside world, the moon being at once the reflection of that image (like the inverted image on the retina of the eye) and the eye that sees it. This analogy won't work beyond a certain point as sound rather than light comes through the lens. In a MS. A variant of this passage, Wordsworth furthers the idea of a camera obscura yet rests it on a Berkeleyan ontology. The mighty Mind "copes with visible shapes" yet

> hears also
> Through vents and openings in the ideal world
> The astounding chorus of infinity
> Exalted by an underconsciousness

Of depth not faithless, the sustaining thought
Of God in human Being.

(1850 Prel, 483, app. crit.)

The "vents and openings" elaborate the idea of the opening or lens of the camera obscura, but equally importantly Wordsworth sees the mighty Mind as essentially suspended over the abyss of idealism: "depth not faithless, the sustaining thought / Of God in human Being" suggest the Berkeleyan God who sustains phenomena.

Another significant analogy suggests links between the Snowdon sequence and the "Immortality" Ode. Quietly gazing at the "sea of mist" and at "the real Sea" beyond, Wordsworth resembles the immortal child of stanza 8 of the Ode: "silent" (but not deaf) he reads the "deep," "Haunted" at this moment by a mighty Mind. "Though inland" some distance, moreover, Wordsworth hears from "the shore / Of . . . [this] huge sea of mist" (13: 42–43) "the mighty waters rolling evermore." As in other instances, the topographical and dramatic repetitions work to promote continuity, demonstration, revision and elaboration of a philosophical belief.

Chapter 5

1. Jonathan Wordsworth asks, "[H]ow far had Wordsworth planned his song's appointed path? . . . how, and how soon, did he at this stage expect to link through to Snowdon and the 'spots of time' (set aside in March, after forming the conclusion to the five-Book *Prelude*)?" (*The Borders of Vision*, 281). Presumably Wordsworth did see these passages as the poem's eventual climax, even if he may have been undecided about where, how and when they would fall into place.

2. On the chronology of composition, see Reed, *Middle Years*, 645–53.

3. Reed, *Middle Years*, 649.

4. *The Prelude: 1799, 1805, 1850*, 504.

5. *Wordsworth's Poetry*, 234. Hartman also discusses parallels with *Paradise Lost* at this point (234–38).

6. Mary Jacobus discusses the connections between Paris and London and how the theater becomes the medium through which Wordsworth confronts the politics of his time and his own political engagement. See "'That Great Stage Where Senators Perform': *Macbeth* and the Politics of Romantic Theatre," *Studies in Romanticism* 22 (1983): 353–87. Jacobus stresses that "The London of Book VII of *The Prelude* is a city of representation" (371).

7. See, for example, Jonathan Wordsworth, 295–307.

8. In chapter 24 ("Of Collective Ideas of Substances") in *An Essay Concerning Human Understanding*, Locke discusses *"complex collective Ideas* of Substances" which are "made up of many particular Substances considered together, as united into one *Idea*, and which so joined, are looked on as one" (317). Though Locke's examples are an army and the world, what he argues applies to the idea of a city as well. Hume further elaborates what Locke suggests in *A Treatise of Human Nature*: "I observe, that many of our complex ideas never had impressions, that corresponded to them, and that many of our complex impressions never are exactly copied in ideas. I can imagine to myself such a city as the *New Jerusalem*, whose pavement is gold and walls are rubies, tho' I never saw any such. I have seen *Paris;* but shall I affirm I can form such an idea of that city, as will perfectly represent all its streets and houses in their real and just proportions?" David Hume, *A Treatise of Human Nature*, ed. L. A. Selby-Bigge (1888;

rpt. Oxford: Clarendon Press, 1975), 3. Hume accurately analyzes the problem facing Wordsworth in book 7. David Simpson mentions that "The city is a shifting assemblage of incoherent significations. There is an overbalance of signifiers over potential things signified, and the one is often at odds with the other." See *Wordsworth and the Figurings of the Real* (Atlantic Highlands: Humanities Press, 1982), 52.

9. Herbert Lindenberger writes that Wordsworth "maintains a stance of almost total aloofness from the urban inferno which he describes." See *On Wordsworth's "Prelude"* (Princeton: Princeton University Press, 1963), 235. This aloofness is literalized in Wordsworth's elevation on the causeway above the upturned face. If he is indeed like Aeneas, then on this occasion he resembles the Aeneas of canto 32 of Dante's *Inferno,* where souls, buried up to their heads in ice, look up at Aeneas and weep tears which freeze as they descend.

10. For a full discussion of what Wordsworth actually saw in London, see Richard D. Altick, *The Shows of London* (Cambridge: Belknap Press of Harvard University Press, 1978), 35–36 (*Bartholomew Fair*), 116 ff. (models and exhibitions), and 184 ff. (panoramas).

11. For a different discussion of issues Jack the Giant-killer raises and their bearing on the questions of vision, silence and textuality in Wordsworth's poetry, see Cynthia Chase, "The Ring of Gyges and the Coat of Darkness: Reading Rousseau with Wordsworth," in *Decomposing Figures: Rhetorical Readings in the Romantic Tradition* (Baltimore: Johns Hopkins University Press, 1986), 32–64.

12. See Mary Lamb's letter to Dorothy Wordsworth of 9 July 1803, *Letters of Charles and Mary Lamb,* 2: 117.

13. As de Selincourt mentions in his notes to book 7 (1850 *Prel,* 563–64), Coleridge and Wordsworth visited Buttermere about the middle of November 1799 when making a tour of the Lake District. The fraud perpetrated on Mary Robinson and popularized in the play evidently captivated Coleridge's interest in particular. Coleridge contributed three articles on the event to *The Morning Post* in 1802. See *Essays on His Times,* ed. David V. Erdman, vol. 3 of *The Collected Works of Samuel Taylor Coleridge,* ed. Kathleen Coburn (Princeton: Princeton University Press, 1978), 1; 357–58; 374–76; 390–91.

14. *Treatise,* 253.

15. *Essay,* 163.

16. Ferguson explores this point in *Wordsworth: Language as Counter-Spirit,* 142–43.

17. See Frank D. McConnell, *The Confessional Imagination: A Reading of Wordsworth's "Prelude"* (Baltimore: Johns Hopkins University Press, 1974), 105–8.

18. Ferguson makes a parallel point in stressing the beggar's dependence on other people—on the *human*—to communicate his meanings and intentions: "Outward form presents itself as the blind man's only hold on the world, as 'his story' as it has been translated into the external form of writing which he cannot read to affirm or deny. The blind beggar is absolutely a beggar, in having to hope that the words written for him and his sightless face will arouse an imagination of his inward existence, a pity which can only be communicated through the giving of alms, another excursion into outward form" (143).

19. The "utmost" almost amounts to a Kantian category, or certainly to the dialectical movement implicit in the triadic structure of the categories; in fact, the "utmost" seems to conflate the categories of quantity and quality:

Of Quantity	*Of Quality*
Unity	Reality
Plurality	Negation
Totality	Limitation

See *Critique of Pure Reason*, 113. The entire blind Beggar episode, in fact, possesses a very Kantian ring, in that the voiding of content as thoughts are made empty leads to "intuitions *without* concepts" (93; emphasis added) which are "blind." Kant's famous sentence is fortuitous here, of course, but it nevertheless describes the exact movement of Wordsworth's discourse at this point.

Chapter 6

1. Coleridge, *Table Talk*, 188.

2. Johnston points out that Wordsworth's scheme is "nominally Christian. . . . The Pastor's flock certainly led lives based on Christian assumptions, but their author stresses their paramount virtue as strength of mind, the sheer mental effort with which they met—or failed to meet—the conditions of their lives." *Wordsworth and "The Recluse,"* 286. Simpson points out that "the terms of the Wanderer's faith seem remarkably basic and inter-denominational, so much so that they have been felt to approach heterodoxy." *Wordsworth's Historical Imagination*, 199.

3. Coleridge, *Table Talk*, 188.

4. The full title of *Alciphron* (1732) is *Alciphron: Or, The Minute Philosopher. In Seven Dialogues. Containing An Apology for the Christian Religion, against Those Who Are Called Free-Thinkers*. The setting is Crito's house in the country, where the participants' "conversation sometimes turns to "the beauty of this rural scene, [and] the fine season of the year." *Alciphron, or The Minute Philosopher, The Works of George Berkeley, Bishop of Cloyne*, ed. A.A. Luce and T.E. Jessop, 9 vols. (London: Thomas Nelson, 1950), 3: 33. Crito, the witty host, and Euphranor, "a farmer who had been through the university and retained his habits of study" (*Alciphron*, 14), share between them the roles of the Wanderer and Pastor, while the free-thinkers Alciphron and Lysicles correspond to the Solitary. "The Reporter, Dion, who does not take part in the conversations" (14) fulfills the role of the Poet.

5. Hodgson writes that "The Solitary's resistance to the combined and blended arguments of the Wanderer and the Pastor represents a lingering philosophical honesty by which Wordsworth at least preserves, almost in spite of himself, a strong core of intellectual respectability." The Solitary's resistance represents Wordsworth's "own persistently honest skepticism"—surely a stance that calls the transcendentalism into question (169).

6. On the "Mechanic Dogmatists," see Coleridge's letter, quoted below (*Collected Letters*, 4: 574). The Wanderer expresses his antipathy for Voltaire and *Candide* at 2. 444–91 and 4. 995–1028. In the second denunciation he characterizes the French as "a most frivolous people" (4. 1005). As mentioned in the introduction, note 28, Wordsworth had several works by the likes of Burnet, Cudworth and More on his shelves. Their Neoplatonic strain may have predisposed him toward Berkeley, if he had not already conceived a liking for his ideas or works either on his own or through conversations with Coleridge in the late 1790s. Of the empiricists in general, only Hume would have been seen as explicitly atheistic (Locke expresses belief in God at several points in the *Essay*).

7. Johnston, 265. Books 2–9 of *The Excursion* were composed between 1809 and 1814. See Reed, *Middle Years,* 666. I omit discussion here of book 1 of *The Excursion* because I have already discussed at length *The Pedlar,* which, together with *The Ruined Cottage,* was transformed into book 1 of the later poem. On the differences between *The Ruined Cottage* and book 1, see William Galperin, "'Then the Voice Was Silent': 'The Wanderer' vs. *The Ruined Cottage,*" *ELH* 51 (1984): 343–63. On the relation of *The Pedlar* to *The Ruined Cottage,* see Peter J. Manning, "Wordsworth, Margaret, and The Pedlar," *Studies in Romanticism* 15 (1976): 195–220.

8. Johnston, 265–66.

9. On the quest romance and Fichtean striving see Kipperman, 61–96.

10. Coleridge, *Collected Letters,* 4: 574–75.

11. Johnston, 345.

12. Wordsworth seems close to Berkeley here in the way he conceives the differences between distance and proximity. At the beginning of *An Essay towards a New Theory of Vision* (1709), Berkeley announces: "My design is to shew the manner wherein we perceive by sight the distance, magnitude, and situation of objects. Also to consider the difference there is betwixt the ideas of sight and touch, and whether there by any idea common to both senses." *Works,* 1: 171.

13. Hartman, *Wordsworth's Poetry,* 293.

14. See Hartman on the "heaping up of exempla" in *The Excursion* (319). See Wolfson on questioning (and the lack of questioning) in *The Excursion* (and in Wordsworth in general): *The Questioning Presence: Wordsworth, Keats, and the Interrogative Mode in Romantic Poetry* (Ithaca: Cornell University Press, 1986), 116–30.

15. On the renunciation of the apocalyptic imagination, see Hartman, *Wordsworth's Poetry,* 293–95, 308–12; Johnston, 283–89 (Johnston talks here of Wordsworth's conscious choice of the "unheroic," the "democratic" and the "non-visionary"); and Ferguson, *Wordsworth: Language as Counter-Spirit,* 238–41.

16. Hartman mentions that the Pensioner seems to have had much the same vision that the Solitary had, that the Solitary's questions about "wherefore do I live?" apply to the Pensioner and that for both "vision, or Imagination, is death-dealing" (*Wordsworth's Poetry,* 309–10). Ferguson mentions that the Solitary's and Wanderer's biographies mirror one another (211), as do their visions (i.e., the Pedlar's sunrise vision), and that when the two men meet in book 2 they each address the other as if he were returning from the dead (223–30).

17. Kant discusses the concept of "purposiveness" in nature in the "Analytic" and "Dialectic" "Divisions" in the "Critique of the Teleological Judgment" in *The Critique of Judgment.* See Immanuel Kant, *Critique of Judgment,* trans. J.H. Bernard (New York: Macmillan, 1951), 205–64.

18. For a definitive discussion of the historical and socio-economic conditions of the Lake District and Wordsworth's treatment of them in *The Excursion,* see Simpson, *Wordsworth's Historical Imagination,* 185–208.

19. Wordsworth makes it clear that it is urban churchyards he is contrasting with rural ones in the first "Essay upon Epitaphs," published as a note to book 6 of *The Excursion* (the essay was originally published in Coleridge's *The Friend,* in the issue of 22 February 1810). See *PrW,* 2: 54–55, and 45.

20. Ferguson discusses the epitaph as the essential paradigm of language itself for Wordsworth (28–34).

21. Ferguson, 227.

22. Ferguson, 226.

23. Ferguson, 225.

24. Ferguson, 228.

25. Hartman, *Wordsworth's Poetry,* 310.

26. For Coleridge's famous definition of the distinction between symbol and allegory, see *The Statesman's Manual* in *Lay Sermons,* ed. R.J. White, *The Collected Works of Samuel Taylor Coleridge,* vol. 6 (Princeton: Princeton University Press, 1972), 30.

27. See Hartman, *Wordsworth's Poetry,* 308–10.

28. Johnston discusses the way these emblems work (282–84). See also Hodgson, 165–67, who makes this point about the monitor shell.

29. See *Siris,* in *Works,* 5: 130, 162–63.

30. On Coleridge's discussion of "I AM" and "it is" and the "chasm" that falls between them, see *The Friend,* 1: 523. See also McFarland, *Coleridge and the Pantheist Tradition,* 107–90.

Bibliography

Abrams, M.H. *The Mirror and the Lamp: Romantic Theory and the Critical Tradition*. 1953; rpt. New York: W.W. Norton, 1958.

———. *Natural Supernaturalism: Tradition and Revolution in Romantic Literature*. New York: W.W. Norton, 1973.

Altick, Richard D. *The Shows of London*. Cambridge: Belknap Press of Harvard University Press, 1978.

Averill, James H. *Wordsworth and the Poetry of Human Suffering*. Ithaca: Cornell University Press, 1980.

Bahti, Timothy. "Figures of Interpretation, the Interpretation of Figures: A Reading of Wordsworth's 'Dream of the Arab.'" *Studies in Romanticism* 18 (1979): 601–27.

Beach, Joseph Warren. *The Concept of Nature in Nineteenth-Century English Poetry*. New York: Macmillan, 1936.

Beatty, Arthur. *William Wordsworth: His Doctrine and Art in Their Historical Relations*. Madison: University of Wisconsin Press, 1922.

Beer, John. *Wordsworth and the Human Heart*. New York: Columbia University Press, 1978.

Bennet, Jonathan. *Locke, Berkeley, Hume: Central Themes*. Oxford: Clarendon Press, 1971.

Berkeley, George. *Alciphron*. Ed. by T.E. Jessop. Vol. 3 of *The Works of George Berkeley, Bishop of Cloyne*. 9 vols. London: Thomas Nelson, 1950.

———. *Essay towards a New Theory of Vision*. Ed. by A.A. Luce. Vol. 1 of *The Works of George Berkeley, Bishop of Cloyne*. 9 vols. London: Thomas Nelson, 1948.

———. *Siris*. Ed. by T.E. Jessop. Vol. 5 of *The Works of George Berkeley, Bishop of Cloyne*. 9 vols. London: Thomas Nelson, 1953.

———. *Three Dialogues between Hylas and Philonous*. Ed. by T.E. Jessop. Vol. 2 of *The Works of George Berkeley, Bishop of Cloyne*. 9 vols. London: Thomas Nelson, 1949.

Bernhardt-Kabisch, Ernest. "Wordsworth and the Simplon Pass Revisited." *The Wordsworth Circle* 10 (1979): 381–85.

Bloom, Harold. *The Anxiety of Influence: A Theory of Poetry*. New York: Oxford University Press, 1973.

———. *A Map of Misreading*. Oxford: Oxford University Press, 1975.

———. *Poetry and Repression*. New Haven: Yale University Press, 1976.

Brooks, Cleanth. *The Well-Wrought Urn: Studies in the Structure of Poetry*. 1947; rpt. London: Methuen, 1968.

Butler, James, ed. *"The Ruined Cottage" and "The Pedlar."* The Cornell Wordsworth. Ithaca: Cornell University Press, 1979.

Cascardi, Anthony J., ed. *Literature and the Question of Philosophy*. Baltimore: Johns Hopkins University Press, 1987.

Chandler, James K. *Wordsworth's Second Nature: A Study of the Poetry and Politics*. Chicago: University of Chicago Press, 1984.

Chase, Cynthia. *Decomposing Figures: Rhetorical Readings in the Romantic Tradition*. Baltimore: Johns Hopkins University Press, 1986.

Christensen, Jerome. *Practicing Enlightenment: Hume and the Formation of a Literary Career*. Madison: University of Wisconsin Press, 1987.

—————. " 'Thoughts That Do Often Lie Too Deep for Tears': Toward a Romantic Concept of Lyrical Drama." *The Wordsworth Circle* 12 (1981): 52–64.

Clarke, Colin C. *Romantic Paradox: An Essay on the Poetry of Wordsworth*. New York: Barnes & Noble, 1963.

Coe, Charles Norton. *Wordsworth and the Literature of Travel*. New York: Bookman Associates, 1953.

Cohen, Ralph, ed. *Studies in Eighteenth-Century British Art and Aesthetics*. Berkeley: University of California Press, 1985.

Coleridge, Samuel Taylor. *Biographia Literaria*. Ed. by James Engell and W. Jackson Bate. 2 vols. Vol. 7 of *The Collected Works of Samuel Taylor Coleridge*. 16 vols. Princeton: Princeton University Press, 1983.

—————. *Collected Letters of Samuel Taylor Coleridge*. Ed. by Earl Leslie Griggs. 6 vols. Oxford: Clarendon Press, 1956–71.

—————. *The Complete Poetical Works of Samuel Taylor Coleridge*. Ed. by Ernest Hartley Coleridge. 2 vols. Oxford: Clarendon Press, 1912.

—————. *Essay on His Times*. Ed. by David B. Erdman. 3 vols. Vol. 3 of *The Collected Works of Samuel Taylor Coleridge*. 16 vols. Princeton: Princeton University Press, 1978.

—————. *The Friend*. Ed. by Barbara E. Rooke. 2 vols. Vol. 4 of *The Collected Works of Samuel Taylor Coleridge*. 16 vols. Princeton: Princeton University Press, 1969.

—————. *Lay Sermons*. Ed. by R.J. White. Vol. 6 of *The Collected Works of Samuel Taylor Coleridge*. 16 vols. Princeton: Princeton University Press, 1972.

—————. *The Notebooks of Samuel Taylor Coleridge*. Ed. by Kathleen Coburn. 3 vols. Princeton: Princeton University Press, 1957–73.

—————. *The Table Talk and Omniana of Samuel Taylor Coleridge*. Ed. by Henry Nelson Coleridge. London: Oxford University Press, 1917.

Cooper, Andrew M. *Doubt and Identity in Romantic Poetry*. New Haven: Yale University Press, 1988.

Culler, Jonathan. *The Pursuit of Signs: Semiotics, Literature, Deconstruction*. Ithaca: Cornell University Press, 1981.

Derrida, Jacques. *Dissemination*. Trans. by Barbara Johnson. Chicago: University of Chicago Press, 1981 (1972).

—————. *Glas*. Trans. by John P. Leavey and Richard Rand. Lincoln: University of Nebraska Press, 1987 (1974).

—————. *Margins of Philosophy*. Trans. by Alan Bass. Chicago: University of Chicago Press, 1982 (1972).

—————. *Of Grammatology*. Trans. by Gayatri Chakravorty Spivak. Baltimore: Johns Hopkins University Press, 1977 (1967).

—————. " 'Ousia and Grammè': A Note to a Footnote in *Being and Time*." Trans. by Edward S. Casey in *Phenomenology in Perspective*, ed. by F.J. Smith. The Hague: Martinus Nijhoff, 1970.

—————. "The Retrait of Metaphor." *enclitic* 2 (1978): 5–34.

—————. *Speech and Phenomena; And Other Essays on Husserl's Theory of Signs*. Trans. by David B. Allison. Evanston: Northwestern University Press, 1973 (1967).

—————. *Writing and Difference*. Trans. by Alan Bass. Chicago: University of Chicago Press, 1978 (1967).

Descartes, René. *Meditations on First Philosophy.* Trans. by Laurence J. Lafleur. 1951; rpt. Indianapolis: Bobbs-Merrill, 1980.

Ferguson, Frances. "Legislating the Sublime." In *Studies in Eighteenth-Century Art and Aesthetics,* ed. by Ralph Cohen. Berkeley: University of California Press, 1985.

———. "The Sublime of Edmund Burke, or the Bathos of Experience." *Glyph* 8 (1981): 62–78.

———. *Wordsworth: Language as Counter-Spirit.* New Haven: Yale University Press, 1977.

Fichte, J.G. *Fichte: Science of Knowledge (Wissenschaftslehre) with the First and Second Introductions.* Trans. and ed. by Peter Heath and John Lachs. New York: Appleton-Century-Crofts, 1970.

Galperin, William. "'Then the Voice Was Silent': 'The Wanderer' vs. *The Ruined Cottage.*" *English Literary History* 51 (1984): 343–63.

Gasché, Rodolphe. *The Tain of the Mirror: Derrida and the Philosophy of Reflection.* Cambridge: Harvard University Press, 1986.

Grob, Alan. *The Philosophic Mind: A Study of Wordsworth's Poetry and Thought, 1797–1805.* Columbus: Ohio State University Press, 1973.

Gutierrez, Donald. *Subject-Object Relations in Wordsworth and Lawrence.* Ann Arbor: UMI Research Press, 1987.

Harris, Wendell V. *The Omnipresent Debate: Empiricism and Transcendentalism in Nineteenth-Century English Prose.* DeKalb: Northern Illinois University Press, 1981.

Hartley, David. *Observations on Man, His Frame, His Duty, and His Expectations.* Introd. by Theodore L. Huguelet. Gainesville: Scholars' Facsimiles and Reprints, 1966.

Hartman, Geoffrey H. *Saving the Text: Literature, Derrida, Philosophy.* Baltimore: Johns Hopkins University Press, 1981.

———. *Wordsworth's Poetry, 1787–1814.* 1964; rpt. New Haven: Yale University Press, 1977.

Hayden, Donald E. *Wordsworth's Walking Tour of 1790.* Monograph Series No. 19. Tulsa: University of Tulsa, 1983.

Hirsch, E.D., Jr. *Wordsworth and Schelling: A Typological Study in Romanticism.* New Haven: Yale University Press, 1960.

Hodgson, John A. *Wordsworth's Philosophical Poetry, 1797–1814.* Lincoln: University of Nebraska Press, 1980.

Hume, David. *A Treatise of Human Nature.* Ed. by L.A. Selby-Bigge. 1888; rpt. Oxford: Clarendon Press, 1975.

Jacobus, Mary. "'That Great Stage Where Senators Perform': *Macbeth* and the Politics of Romantic Theatre." *Studies in Romanticism* 22 (1983): 353–87.

———. *Tradition and Experiment in Wordsworth's "Lyrical Ballads" (1798).* Oxford: Clarendon Press, 1976.

Jaye, Michael C. "William Wordsworth's Alfoxden Notebook: 1798." In *The Evidence of the Imagination: Studies of Interactions between Life and Art in British Romantic Literature.* Ed. by Donald H. Reiman, Michael C. Jaye, et al. New York: New York University Press, 1978.

Johnston, Kenneth R. "Recollecting Forgetting: Forcing Paradox to the Limit in the 'Intimations' Ode." *The Wordsworth Circle* 2 (1971): 59–64.

———. *Wordsworth and "The Recluse."* New Haven: Yale University Press, 1984.

Jordan, Frank, Jr., ed. *The English Romantic Poets: A Review of Research and Criticism.* New York: MLA, 1972.

Kant, Immanuel. *Critique of Judgment.* Trans. by J.H. Bernard. New York: Macmillan, 1951.

———. *Immanuel Kant's Critique of Pure Reason.* Trans. by Norman Kemp Smith. 1929; rpt. London: Macmillan, 1964.

Keats, John. *Letters of John Keats.* Ed. by Robert E. Gittings. London: Oxford University Press, 1970.

Kelley, Theresa M. "Wordsworth, Kant, and the Romantic Sublime." *Philological Quarterly* 63 (1984): 130–40.

Kishel, Joseph F. "The 'Analogy' Passage from Wordsworth's Five-Book *Prelude*." *Studies in Romanticism* 18 (1979): 271–85.

Kipperman, Mark. *Beyond Enchantment: German Idealism and English Romantic Poetry*. Philadelphia: University of Pennsylvania Press, 1986.

Knapp, Steven. *Personification and the Sublime: Milton to Coleridge*. Cambridge: Harvard University Press, 1985.

Kofman, Sarah. *Lectures de Derrida*. Paris: Galilée, 1984.

Lamb, Charles and Mary Anne. *The Letters of Charles and Mary Anne Lamb*. Ed. by Edwin W. Marrs, Jr. 3 vols. Ithaca: Cornell University Press, 1975–78.

Levinson, Marjorie. *Wordsworth's Great Period Poems: Four Essays*. Cambridge: Cambridge University Press, 1986.

Lindenberger, Herbert. *On Wordsworth's "Prelude."* Princeton: Princeton University Press, 1963.

Liu, Alan. "Wordsworth: The History in 'Imagination.'" *English Literary History* 51 (1984): 505–48.

Llewelyn, John. *Derrida on the Threshold of Sense*. London: Macmillan, 1986.

Locke, John. *An Essay concerning Human Understanding*. Ed. by Peter H. Nidditch. Oxford: Clarendon Press, 1975.

McConnell, Frank D. *The Confessional Imagination: A Reading of Wordsworth's "Prelude."* Baltimore: Johns Hopkins University Press, 1974.

McFarland, Thomas. *Coleridge and the Pantheist Tradition*. Oxford: Clarendon Press, 1969.

——— . *Originality and Imagination*. Baltimore: Johns Hopkins University Press, 1985.

——— . *Romanticism and the Forms of Ruin: Wordsworth, Coleridge, and the Modalities of Fragmentation*. Princeton: Princeton University Press, 1981.

McGann, Jerome J. *The Romantic Ideology: A Critical Investigation*. Chicago: University of Chicago Press, 1983.

McInerney, Peter F. "Natural Wisdom in Wordsworth's *The Excursion*." *The Wordsworth Circle* 9 (1978): 188–99.

Manning, Peter J. "Placing Poor Susan: Wordsworth and the New Historicism." *Studies in Romanticism* 25 (1986): 351–69.

——— . "Wordsworth, Margaret, and The Pedlar." *Studies in Romanticism* 15 (1976): 195–220.

Marshall, Donald G., ed. *Literature as Philosophy/Philosophy as Literature*. Iowa City: University of Iowa Press, 1987.

Modiano, Raimonda. *Coleridge and the Concept of Nature*. Tallahassee: Florida State University Press, 1985.

Moorman, Mary. *William Wordsworth, a Biography: The Early Years, 1770–1803*. 1957; rpt. Oxford: Clarendon Press, 1965.

Norris, Christopher. *Derrida*. Cambridge: Harvard University Press, 1987.

Onorato, Richard. *The Character of the Poet: Wordsworth in "The Prelude."* Princeton: Princeton University Press, 1971.

Orsini, G.N.G. *Coleridge and German Idealism: A Study in the History of Philosophy with Unpublished Materials from Coleridge's Manuscripts*. Carbondale: Southern Illinois University Press, 1969.

Owen, W.J.B. "The Perfect Image of a Mighty Mind." *The Wordsworth Circle* 10 (1979): 2–20.

Parrish, Stephen, ed. *The Prelude, 1798–1799*. The Cornell Wordsworth. Ithaca: Cornell University Press, 1977.

Pearsall, Robert Brainard. "Wordsworth Reworks His Hartley." *RMMLA Bulletin* (1970): 73–83.

Phillips Griffiths, ed. *Philosophy and Literature*. Cambridge: Cambridge University Press, 1984.

Piper, H.W. *The Active Universe: Pantheism and the Concept of Imagination in the English Romantic Poets*. London: Athlone Press, 1962.

Price, John Valdimir. "The Reading of Philosophical Literature." In *Books and Their Readers in Eighteenth-Century England*. Ed. by Isabel Rivers. New York: St. Martin's Press, 1982.

Rader, Melvin. *Wordsworth: A Philosophical Approach*. Oxford: Clarendon Press, 1967.

Reed, Mark L. "The Speaker in *The Prelude*." In *Bicentenary Wordsworth Studies in Memory of John Alban Finch*. Ed. by Jonathan Wordsworth. Ithaca: Cornell University Press, 1970.

———. *Wordsworth: The Chronology of the Early Years, 1770–1799*. Cambridge: Harvard University Press, 1967.

———. *Wordsworth: The Chronology of the Middle Years, 1800–1815*. Cambridge: Harvard University Press, 1975.

Reiman, Donald H., ed. *The Evidence of the Imagination: Studies of Interactions between Life and Art in British Romantic Literature*. New York: New York University Press, 1978.

Rivers, Isabel, ed. *Books and Their Readers in the Eighteenth-Century*. New York: St. Martin's Press, 1982.

Robinson, Henry Crabb. *Correspondence of Crabb Robinson with the Wordsworth Circle*. ed. Edith Morley. 2 vols. Oxford: Clarendon Press, 1927.

Rorty, Richard. *Philosophy and the Mirror of Nature*. Princeton: Princeton University Press, 1979.

Rousseau, G.S. "Science Books and Their Readers in the Eighteenth Century." In *Books and Their Readers in Eighteenth-Century England*. Ed. by Isabel Rivers. New York: St. Martin's Press, 1982.

Rzepka, Charles J. *The Self as Mind: Vision and Identity in Wordsworth, Coleridge, and Keats*. Cambridge: Harvard University Press, 1986.

Schneider, Ben Ross, Jr. *Wordsworth's Cambridge Education*. Cambridge: Cambridge University Press, 1957.

Shakespeare, William. *King Lear*. Ed. by Kenneth Muir. *The Arden Shakespeare*. 1952; rpt. London: Methuen, 1966.

Shaver, Chester L., and Alice C. Shaver. *Wordsworth's Library: A Catalogue*. New York: Garland, 1979.

Sheats, Paul. *The Making of Wordsworth's Poetry, 1785–98*. Cambridge: Harvard University Press, 1973.

Sherry, Charles. *Wordsworth's Poetry of the Imagination*. Oxford: Clarendon Press, 1980.

Simpson, David. "What Bothered Charles Lamb about Poor Susan?" *Studies in English Literature* 26 (1986): 589–612.

———. *Wordsworth and the Figurings of the Real*. Atlantic Highlands: Humanities Press, 1982.

———. *Wordsworth's Historical Imagination: The Poetry of Displacement*. New York: Methuen, 1987.

Stallknecht, Newton P. *Strange Seas of Thought: Studies in William Wordsworth's Philosophy of Man and Nature*. Bloomington: Indiana University Press, 1958.

Stempel, Daniel. "Revelation on Mount Snowdon: Wordsworth, Coleridge, and the Fichtean Imagination." *Journal of Aesthetics and Art Criticism* 29 (1971): 371–84.

Stroud, Barry. *The Significance of Philosophical Scepticism*. Oxford: Clarendon Press, 1984.

Trilling, Lionel. *The Liberal Imagination*. 1950; rpt. Garden City: Doubleday Anchor, n.d.

Vendler, Helen. "Lionel Trilling and the Immortality Ode." *Salmagundi* 47 (1978): 66–86.

Wasserman, Earl R. "The English Romantics: The Grounds of Knowledge." *Studies in Romanticism* 4 (1964): 17–34.

Weiskel, Thomas. *The Romantic Sublime: Studies in the Structure and Psychology of Transcendence*. Baltimore: Johns Hopkins University Press, 1976.

Wesling, Donald. *Wordsworth and the Adequacy of Landscape*. London: Routledge & Kegan Paul, 1970.

Wildi, Max. "Wordsworth and the Simplon Pass." *English Studies* 40 (1959): 224–32.

———. "Wordsworth and the Simplon Pass." *English Studies* 43 (1962): 359–77.

Wolfson, Susan J. *The Questioning Presence: Wordsworth, Keats, and the Interrogative Mode in Romantic Poetry*. Ithaca: Cornell University Press, 1986.

――――― . "The Speaker as Questioner in *Lyrical Ballads*." *Journal of English and Germanic Philology* 77 (1978): 546–68.

Wordsworth, Jonathan. "The Five-Book *Prelude* of Early Spring 1804." *Journal of English and Germanic Philology* 76 (1977): 1–25.

――――― . *The Music of Humanity: A Critical Study of Wordsworth's "Ruined Cottage."* London: Thomas Nelson, 1969.

――――― . *William Wordsworth: The Borders of Vision*. Oxford: Clarendon Press, 1982.

―――――, ed. *Bicentenary Wordsworth Studies in Memory of John Alban Finch*. Ithaca: Cornell University Press, 1970.

Wordsworth, William. *The Letters of William and Dorothy Wordsworth: The Early Years, 1787– 1805*. 2nd. ed. Rev. by Chester L. Shaver. Oxford: Clarendon Press, 1967.

――――― . *The Letters of William and Dorothy Wordsworth: The Middle Years, 1806–1820*. Part 2, 1812–1820, rev. by Mary Moorman and Alan G. Hill. Oxford: Clarendon Press, 1970.

――――― . *The Poetical Works of William Wordsworth*. Ed. by Ernest de Selincourt and Helen Darbishire. 5 vols. Oxford: Clarendon Press, 1940–49.

――――― . *The Prelude; or, Growth of a Poet's Mind*. Ed. by Ernest de Selincourt. 2nd ed. rev. by Helen Darbishire. Oxford: Clarendon Press, 1959.

――――― . *The Prelude; or, Growth of a Poet's Mind (Text of 1805)*. Ed. by Ernest de Selincourt. Rev. by Stephen Gill. London: Oxford University Press, 1970.

――――― . *The Prelude, 1798–1799*. Ed. by Stephen Parrish. *The Cornell Wordsworth*. Ithaca: Cornell University Press, 1977.

――――― . *The Prelude: 1799, 1805, 1850*. Ed. by Jonathan Wordsworth, M.H. Abrams, and Stephen Gill. New York: W.W. Norton, 1979.

――――― . *The Prose Works of William Wordsworth*. 3 vols. Ed. by W.J.B. Owen and Jane Worthington Smyser. Oxford: Clarendon Press, 1974.

――――― . *'The Ruined Cottage" and "The Pedlar."* Ed. by James Butler. *The Cornell Wordsworth*. Ithaca: Cornell University Press, 1979.

Yolton, John W. *Perceptual Acquaintance from Descartes to Reid*. Minneapolis: University of Minnesota Press, 1984.

――――― . *Thinking Matter: Materialism in Eighteenth-Century Britain*. Minneapolis: University of Minnesota Press, 1983.

Index